92-03-16		
NOV 16 1992		
MAY 29 1993		
APR 13 2009		
261-2500		Printed in USA

Recent Titles from Quorum Books

The Evolution of Foreign Banking Institutions in the United States: Developments in International Finance
Faramarz Damanpour

Corporate Planning, Human Behavior, and Computer Simulation: Forecasting Business Cycles
Roy L. Nersesian

The Valuation and Investment Merits of Diamonds
Sarkis J. Khoury

Market-Oriented Pricing: Strategies for Management
Michael H. Morris and Gene Morris

The Divestiture Option: A Guide for Financial and Corporate Planning Executives
Richard J. Schmidt

International Perspectives on Trade Promotion and Assistance
S. Tamer Cavusgil and Michael R. Czinkota, editors

The Promise of American Industry: An Alternative Assessment of Problems and Prospects
Donald L. Losman and Shu-Jan Liang

Global Corporate Intelligence: Opportunities, Technologies, and Threats in the 1990s
George S. Roukis, Hugh Conway, and Bruce Charnov, editors

The Process of Change in American Banking: Political Economy and the Public Purpose
Jeremy F. Taylor

Drop Shipping as a Marketing Function: A Handbook of Methods and Policies
Nicholas T. Scheel

Manufacturing for the Security of the United States: Reviving Competitiveness and Reducing Deficits
Robert E. McGarrah

Employee Complaint Handling: Tested Techniques for Human Resource Managers
D. Keith Denton and Charles Boyd

Alcohol Problem Intervention in the Workplace: Employee Assistance Programs and Strategic Alternatives
Paul M. Roman, editor

PROBLEM
EMPLOYEE
MANAGEMENT

Proactive Strategies
for Human Resource Managers

WILLA M. BRUCE

QUORUM BOOKS
New York • Westport, Connecticut • London

Library of Congress Cataloging-in-Publication Data

Bruce, Willa M.
  Problem employee management : proactive strategies for human
resource managers / Willa M. Bruce.
    p. cm.
  ISBN 0–89930–501–6 (lib. bdg. : alk. paper)
  1. Problem employees.   I. Title.
HF5549.5.E42B78   1990
658.3'043—dc20   89–24330

British Library Cataloguing in Publication Data is available.

Library of Congress Catalog Card Number: 89–24330
ISBN: 0–89930–501–6

First published in 1990

Quorum Books, 88 Post Road West, Westport, CT   06881
An imprint of Greenwood Publishing Group, Inc.

Printed in the United States of America

The paper used in this book complies with the
Permanent Paper Standard issued by the National
Information Standards Organization (Z39.48–1984).

10 9 8 7 6 5 4 3 2 1

Copyright Acknowledgment

The author gratefully acknowledges permission to quote from the following:

From Dawn Marie Warfle, ed., *Advanced Supervisory Practices*, 1990. Reprinted with
permission of the International City Management Association, 777 North Capitol Street,
Washington, DC   20001. All rights reserved.

If you can keep your head when all about
you
    Are losing theirs and blaming it on you,
If you can trust yourself when all men doubt
you,
    But make allowance for their doubting too;
                        Rudyard Kipling

Contents

    METHOD THAT DOES WORK   59

    Reality Therapy   59
    Performance Monitoring   61
    Active Listening   81
    Precautions   85
    Summary   86
    Appendix:
      4.A Using Performance Monitoring   87

5. OTHER METHODS FOR DEALING WITH THE
    PROBLEM EMPLOYEE   93

    Promote a Healthy Organization   93
    Policies and Procedures   96
    Wellness Programs   100
    Help Prevent Family Crises   101
    Educate Supervisors   104
    Support Supervisors   106
    Summary   108
    Appendix:
      5.A Corrective Action Report   110
      5.B Sample Drug Policy   111
      5.C "Managing the Problem Employee": A Training
           Workshop Outline   116

6. WHEN THE METHODS FAIL: GET OUTSIDE HELP   121

    The Ideal Employee Assistance Program   123
    Evaluating an Employee Assistance Program   132
    Establishing an Employee Assistance Program   135
    Utilizing an Employee Assistance Program   137
    Criticisms of Employee Assistance Programs   142
    Summary   144
    Appendix:
      6.A Directions for Issuing and Evaluating RFPs   145
      6.B Summary of Elements and Standards for EAP
           Programs in Federal Agencies   149
      6.C "Utilizing the EAP": A Training Workshop Outline 151

7. DON'T BECOME A PROBLEM TOO: HELP YOURSELF   157

    Understand Transition   158
    Help Yourself   162

Illustrations

Acknowledgments

To thank all of the people whose inspiration, assistance, and support encouraged and helped me through the preparation and completion of this book would require a list almost as long as the book itself. So I will not make the list. On that list, however, are a few special people who are named herein because of the significance of the contribution they made to this book.

First, my deepest appreciation must be expressed to Dr. J. Walton Blackburn, my spouse, my friend, my confidant, and my most synergistic colleague. His willingness to spend long hours discussing the issues of problem employee management during both the conception and the birth of this book have contributed immeasurably to its content. When I was dealing with my own problem employees he was my support. When I was discouraged he cheered me. When the manuscript was done he celebrated with me.

I also want to thank Dr. Christine Reed, my colleague who carefully read and edited the chapter that deals with legal issues. She is an expert in administrative law, and her knowledge and insights made an immeasurable contribution to the value of this book.

Others who clearly went above and beyond the call of duty in the contributions they made to this book are Neal Truitt, who read and edited the first six chapters, Nancy Krzycki, who prepared the manuscript in its final format, Kim Barnes, who helped me find appropriate films to recommend, and Barbara Frohlich, whose assistance in the final stages of manuscript preparation was invaluable.

Finally, I want to thank the many graduate students in my classes at the University of Nebraska at Omaha. Over 90 percent of them are full-time employed managers who know the importance of learning to deal with the problem employee. Their questions and their demands for more information were the impetus for the development of proactive strategies for problem employee management.

PROBLEM
EMPLOYEE
MANAGEMENT

Chapter 1

One Bad Apple

Have you ever had to deal with a problem employee—an employee whose behavior disrupted the work of your organization? If you have not, consider yourself lucky, but realize that the odds are that your time will come, and that the effects of problem employees can be devastating. This book will prepare you to deal with them. If you are currently trying to cope with a problem employee, read on. This book will teach you how.

It is currently estimated that, at any one time, from 10 percent to 20 percent of the work force are problem employees and that this same 10 to 20 percent can require as much as 80 percent of your time in trying to motivate and deal with them.[1] In this country alone, the costs to employers in lost time, reduced productivity, and spillover effects on other employees is now thought to be over 195 billion dollars per year.[2] Yet for the most part, a manager, when faced with a problem employee, is hard-pressed to know how to act. This book provides a guide on how to reduce both the numbers of problem employees in your work group and how to decrease the time required to manage them.

If you have worked in any organization for any length of time, you can probably attest to the existence of the problem employee. Yet an awareness of this problem has somehow not found its way into most of the books on managing employees, whether those employees are in the public or the private sector. Although it is generally accepted that on any street, in Anytown, USA, there lives a diverse, not equally successful, but equally healthy, equally productive group of people with equal standards and equal goals, this obvious phenomenon seems to have been left out of most of our books.

Rather, the implicit assumption prevailing in the "how-to-manage" books suggests that some mystical transformation takes place when recognizably different people enter employment. Walking through the door of an organization somehow seems to be considered a rite of passage by which obviously different people all become equally desirous and capable of maximum competent production. When the rite doesn't "take," it is usually assumed that the manager, or the organization, or a lack of training is at fault. The prescriptions then offered typically take the form of organizational or job redesign; or the application of "magic management" in some guise. The organization is thought to have a human relations or a communication problem. A consultant is frequently brought in to apply an eclectic bag of tricks to all members of the work unit.

This is not to say that the writers on how to manage do not recognize that the work place is composed of people with different personalities, backgrounds, experiences, values, and styles. Rather, it is to point out that not all employees in the work place will, or want to, apply themselves toward accomplishing the goals of the organization, or to ranking those goals first among their personal priorities. These workers, then, are the problem employees, and recognizing their existence is a crucial prerequisite to developing the skills necessary for dealing with them.

It seems that almost every manager has a story to tell about a problem employee. Unfortunately, none of the storytellers I have met had a happy ending to his or her story. One manager in a public agency bemoaned the employee who, he claims, was "like an old gun—she wouldn't work and I couldn't fire her." His solution was to assign the woman to sit on a stool in the hall all day. He hoped that the monotony and the embarrassment would prompt her to resign. They didn't.

While action such as this sounds extreme, the story is told as true. It is a graphic example of a manager who simply had no skills for dealing with a problem employee and so resorted to desperate measures.

There are simply a multitude of problems in the work place that are not amenable to solution by traditional management practices. One has only to look at the over 5,000 Employee Assistance Programs in the United States to realize that something is lacking in management practice.[3] I believe this lack is created because the theories we learn do not recognize the reality of employees whose behavior is creating problems in the work place, nor do they provide strategies for dealing with these problems. A basic task of management is to get employees to contribute to the accomplishment of organizational goals. Unfortunately, not all employees are ready to contribute.

Traditional books on human resource management presuppose a willingness on the part of the employee to contribute to the accomplishment of organizational goals. When they don't, the manager is frequently accused of "bad" management, or viewed as incompetent. Yet the fact remains that some employees do not contribute (or contribute minimally) no matter what a manager does. That this failure on the part of all employees to contribute to organizational goal accomplishment is a real problem for managers was identified as early as 1938 by Chester Barnard. His now-classic treatise, *The Functions of the Executive*, emphasized that an organization can operate efficiently and survive only when both the organization's goals and the aims and needs of the employees are kept in balance.[4] In the almost half-century since Barnard wrote, management theorists have yet to provide a means by which managers can successfully accomplish this "function" with employees whose personal goals are paramount for them.

During the past decade, there has been an increasing emphasis on the importance of learning how to deal with the problem employee.[5] Many organizations consider this a part of their ethical responsibility.[5] Others want to deal with these employees because the problems they create can adversely impact the job performance of fellow employees, including the manager.[6] Still others recognize that problem employees put an extra burden on managers who must learn to deal with them.[7]

Whatever the reason, the issue to be considered is that in spite of the formal planning, paper work, and emphasis on the proverbial bottom line, management still ends up being a relationship of people.

The chief executive has essentially the same employee difficulties as the line supervisor, and must be able to deal with these problems openly. Both executive and supervisor must interact on a daily basis with other human beings upon whom they must rely for the accomplishment of organizational objectives. The numbers of subordinates may differ, as may responsibilities and activities. No matter what level of the organization is involved, relationships between individuals are a critical part of everyday organizational life.

Traditionally, organizations did not even attempt to deal with the problem employee. Rather, the problem employee was laid off, transferred, or discharged. Gradually an attempt at helping emerged, and many organizations have moved to establish Employee Assistance Programs, which are usually coordinated by a human resource manager or a personnel officer and typically utilize the services of mental health professionals housed away from the job site. However, this book calls for a proactive approach, which will develop means of managing the problem employee through prevention and skillful management.

Articles on managing problem employees are appearing more frequently in our journals. A typical article cites numbers and costs, sympathizes with the manager who is trying to cope, provides a list of ways to recognize the problem employee, then a prescription of from three to ten steps to tell a manager what to do. These articles often end with a sales pitch for the establishment of an Employee Assistance Program. While these articles are frequently a consolation for the manager and the information they provide helpful, they are generally insufficient in the provision of practical help for day-to-day management of a problem employee. Their existence illustrates the current "crisis of usefulness" in organizational literature, a crisis created because "academicians do not address the practical needs of managers."[8] The book you hold in your hand is an attempt to remedy this crisis by providing a practical handbook for dealing with the problem employee.

Learning to deal with the problem employee has become a *must* in today's organization. If you're reading this book, you probably already know this; but do you know the following statistics about the cost of problem employees? I've already told you that the costs to employers in lost time, reduced productivity, and spillover effects on other employees is now estimated at over 195 billion dollars a year. What's really scary is that this figure does not include the costs of any rehabilitation program that may be instituted. Such costs were calculated to be an additional $3,000 per employee in 1975.[9] In 1990, one can estimate that this figure has almost doubled. A problem employee can be expected to earn only 75 percent of annual salary,[10] and problem behavior can foster escalating insurance costs, rising accident rates, and increasing litigation and grievance administration.[11]

In fact, one supervisor observed, "It would be interesting to actually 'clock' my problem employee. I'd bet she doesn't earn 50 percent of her salary some weeks!!" Thus, it seems incumbent upon you to know how to recognize, prevent, and intervene with the problem employee.

WHO IS THE PROBLEM EMPLOYEE?

As we begin this discussion of the problem employee, it is important that we all be operating from the same frame of reference. First, I want to define the term "problem employee" as it will be used in this book. The terms "problem employee" and "troubled employee" are often used synonymously. However, in this book, the term "problem employee" will be used to describe an employee whose behavior in the work place causes reduced productivity and lowered morale for self, co-workers, or supervisor. An employee can be troubled by personal problems as minor as a stubbed toe or as major as the death of a spouse; but unless those troubles spill over into the work place as behaviors that lessen effectiveness and detract from the achievement of organizational goals, that employee will not be considered a problem employee. Conversely, an employee whose behavior at work consistently detracts from organizational goal accomplishment, but has no known troubles, will also be viewed as a problem employee.

It is important here to acknowledge a situation that is unique to the public sector where goals may be ambiguous or in contention. In the public sector it is possible for employees to become what a manager may call a problem for all the right reasons. To understand this, think for a minute about the 1984 Environmental Protection Agency scandal in which the manager (Ann Burford) was called to task because employees recognized that her actions deviated from congressional intent with regard to environmental protection. In the private sector top management sets organizational goals. In the public sector, things are not so simple.

Both employees and managers in the public sector are affected by a volatile environment in which they are accountable, not only to their managerial superiors, but to the president, the Congress, the courts, interest groups and clientele, and citizens in general. In such an environment, where organizational goals must reflect public sentiment, both managers and employees are expected to act on behalf of the people and their representatives, rather than on some privately determined philosophy. Within this highly complex environment, public managers are delegated the task of ensuring that those goals, as determined for an agency, are met.

To define a problem employee as one whose behavior detracts from organizational goal accomplishment is to assume that the managers in the organization are actively working toward this goal accomplishment as well. In the private sector, managers are accountable to their own supervisor and, ultimately, to the stockholders for meeting organizational objectives. In the public sector they are accountable not only to their own manager, but also for ensuring that those goals determined for their agency by the public and its representatives are met. Supervisors and the majority of employees work toward achieving the goals on which there is consensus both within and without the organization. An employee who is thwarting these goals by performing at odds with organization purposes is a problem employee.

Focusing on observed behavior is crucial to both the development of understanding and the identification of possible interventions. So long as employee behaviors contribute positively to production (whether of service or products), neither you nor the employee has a problem. An employee's troubles are relevant only if they affect job performance.

CLUES THAT ALERT THE MANAGER TO PROBLEMS AHEAD

A number of indicators have been identified to alert the manager that a worker has troubles that will soon create a problem in the work place. These include:

1. Excessive, unexcused, or frequent absences
2. Tardiness and early departures
3. Altercations with fellow employees

4. Causing other employees injuries through negligence
5. Poor judgment and bad decisions
6. Unusual on-the-job accidents
7. Increased spoilage and breakage of equipment
8. Involvements with the law
9. Deteriorating personal appearance
10. Mood shifts[12]

This list is a list of symptoms. The more symptoms present, the more likely is the employee to become a problem in the work place. Almost everyone is absent sometimes, and, yes, people really do get sick on Monday or have an important errand that causes them to leave early on a Friday afternoon. But when numbers of absences begin to exceed the number of hours of approved leave available, the employee may be on the road to becoming a problem. In the same vein, most people lose their temper once in a while, and few of us are able to be 100 percent correct in all our judgments. Everyone has a bad day once in a while. I do. I expect you do. The key to this list of clues is to alert you that when they occur frequently or inexplicably a problem employee is in the making.

Other indicators of problem behavior have been identified in recent books. In *Coping with Difficult People*, Robert Bramson calls these indicators "patterns of difficult behavior."[13] The patterns reflect those behaviors that all of us who have had to deal with difficult people recognize. They are "Hostile-Aggressives, Complainers, Silent and Unresponsives, Super-Agreeables, Negativists, Know-It-All Experts, and Indecisives." Another writer, Delaney, describes similar behaviors, calling them "attitude problems" and confessing to a "100 percent failure rate" in dealing with them.[14] Masi blames substance abuse, particularly alcohol abuse, for all problem employee behaviors and believes that chronic absenteeism and tardiness are, in fact, symptoms of a substance abuser.[15]

I prefer to provide you with clues to help you recognize problem employees by describing their behaviors as "Response Patterns." I first identified these response patterns when I was a social worker assigned to counsel problem employees. Later, as a manager, I acquired my very own problem employees. When that happened, I felt as helpless as you probably do right now. Finally, I turned my attention to figuring out what I, as a manager, could do to deal with these employees. I devoted several years of research to the subject. It seemed that every manager with whom I talked had at least one problem employee, and could tell stories about others. I read cases that had come up as appeals before the federal government's Merit Systems Protection Board and I saw these same response patterns—patterns that had left managers helpless. In most cases these responses were not related to substance abuse. Then I began to focus on what could be done to manage the problem employee. What I learned I considered worth sharing, and I developed workshops that I have presented to various groups of human resource managers. In this book I present the information to you.

PROBLEM EMPLOYEE RESPONSE PATTERNS

Whether you are a manager of a few or many employees, the classic problem employee response patterns can literally drive you up the wall. They occur in both the private and the public sectors. None of us is immune. If you have had to deal with a problem employee you will instantly know what I mean. You may be reassured to know that such people come into all of our lives—that you are not to blame. If you have so far been spared an encounter with these response patterns, I tip my hat. You've been lucky! These response patterns are those that cause managers to wring their hands, tear out their hair, and literally want to write the employees off as "impossible." However, these response patterns can be dealt with successfully.

First, let's think about some of them.

"It's Not My Fault"

Some employees make mistake after mistake, but always manage to find some excuse or someone else to blame for the mistake. The excuse is usually that you or a co-worker is to blame. An example that perfectly illustrates this type of employee is the recruiter who was required to enlist 100 new people every three months. At the end of ten weeks, he had recruited one person, although his co-workers had exceeded the goal of 100. During this ten-week period he had weekly conferences with his supervisor but rejected every suggestion made. He managed to alienate several agency officials, failed to keep appointments, and refused to take phone calls. His explanation for his failure was to blame his co-workers and supervisors. He said he had been "set up" to fail and used as his "proof" that a co-worker had said "good luck" to him as he left one day. He also said that people in his recruitment area had said "bad" things about him and that his co-workers used racial slurs when talking with him. When asked to be specific about the racial slurs, he pointed to a co-worker who had joked about spooks on Halloween.

"I Don't Have to Punch a Time Clock"

Jobs that lend themselves to the "I don't have to punch a time clock" response are found in both the private and public sector. Some employees get the mistaken idea that they have the right to set their own job performance standards *and* their own hours. It goes without saying that these standards are lower than yours and the hours they set less than a forty-hour week. These responses fit very well for problem social workers and salesmen, especially when they are on salary and not commission. Anyone whose job requires time spent outside the office and beyond your line of vision can exhibit this type of response.

Jason was a social worker who was also a preacher for a small church. He received a base salary and was reimbursed for mileage expense in his assigned territory. He was rarely in the office, claiming that his clients required extra "care and feeding." A routine check of mileage charges revealed that he had, on numerous occasions, charged over 300 miles for 50-mile trips. About the same time, a newspaper article reported him conducting a revival at a time he was ostensibly visiting clients. When confronted with the mileage audit and newspaper evidence, his response was that he was a professional, and that so long as he did his job, he didn't have to "punch a time clock." He saw the freedom of his position as God's way of assisting him to preach.

"Let Me Alone"

Employees who don't want to be bothered with supervisory contact are usually on the way to becoming problem employees. Donna was such a person. She had worked as an accountant for the past four years when she started making expensive mistakes. She began refusing to talk with her co-workers. She ignored appointments for supervisory conferences. If she was in a room and others entered, she left abruptly. Her supervisor did not know what she was working on yet frequently had to respond to complaints about her. When her supervisor approached, she left her desk and went into the rest room. Finally, her supervisor followed her into the rest room and said, "We've got to talk." At this, Donna burst into tears, shouted "You don't care about me, let me alone," and raced from the room, slamming the door.

"I'm Not Crazy, You Are"

Some employees exhibit behavior that is so odd, bizarre, grotesque, and/or eccentric that it greatly detracts from organizational goal accomplishment. Henry is a good example of this. Although he shared an office, he kept the door locked and wouldn't admit his office mate. Since the office mate had a key, she unlocked the door and went in. He refused to speak. Thinking she had offended him in some way, the next day she brought him a plate of homemade cookies. He accused her of trying to poison him. Her nervous response was to laugh and say:

"Are you crazy?"

"I'm not crazy, you are."

Still another example of "crazy" behavior was demonstrated by Mary, a typist in an office secretarial pool. During the summer months a large fan was used to supplement the office air conditioning. One day, with no apparent provocation, Mary jumped up from her desk, grabbed a pair of scissors, cut the fan cord, and ran screaming from the room. No work was accomplished that day as co-workers sat and compared "crazy" behavior stories about Mary.

"You Can't Tell Me What To Do"

Some employees attempt to control their supervisor with intimidation. When questioned, the employee often becomes verbally or physically abusive and usually leaves the supervisor speechless, if not helpless. These employees frequently perceive themselves as "experts" who do not need to follow some agency requirement or supervisory direction. Lewis was an "expert" counselor in a local public agency that received funding from a federal grant. In order to regularly draw down the funding, the agency was required to submit a monthly bill prepared from data submitted by each counselor. The bill was due in Washington on the tenth of each month and prepared at the agency level on the fifth.

Lewis decided that he had more important things to do than compile data. In vain the supervisor tried to explain the reasons for the data requirement and the necessity of prompt billing. Finally, five days after the due date, about 4:30 in the afternoon, Lewis arrived in his supervisor's office. Shouting an obscenity, he threw the reports in her face.

Steve was another employee who refused to be told what to do. Because he did not agree with a decision his supervisor made, he prepared and distributed a flyer criticizing his supervisor. When he was suspended for this, he filed a grievance. During the grievance procedure, he shouted that he despised the supervisor and called him a "pompous ass" and a "baby." Then Steve grabbed the supervisor's files and threw them at him; next he took the supervisor's keys and threw them in a wastebasket; then he ended the performance by grabbing a pencil from behind his supervisor's ear and throwing it across the room.

"Who do you think you are? You can't tell me what to do!" he shouted.

"Quit Laughing!"

While one might argue that being able to smile is not a requisite for productive behavior, any manager who has tried to deal with an employee for whom life is too serious for laughter can attest to this employee's ability to detract from organizational effectiveness. Michael was such an employee. Not only did he not smile or joke, he took others' joking seriously. During staff meetings in his organization, it was the custom for employees to take turns keeping the minutes. After two women had taken notes, it was his turn. One of the women joked, "We are an equal opportunity employer." He interpreted this as a slur. Later, someone joked about his coming to work early every day. He believed this was a sign his fellow employees didn't like him. He dealt with joking by withdrawing, until the day he submitted his resignation. The reason he gave was that he was constantly subjected to insults.

"My Personal Life Is My Own Business"

Indeed an employee's personal life is his or her own business *until* it spills over into the work place as it did with Pete and Karen. Their supervisor became aware of their personal relationship when Pete, a forklift operator, struck Karen in the stomach and then shoved her into one of the storage bins. As she lay screaming, other employees rushed to her aid, took sides, and a fight ensued. When the supervisor finally got the fighting stopped, he learned that Pete was the father of Karen's child, but that she had broken off their relationship and started seeing someone else. When he instituted disciplinary action for the fighting, he was told by both Pete and Karen that he had no business meddling in their personal lives.

"I'll Decide What My Job Tasks Are"

The employee who arbitrarily decides which of his or her job responsibilities he or she will perform and which he or she will not can disrupt an entire organization and subvert its purposes. Patrick was a mail carrier who literally sabotaged the delivery of mail. For whatever reason, he arbitrarily decided that third class mail was not worth the time and effort it took to deliver. Instead, he disposed of it by hiding it under a U-Haul trailer next to a trash dumpster in the parking lot of an apartment complex. His behavior was discovered and reported when the trailer was moved. When confronted he denied the action. He then filed a grievance because of the resultant disciplinary action of his supervisor.

Mark was another employee who decided his own responsibilities. He was a service coordinator for a hospital, and as such was entrusted with keys to the hospital pool, which, policy dictated, was reserved for patients receiving prescribed physical therapy. Mark decided that the "for patient only" rule was one that should not have been made, so he admitted his friends. When the friends were caught using the pool, Mark was called in to explain. At that point, he claimed he thought they were patients and produced forged prescriptions authorizing their pool use.

While not all of these responses will occur in every organization, and while every problem employee response will be uniquely different, these response patterns do provide clues to alert you to a potential problem situation. You've, of course, heard the folk wisdom that "one bad apple can spoil the whole barrel." It's been my experience that in the case of problem employees this expression is also true. Finding the bad apple can save the barrelful. Identifying the problem employee and dealing with that employee can save your organization.

PROBLEM EMPLOYEE MANAGEMENT PREVIEWED

You have just been introduced to the problem employee, that worker with whom, at one time or another, we are all confronted. The rest of this book will provide you with the means of dealing with those you will encounter.

In chapter 2, "Why Problems Develop," a theoretical explanation of the causes of problem behavior in the work place is provided. This chapter offers the premise that the recruitment and hiring process generally acquires persons capable of performing their jobs, but that a life or work crisis will precipitate problem behavior, including substance abuse. Ways of minimizing work-related crises are discussed.

In chapter 3, "Traditional Remedies and Why They Fail," traditional methods of dealing with the problem employee are discussed along with explanations of why they typically do not improve performance. This chapter will assure you that most managers make the same mistakes and offers reasons for these mistakes.

In chapter 4, "Performance Monitoring: An Interpersonal Method That Does Work," a successful method for dealing with the problem employee is offered. This method is based on a counseling psychology model that is easily learned and provides a means for manager and employee to share joint responsibilty for improving performance and changing behavior.

In chapter 5, "Other Methods for Dealing with the Problem Employee," other effective methods will be explained. These include developing a healthy organization, policies and procedures for dealing with the problem employee in general and substance abusers in particular, wellness programs, family crises prevention programs, and supervisory education and support systems.

In chapter 6, "When the Methods Fail: Get Outside Help," the utilization or the establishment of an Employee Assistance Program is recommended as a means of seeking professional help for the problem employee when your own efforts fail, or when you realize that the employee is deeply troubled or a substance abuser. Chapter 6 provides a step-by-step procedure for both establishing an Employee Assistance Program and utilizing an existing one.

In chapter 7, "Don't Become a Problem Too: Help Yourself," you are reassured that while dealing with a problem employee is never easy, you can survive the experience. This chapter presents the experiences of other managers in learning to survive a problem employee and provides you with a technique for helping yourself.

In chapter 8, "Legal Issues in Problem Employee Management," the legal rights of the employee, the supervisor, and the organization are explained. This chapter also presents relevant court decisions and instructs you on how to work within the law for the protection of yourself, the employee, and the organization.

NOTES

1. John Hall and Ben Fletcher, "Coping with Personal Problems at Work," *Personnel Management* 16, no. 2 (February 1984), 30–33; and Philip Schneider, "There Is a Better Way to Help Troubled Employees," *Office* 89, no. 5 (May 1979), 46, 50, 146.

2. Hall and Fletcher, "EAP Potential to Save Money Unknown," *Business Insurance* 17, no. 35 (29 August 1983), 14.

3. Ibid.

4. Chester Barnard, *The Functions of the Executive* (Cambridge, Mass.: Harvard University Press, 1938 and 1968).

5. Robert Hollman, "Managing Troubled Employees: Meeting the Challenge," *Journal of Contemporary Business* 8, no. 4 (October 1979), 43–57.

6. Peter Cairo, "Counseling in Industry: A Selected Review of the Literature," *Personnel Psychology* 36, no. 1, (Spring 1983), 1–18.

7. W. Randolph Flynn and William E. Stratton, "Managing Problem Employees," *Human Resource Management*, 20, no. 2 (Summer 1981), 28–32.

8. Stephen Strasser and Thomas Bateman, "What We Should Study, Problems We Should Solve," *Personnel Psychology* 37, no. 1 (Spring 1984), 77–92.

9. Robert F. Reardon, "Tackling the Problem of Problem Employees," *New Englander*, 22, no. 8 (December 1975), 50–52.

10. See Philip V. Schneider, "There Is a Better Way to Help Troubled Employees," *Office* 89, no. 5 (May 1979), 46, 50, 146.

11. William Kandel, "Alcoholism and Employment Law," *Employee Relations Law Journal* 9, no. 3 (Winter 1983/84), 500–503.

12. The first ten items in this list were identified by Christine Filipowicz, "The Troubled Employee: Whose Responsibility," *Personnel Administrator* 24, no. 6 (June 1979), 17–22, 33. See also Hollman, "Managing Troubled Employees," added "mood shifts."

13. See Robert Bramson, *Coping with Difficult People* (Garden City, N.Y.: Anchor Press/Doubleday, 1981).

14. See William Delaney, *Thirty Most Common Problems in Management and How to Solve Them* (New York: AMACOM, 1982).

15. See Dale Masi, *Human Services in Industry* (Lexington, Mass.: Lexington Books, D.C. Heath, 1982).

Chapter 2

Why Problems Develop

The purpose of this chapter is to enable you to understand why seemingly capable people, carefully selected by a screening process that has proven adequate again and again, become problems in the work force. As you begin to understand why problems develop, you will be able to acquire the skills you need to prevent problem behavior when possible and to manage problem behavior when it occurs. You will also learn what causes those situations over which you have no control.

Understanding why problems develop will help you prevent many of them. Far too often an employee becomes a problem employee because of a work-related crisis. Work-related crises can occur because of inadequate or inappropriate training, an organization that is dysfunctional, or a supervisor who is insecure and ill-equipped to deal with his or her subordinates. Sometimes employees become problems because of job dissatisfaction and sometimes they become problems because their personality type simply doesn't fit with their superiors or co-workers. Most work-related crises are preventable.

When an employee experiences a family crisis, becomes ill, or abuses alcohol or drugs, that employee is likely to become a problem employee. Still other problems develop because an employee gives up, doesn't "give a damn," or gets caught up in office politics. You cannot prevent these problems and you cannot change the cause of these types of problems. You can, however, learn to change the impact of these problems on you and on your organization.

You hope that you never hire a problem employee. Rather, you choose new employees after thorough consideration. You try to select the best, leaving the problems for someone else in some other organization. When you hire an employee, you carefully screen the many forms and resumes that have been submitted as applications for the one vacancy you are trying to fill. One author has identified eight steps in the employee selection process: job specifications, applications, tests, interviews, reference checks, physical examinations, employment decisions, and finally, offer of employment.[1] At each of these steps, if the information you obtain raises any cautionary questions, you can and do stop the selection process for that person. One of the purposes of the elaborate selection processes in place in most organizations today is to screen out problem employees.

The reality is, however, that the selection process usually screens out only those who are not capable of performing the job. The "Uniform Guidelines" on employee hiring emphasize that valid selection procedures must relate to job performance, and Title VII of the Civil Rights Act offers a framework of lawful questions that can be asked in a job interview.[2] This framework permits only performance-related questions and does not allow for inquiries about how one handles frustrations or family problems, how one responds to supervisory direction, or how one relates to co-workers.

The basic rule of thumb for conducting a pre-employment interview is that no questions may be asked that directly or indirectly result in limitation of job opportunity in any way. Thus, in protecting the job applicant against discrimination, federal laws literally tie the hands of the employer who hopes to screen potential problems from the work force.

There are, of course, many strengths in the personnel selection process; but it is not the purpose of this book to discuss them. Rather, the emphasis here is on managing the problem employee—those persons whose knowledge, skills, and abilities are sufficient for the hiring process, but who, after some time on the job, become inadequate performers. We all know that this happens, and you wouldn't be reading this book if you didn't want to know what to do about it.

Certainly, managing problem employees is a challenge for a number of reasons. Hollman has identified the following:

1. Management practices are based on the assumption that the employee is both mentally and physically fit to perform the job, therefore traditional management practices may not work with the problem employee
2. In a recent survey of members of the American Society for Personnel Administration, 90 percent of the respondents rate their current methods of dealing with problem employees as only "fair"
3. Managing problem employees requires resolution of some difficult philosophical and economic issues
4. An organization cannot rely on its selection process to weed out problem employees
5. The organization itself may be a contributing cause of the employee's behavior[3]

Other challenges to the manager presented by problem employees include learning to deal with their disruptive behavior and the costs incurred by the organization as a result of this disruptive behavior.[4]

The basic philosophy of this chapter is that "prevention is the better part of cure." With that in mind, let's examine the reasons employees become problems so that you can rise to the challenge of preventing these problems from occurring.

PERSONS AND EVENTS IN THE WORK PLACE

In this section I will help you understand why problems develop in the work place by describing situations and conditions that can precipitate a work crisis. I will also explain how personality can impact performance. As I explain how each problem can develop, I will give you tips for preventing that problem.

Frustration

A common thread running through all problem behavior in the work place is frustration.[5] The cause of frustration may occur at home. It may occur at work. Perfectly capable employees, when confronted with a frustrating situation, will frequently let their emotional response to frustration override their ability to perform. They will react to frustration with behaviors that hurt their performance, reduce organizational goal accomplishment, and, literally, drive you and their supervisor to distraction. Let's think a minute about why.

When people are frustrated, or hurt, or angry, they develop defense mechanisms to protect themselves. What they don't often do is realize that these same defense mechanisms may result in behaviors that a manager will define as "problem." In fact, defense mechanisms that detract from work performance have been characterized as "frustration-instigated behaviors."[6] These behaviors include: aggression, rationalization, fixation, repression, regression, and avoidance. These actions are also referred to as "deviant behaviors."[7]

Aggression can manifest itself in fighting, belligerence, and temper tantrums. People who behave aggressively usually perceive themselves as having to fight to survive. They attack before they are attacked. Sometimes a supervisor bares the brunt of the attack, sometimes other workers suffer. In either event, the adrenalin surge required to fight or defend will leave everyone involved in the encounter both emotionally and physically drained. When this happens, ability to perform is diminished. Supervisors, as well as employees, can express frustration with aggression. Recently, an employee told me about a supervisor who threw a typewriter at her because she hadn't completed an assignment on time.

Repression is the opposite of aggression. Instead of fighting, repressed people will force painful events into their subconscious. Here they do not have to deal with the hurt. What happens, however, is that as repressed memories seek to surface, they can manifest themselves in physiological ways such as severe headaches, general malaise, or aches and pains. These psysiological manifestations can give a person an excuse for not performing and have the added benefit of soliciting sympathy rather than discipline from a supervisor.

Many people are skilled rationalizers. No matter what happens, it's always "your" fault, not "mine." Rationalizers defend themselves with elaborate excuses designed to elicit your sympathy, not your discipline. One supervisor told me about a worker we'll call Mark. Mark was chronically late for work. His first excuse was a broken alarm clock. His second was that he did not hear the ring of his new alarm. The supervisor, in a rush of sympathy, offered to call him every morning at 6:00 A.M. to help him wake up. He still arrived later and later for work, until three days in a row he appeared at 2:00 P.M. His excuse was that the supervisor had called him so early that he had gone back to sleep!

Fixation occurs when people get so devastated by a single event in their past that they become obsessed with the event and its results and fail to see that situations and persons change. Henry was such an employee. Ten years ago, he had been passed over for a promotion. He became so obsessed with his hurt that his performance deteriorated, he constantly told new workers and customers about the incompetence of management, and filed frequent complaints about his supervisor's treatment of him and others.

Regression occurs when a frustrated person deals with that frustration by retreating to earlier, often childlike behaviors as a means of coping. This person may cry or throw temper tantrums. He or she will retreat from responsibility and expect many favors and special considerations.

Avoidance behaviors occur when a person withdraws from contact with you and fellow employees. People who are avoiding will fail to attend staff meetings, sit alone at coffee breaks, and often "forget" appointments.

No matter how we label problem behaviors, however, the bottom line is that they are disruptive and take up time that you, as a manager, would rather spend in other pursuits. That's why it's so important for you to understand what causes frustration-instigated behavior. Once you understand its causes, you can take steps to minimize the frustration created by you or by your organization.

Now, if you and I were psychologists, we would want to delve into the employee's subconscious, place a medical label on the employee's behavior, and seek to psychoanalyze or to understand why one employee responds to frustration in a negative way and another manages to cope effectively. We are, however, managers; and our concern must be with the work place and the successful accomplishment of organizational goals. Thus we need to understand what causes problem behavior only to the extent that those causes occur in the work setting, a setting over which we have some measure of control.

Supervisory Actions

A number of writers have demonstrated that problem behavior in the work place is job or organization related and that employees often have rational and sound motivation for poor performance.[8] Your role must be to ensure that neither your behavior nor that of supervisors is the cause of a problem employee. While "preventing problem employees" is probably not a part of your official position description, the efforts you make in this direction are truly an investment in ensuring that you are able to effectively perform your identified responsibilities. Let's talk about actions taken by supervisors that either created or worsened problem behavior.

One of the quickest ways to produce frustration-instigated behavior in your employees is to change your rules, change the way you treat them, or violate their expectations of you or your organization. It has been found that if the manager, as the employee's representative of the organization, abruptly changes the work structure, job definition, or breadth of discretion, the employee will react with problem behavior. Such management action threatens the employee's sense of self, and thereby undermines dignity and identity.[9]

When this happens, the employee will try to cope in some way. Coping activities may take the form of either "adaptive" or "deviant" behavior. Adaptive behavior will not be a problem for you. Deviant behavior will. Deviant behavior occurs "when people use illegitimate means, or methods, not sanctioned by the organization, to accomplish *their* goals."[10] Deviant behavior is behavior which, from your and my perspective, reduces the ability of the organization to provide the level of goods or services necessary. Figure 2.1 shows the continua of deviant/adaptive behaviors, behaviors that can alert you that something has happened to create dissatisfaction for your employee.

When employees experience conflicting expectations between themselves and you, they will demonstrate coping mechanisms. These mechanisms will be vis-a-vis you, the job, themselves, or their careers. They occur as a survival technique in a dissatisfied employee. They may manifest themselves in a way that you will consider a problem, such as poor performance, or absenteeism, or tardiness. They may be behaviors that do not affect job performance but lead the way for an employee to leave the organization. The point here is that when conflicting expectations

Figure 2.1
Continua of Deviant/Adaptive Behaviors

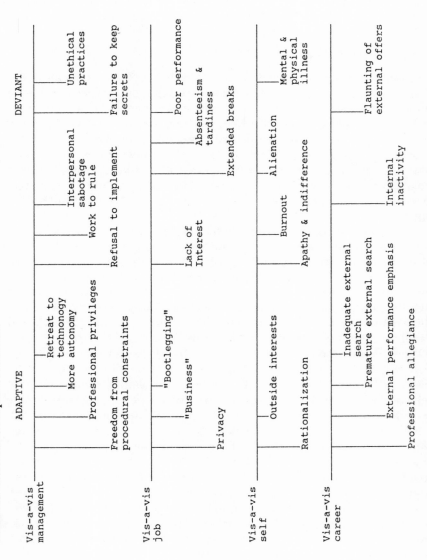

Source: Reprinted with permission from J. Raelin, "An Examination of Deviant/Adaptive Behaviors in the Careers of Professionals," *Academy of Management Review* 9, no. 3 (July 1984), 422.

do occur, an employee will take some action to deal with the situation. If you do not want to risk that the action will be deviant, don't abruptly change the rules or your methods for relating to the employee.

One way to prevent an abrupt change in employee expectations is to carefully train personnel recruiters and those who conduct new employee orientation to minimize employee expectations of the company and the job. A tendency of personnel recruitment is often to sugarcoat terms and conditions of employment. Research has indicated, however, that sugarcoating can have dysfunctional consequences. People who join the organization may not fit it as it actually is, and/or they may have such unrealistic expectations that they soon become dissatisfied and leave, or become problem employees.[11]

Another way to prevent these types of problems is to not give false hopes of promotion. I have known a number of people (and you probably have too) who were exemplary employees *until* their immediate supervisor left and they were assigned as "acting" supervisor or director. When that same employee applied for the position, and did not get it on a permanent basis, the employee demonstrated *every* deviant behavior in the continua. (See Figure 2.1.)

I particularly remember Marcella. She had been the assistant director of a federal government office for several years when the director resigned. Marcella was asked to serve as interim director and, as a part of the agency's Affirmative Action program, Marcella was encouraged to apply for the director's position. She did. So did fifty others. During the six months it took to fill the vacant position, Marcella ran the department, and ran it well. When Max was hired as director, she was devastated and her reaction soon became deviant behavior.

Vis-a-vis management, she conducted interpersonal sabotage in three ways: She failed to follow instructions, then claimed that Max had been unclear and ambiguous. She instituted secret meetings with his superior, Naomi, and reported imagined incidents of discrimination, incompetence, and inefficiency. She also began to spread uncomplimentary lies about Max to other members of the department. Soon factions formed and productivity went to near zero.

Vis-a-vis her job, Marcella's performance became minimal. She was frequently late for work and vanished for long periods during the day. When Max talked with her about it she claimed he was insensitive. As though to prove it, on a day when she was really sick, she came to work on time and fainted in his office door. Emergency medical personnel revived her. As they carried her to the ambulance, she screamed, "Don't take me to the hospital. If I'm not at work, I'll get fired."

Vis-a-vis herself, Marcella first became indifferent and apathetic toward her job, then began to report real and imagined illnesses. She became so paranoid that she erected a six-foot chain link fence topped with barbed wire around her home and bought a vicious guard dog. Within three months she became pregnant. Within six months she had a miscarriage, which she blamed on poor Max.

Vis-a-vis her career, Marcella immediately began a job search. After eleven months, she resigned for a position with much less responsibility and a greatly reduced salary.

While Marcella's reaction to her shattered expectations was extreme, it really did happen. She became a problem employee because she was confronted with a job crisis precipitated by a human resource manager giving her false hopes. Don't do that to any of your employees.

COMMUNICATION

"The problems around here are caused by poor communication," is a frequently heard lament. And even as you nod your head in agreement, you often do not stop to think about what is actually involved in successful communication. You may not even be aware of how frequently you must communicate in any given day. This amount of time may be as high as 80 percent or as low as 50 percent.[12] Communication skills may be the most important skills that any manager can possess. Yet we often use a "telephone model" of communication in which directions are transmitted unilaterally, without taking into consideration all the things that can facilitate or impede the process.

The word *communicate* comes from a Latin word meaning "to share," and that's what communication is all about—sharing. It's a sharing of ideas and feelings, as well as a sharing of information, and it is a two-way process.

It is generally agreed that for a message to be received and understood, several ingredients are required. First, the message must be delivered in such a way that the person receiving the message clearly understands it. Second, when you send a message you must allow the person receiving it to give you feedback so that you will know that person did indeed understand what you meant. An employee who does not understand what is expected cannot do what is expected.

As the sender of the message, you have the responsibility to deliver your message in such a way that your receiver understands it. To do this, it is important that you understand the different types of communication styles and learn to use them for your benefit.

Communication Styles

There are a variety of communication theories, but all seem to agree that people remember 25 percent of what they hear, 45 percent of what they see and hear, and 70 percent of what they see, hear, and do.[13]

Although individuals are *always* taking in sensory data at *all* times from the five basic senses, only three are typically *utilized* to retain data and to access it: visual, auditory, and kinesthetic (both visceral touch and affective emotions). . . .

The predominant or preferred mode of representing reality is one's primary "representational system." . . . Effective communication occurs when people communicate in the same representational system. Conflict occurs on one level or another when that rapport doesn't exist; they are, in essence, speaking in different languages.[14]

Understanding the three distinct communication preferences (visual, auditory, and kinesthetic) will help you to adapt the way you send messages so as to maximize the receiver's chances of understanding what you want. It will, in essence, enable you to speak the same language.

People who are visual communicators like to see what you are saying. They need to receive your message in writing. They'll read memos and bulletin boards. If they are at a formal presentation, they will understand it better if visual aids such as flow charts and drawings are used by the communicator. They like to have written summaries of meetings, even though they frequently take copious notes.

People who are auditory communicators are the talkers and the listeners. They rarely read written communication, and even when they do, they are not comfortable until you talk about the subject with them. They need to ask questions and receive explanations. They may even ask you to explain a memorandum you have just written. They probably won't read announcements and memos, so be sure to talk with them about what you want.

Kinesthetic communicators understand better when they are able to handle and examine items and have the opportunity to practice new skills. They learn by doing, not by reading or listening. They need the freedom to move around a lot, and are more likely to understand what you say if you talk with them while walking. They may be disruptive in staff meetings because of their need to get up and move around. They may be perceived as problem employees simply because they cannot sit still for extended periods of time.

Let me illustrate these communication differences by telling you a story about how three different employees learned to use a new word processing program.

Joel is a visual communicator. When I met with him to explain how to use the program, he became frustrated and angry. "Just give me the instruction manual," he said. "I can't make any sense out of your directions."

Bev is auditory. When I handed her a copy of the user's manual she tossed it on the table. "I can't read this thing," she said. "just tell me what to do and I'll do it."

Joanne is kinesthetic. She neither looked at the manual nor listened. I had to sit with her at the computer terminal and show her what to do, then give her time to "play around" and figure the system out for herself.

If an employee's primary representational system is out of sync with the job he or she is expected to perform, that employee can be perceived by you as a "problem." You'll see why as I tell you about Betsy and Peg.

Betsy was the receptionist in an organization to which I had been called as a consultant by the manager. Betsy's job consisted of answering between fifty and seventy phone calls a day and dealing with customers who came into the office. To prove the amount of work she did, Betsy kept a careful phone and visitors log. Peg was the accountant in that same organization. She had a private office and was assigned to work alone.

"Betsy and Peg have become real problems," the manager told me. "Betsy spends a lot of time crying. She is rude to callers and walk-in customers, and she refuses to talk with the other staff. Peg, on the other hand, talks all the time. I can't seem to keep her in her office long enough to do her work. She wants to spend the day visiting."

When I talked with Betsy, she regaled me with complaints about her co-workers and the manager as she showed me her carefully written record of all the calls and clients she received. Tears rolled down her cheeks as she told me how tired she was of, what she called, "interruptions."

When I talked with Peg she told me that she was "literally stir-crazy" and that she couldn't stand "being cooped up in that office all day."

I began to think that the reason both of these employees had become problems was because their jobs required different representational systems than they possessed. Betsy's carefully kept record and complaints about "interruptions" cued me that she was a visual communicator, a person who was not comfortable with interpersonal interaction. Peg's inability to sit at her desk and work with figures without talking indicated that she needed auditory stimulation.

I checked my perceptions with them by asking each one to fantasize for a minute and then to tell me what her ideal job would be.

Betsy was quick to respond. "I'd like to work by myself in a quiet place. I'm a good bookkeeper and I'd like to work with the accounts. I like to see what I've accomplished."

Peg's ideal job was to deal with the clients. She was very critical of Betsy's inability to cope and couldn't understand why Betsy viewed the customers as interruptions. "They're the reason we're here," she said.

My recommendation to the manager was to have Betsy and Peg switch jobs. When I checked back about six months later, I found two happy productive employees.

"They think you're wonderful," the manager told me.

Yet all I had done was to identify each employee's communication style and recommend that they be placed in jobs that utilize them. All communication styles are fine. The key is to figure out an employee's strength and play to it.

Of course some people have a balance of all three types of communication skills. I think they're the lucky ones. They can adapt readily to any communication encounter. I also think that once you understand the three communication styles you can adapt to any of them when appropriate.

Using Your Communication Strengths

Your own communication style is your personal strength. Understanding the style of those with whom you work is an even greater communication strength. You will heighten your ability to manage when you reach out to others in *their* style, rather than your own. You can often eliminate problem employees simply by becoming alert to the clues they provide you.

Visual people usually have an uncluttered working environment. When trying to remember something, they may close their eyes and try to picture it. They are the ones who will ask you for your comments in writing and are likely to say such things as, "I *see* what you mean."

Auditory communicators like to discuss work projects. They literally think out loud. They are sensitive to other sounds and easily distracted by noise. They probably won't read your memos, but they love to sit down and talk about what you want and what they are doing. They are likely to say such things as, "*Listen* to this," or "That *sounds* like a great idea."

Kinesthetic people respond to a pat on the back and a handshake. They are bothered by long periods of having to sit still and may fidget, chew on their pencil, "play" with paper clips, or doodle. They may not listen as closely as you'd like and may jump into a project before they fully understand it. They are likely to say such things as, "I've got a *handle* on the problem," or "It *feels* OK to me."[15]

As you develop an awareness of the communication styles of others, you will enhance your own communication strengths. Once people understand what you're trying to say they are more likely to listen to the reasons you have for making requests. They are less likely to become problem employees.

Zone of Indifference

When a person comes to work for you, there is a kind of unwritten contract that carries the expectation that the employee will devote himself or herself to the accomplishment of organizational goals. This means that, within reason, you can expect that people will respond affirmatively to supervisory requests and direction. For an employee to do as requested, however, the request must fall within his or her "zone of indifference," which has been explained as follows:

If all the orders for actions reasonably practicable be arranged in order of their acceptability to the person affected, it may be conceived that there are a number which are clearly unacceptable, that is, which certainly will not be obeyed; there is another group somewhat more or less on the neutral line, that is barely acceptable or barely unacceptable; and a third group unquestionably acceptable. This last group lies within the "zone of indifference."[16]

In the zone of indifference an employee will comply with requests without questioning. The conditions that create this zone are:

1. The employee can and does understand what is requested
2. At the time of making the decision to do what is requested, the employee believes that the request is in the best interest of the organization
3. At the time of making the decision to do what is requested, the employee believes that such action will be in his or her own best interest
4. The employee is physically and mentally able to comply with the request

This zone can be expanded with education and persuasion through which the employee is helped to understand that a supervisory request falls within the zone. A supervisor who simply issues a directive and expects an employee to act "because I say so," may, in fact, label an employee "problem" because the orders are not within the employee's zone of indifference and the supervisor makes no effort to put them there.[17]

Barriers to Communication

Now that you understand *how* to effectively communicate, you also need to know about the kinds of obstacles that can get in the way of effective communication. These barriers can be divided into three categories: personal factors, organizational structure factors, and attributes of the communication episode.[18]

Personal factors include communication style. They also include such issues as age, race, sex, emotional state, and the degree to which trust exists in the communication event. People who are angry or worried will not as quickly understand what you mean as you might expect. And, if they don't trust you, they won't believe you. One study found that women talk differently to their peers and their supervisors than men do.[19] While the French might shout, "Vive la différence," these differences in the work place can lead to communication breakdowns.

Attributes of the communication episode refers to those physical conditions that are present at the time you are trying to communicate. Such things as noise, excessive heat, time constraints, and complexity of information also make successful communication difficult. You can minimize noise and heat by shutting doors and adjusting thermostats. You also need to be so conscious of the effect of time constraints that you never communicate important information at the end of a day, nor at the end of a meeting, nor when a crucial deadline looms.[20]

Organizational structure factors relate to status differences and the levels of the organization through which communication must travel. As a human resource manager you may unconsciously intimidate employees at lower levels in the organization. Your status in relation to your employees can also impact your communication with them.[21] In a large organization, all employees will not have the same amount of information. The information they do have may have become misinformation as it traveled through organizational levels.

Do you remember the childhood game of "Gossip?" One person whispers a message to a partner, who in turn whispers the news to another, and so on. By the time ten or more people have heard the message, it rarely resembles the initial point at all. This happens in organizations too. The larger your organization, the more likely communiques from you will be garbled in transmittal. Be aware of this. You can take steps to guard against such misinterpretation by always putting important things in writing and/or using a newsletter.

Believe it or not, the very characteristics of the organization in which you work may create barriers to communication that result in problem behavior by employees. Employees often have rational and sound motivational reasons for poor performance as organizations fail to reward and thus, inadvertently, punish productive behavior. The properties of formal organizations, with their bureaucratic structure, chain of command, division of labor, and technological advances and this frequent failure to reward on the basis of merit "often inadvertently condition employee failure."[22] Information provided in chapter 5 will help you establish organizational characteristics that enable you to facilitate employee success.

ORGANIZATIONAL CULTURE

An organization's culture, that is, the shared understandings, sayings, doings, and feelings, may influence the behavior of its members.[23]

A recent book by Kets de Vries and Miller concludes that organizational culture, like people, can become neurotic.[24] When organizations become neurotic, the employees in them are likely to respond with frustration-instigated behavior. Kets de Vries and Miller believe that neurotic organizations will fall into one of five types: paranoid, compulsive, dramatic, depressive, or schizoid.

Paranoid organizations are characterized by suspiciousness and mistrust. People in them are likely to be cold, rational, and unemotional. Like Joe Friday in the old *Dragnet* series, they want "the facts ma'am, just the facts."

Compulsive organizations are perfectionist. Persons in them will often avoid making decisions or taking actions because they fear making a mistake. I always think we're better off to "do something even if it's wrong." In compulsive organizations, employees do little because "it might be wrong."

People in dramatic organizations often alternate between idealization and devaluation of others. Some employees may take action more to get attention than to accomplish organizational goals. Others may feel used or abused. Some people in these organizations may become overcommitted and underwhelmed, others may give up.

Depressive organizations foster a sense of helplessness and hopelessness in their employees. People may lose interest in their job and lack motivation. Time at work is likely to be spent commiserating with one another about how bad things are and people leave each evening feeling like they've been on a treadmill.

Schizoid organizations are characterized by employees who have withdrawn from one another and who are indifferent to either praise or criticism. Employees may become aggressive or bewildered.

If any of these descriptions fit your organization, you can be certain of two things: The organization's culture is inhibiting your communication with your employees and your employees will soon (if they aren't already) demonstrate frustration-instigated behaviors. Kets de Vries and Miller do offer a means of intervening and changing a neurotic organization. If any of the above descriptions fit your organization, I suggest you read and apply the information in their book before you decide that you have a problem employee. In other words, deal with the problem organization first. Then you'll know if you have a problem employee. Making certain that the working environment of your organization is conducive to productive, satisfied employees not only makes good sense, a recent Supreme Court decision ruled that you must. In 1986, the Supreme Court ruled that an offensive work environment may constitute illegal job discrimination (*Meritor Savings Bank v. Vinson*).[25]

Job Dissatisfaction

Numerous researchers have consistently demonstrated the importance of job satisfaction in relation to performance.[26] Simply put, problems can occur when an employee is dissatisfied with the job. Thus, it is important to understand what circumstances lead to job satisfaction, and to learn to create those circumstances in your organization.

The most widely recognized work on job satisfaction identifies five core work dimensions that lead to job satisfaction: task identity, task significance, skill variety, autonomy, and feedback.[27] Task identity, task significance, and skill variety are dimensions of what are called "enriched jobs." These are jobs in which the job holder can be involved with a project from start to finish, can see the end product and point to it with pride.

I recently completed research with the municipal clerks in the United States to attempt to learn what an organization can do to foster job satisfaction in its employees. I learned that workers who are able to balance home and work responsibilities, who are free from stress, who feel respected, and who are proud of their jobs experience significantly more job satisfaction than do others.

This research also indicated that the behavior of a supervisor plays an important role in the job satisfaction of his or her supervisees. Supervisors who help their employees to solve problems, practice effective communication, foster positive relations, are consistent, and encourage their employees to advance themselves both educationally and in their careers are more likely to have satisfied employees than are others.[28]

Now, the interesting thing to me is that these ingredients of job satisfaction are within the purview of a good human resource manager to bring about through training and development activities. Time management skills and stress management skills can be taught in half-day workshops. A series of supervisory training programs can teach problem solving, effective communication, and interpersonal skills.

Supervisors who proactively treat employees with respect, let them know where they stand, assist employees when they need help, and encourage them to better themselves have satisfied employees. A recent supervisory training film points out that too often supervisors see themselves as controllers and directors, rather than as encouragers and facilitators.[29]

Yet for employees to be satisfied, supervisors can neither abdicate nor appropriate responsibility. Rather, the supervisor of a satisfied employee will act as helper, teacher, and encourager; expecting the employee to take over more and more job responsibilities. They consistently treat the employee as an important person, offering encouragement and aid when it is needed.[30]

So another dimension of the issue of why problems develop can be prevented. Problems develop when employees are dissatisfied. Capable and competent supervision can alleviate dissatisfaction, enhance productivity, and decrease the likelihood of an employee becoming a problem employee.

PERSONALITY

An employee's personality may be another reason that he or she is perceived as a problem employee. Often an employee who is "different" from most of the others appears to be a problem. Yet the differences can become assets rather than problems when one understands the value of differences and learns to utilize them to maximize the productivity of a department or of an organization. The two psychological theories of personality that have been of most use for me in working with people in organizations are "type" theory[31] and "identity" theory.[32] The discussion below provides a brief description of each and explains how these theories can enhance your understanding of employees. As you come to understand, you can learn how to build on employee strengths and minimize their weaknesses. You will have another tool for understanding why problems occur.

Type Theory

Type theory, which is rooted in Jungian psychology, provides four sets of personality characteristics that will combine in one of sixteen possible ways in each of us. These combinations are expressed in a series of four letters, each representing one facet of personality. Each characteristic has its own set of strengths and weaknesses. Unfortunately, however, supervisors often view people as problems when, in fact, they are simply different. They are not problems, but rather they have jobs that do not allow them to use their strengths.

The first combination identified in type theory is that of "extrovert" (E) and "introvert" (I) and reflects how the individual deals with the world. Extroverts are those who are interested in the outer world of objects and persons. They get energized by others and are happier in a job where they have ample opportunity to interact with others. Introverts, on the other hand, are interested in the world of concepts and ideas. Their energy is drained by others and they prefer to work alone.

Problems can occur when an extrovert is required to work alone, isolated from human contact, and has no opportunity to reenergize by interactions with others. Problems can also occur in the work place when an introvert has a job that requires long hours of interaction with clients and customers, and provides no opportunity to work alone, think, and reenergize.

The second pair of personality characteristics in type theory is that of "sensing" (S) and "intuiting" (N). This pair refers to how an individual understands new information and gains insights. A sensing person is one who learns by experience, is practical, sensible, and prefers to understand through continuously accessing new data. Thus, a sensing person often appears to be slow and indecisive. An intuitive, on the other hand, is imaginative, spontaneous, and ingenious. This person requires little data and operates from hunches based on past experience. Problems can occur in the work place when one type supervises another. The sensing person will think the intuitive is not thorough. The intuitive is likely to think that the sensing person is too slow.

"Thinking" (T) and "feeling" (F) are the third pair of personality characteristics described in type theory. They explain how people make decisions. The thinkers are the Joe Fridays of the work place. They want "just the facts" and they are innately capable of rational, objective decisions. They are often viewed as critical. They may be accused of not caring by the feeling types who prefer to decide subjectively, carefully weighing values and considering how the decision will affect others.

The final pair of characteristics identified in type theory are "perceiving" (P) and "judging" (J), which indicate how people prefer to live. Perceiving types prefer to live in a flexible way and often start so many projects they have difficulty finishing them. They may be accused of procrastination by judging types who like to plan their life, get things settled and finished quickly, and complete one project after the other. Perceivers are those who are so busy seeing the forest they have trouble focusing on a single tree. Judgers will focus on the tree and lose sight of the forest.

So that you can get a sense of the variety of people in your work force, let me tell you that 75 percent of the population are extroverts and 25 percent are introverts; 75 percent make decisions by sensing and 25 percent are intuitive. Thinking and feeling are divided equally among the population with 50 percent falling in each category. Judging and perceiving are also split equally.[33]

A well-balanced work place needs a combination of types. Unfortunately, however, that balance does not always occur, nor are you really in a position to create it. Type can be determined by administration of the instrument known as the "Myers-Briggs Type Indicator," but this questionnaire has not been validated for employee selection purposes.[34] Its value lies in the understanding it provides about already-hired employees, and in the insight it can give you about yourself.

A person's "Myers-Briggs Type" will be a combination of four letters, each representing one characteristic from each pair described above. The combination represents the personality that the person presents to the world. It represents his or her strengths and comfortable way of operating and relating to others. In times of crisis, heavy demands, or duress, however, a person's type may temporarily change.

To explain the way type theory can help you understand why problems occur, I'd like to tell you about Sam. Sam is an ENTJ (an extroverted, intuitive, thinker, judger) which is a frank, decisive, confident mover and shaker. He was hired to supervise a department that was composed of two ISFPs (exact opposites of Sam) and two ESFPs. These employees were all thorough people who did not force their opinions on others and were relaxed about getting their jobs done. The introverts were reticent, quietly friendly, and modest. The extroverts were outgoing and enjoyed long discussions with their co-workers to enhance the quality of their work.

Sam immediately decided that his work force was composed of procrastinators who spent far too much time doing far too little. His rational, abrupt actions (characteristic of an NT) literally destroyed his employees before Sam's first year had ended. Marsha, at age 43, had a heart attack and had to retire on total disability. Erin, at age 55, resigned, sold his home, and moved to Japan. Lisa spent six months in therapy to try to regain her self-esteem, didn't, and was fired. Bob looked at what had happened to his co-workers, realized that the same things could happen to him, and resigned.

Sam believed that he had inherited a department of problem employees. His employees thought that they had acquired a problem supervisor. Neither was correct. The problem was that no random mix of types existed in the department, and that the employee types were, literally, the exact opposite of Sam in the way they approached their job responsibilities. The employees were so different from Sam that they lacked a common base of understanding.

Sam is still the supervisor in that department. He has surrounded himself with persons of his own type. The department turns out vast numbers of projects, many of which have been poorly thought out and either fail or have to be redone (the S's and the P's are gone). A new set of problems has emerged.

Now this is not to say that an ENTJ is a problem supervisor. It is, rather, to point out that each type has strengths and weaknesses. It is to demonstrate that problems may occur simply because of an inadequate mix of personality types in a work group. Personality types, in and of themselves, are value neutral. Understanding type theory can help you, as a human resource manager, recognize when an employee is truly a problem, and when he or she is simply a fish out of water.

Identity Theory

The second theory about personality that can help you understand why problems occur is identity theory, developed by William Glasser, who defines identity as "the unity and persistence of personality."[35]

Glasser conceives of five types of identities from which people operate. The "success identity" is possessed by those who display flexible, effective behaviors. A person who has a success identity may be either a "fulfilled person" or a "security person." These people are in charge of their lives, responsible, and self-disciplined. Those with success identities believe their needs are best met through socially acceptable activities that bring love, a sense of belonging, and the opportunity to gain recognition for achievement and productivity.

The success identity is the identity with which traditional human resource management literature has dealt. This identity responds positively to motivation and leadership, to training, and to job and organization design. This is the identity that has made possible the Horatio Alger notion of the American dream. Unfortunately, every person in the work force does not possess a success identity.

It is also unfortunate that most (maybe all) academicians and managers can only conceive of persons with success identities because they, themselves, have attained their place in life through a success orientation. It is a typical fallacy of human thinking to view others as thinking or capable of thinking, or doing, only as "I" do. This phenomenon is demonstrated daily by university-educated parents who don't understand why their offspring quit high school, and by judges who return battered kids to abusing parents, thinking "I" spank "my" kids too. But, all persons do not have a success identity.

This is not to say that managers and academicians, or for that matter everyone else, believe that people are clones. Certainly, different personality types are recognized. Certainly, it is also acknowledged that different people have different goals, and that some are procrastinators, some are optimistic, some are pessimistic, etc. The list of differences could go on and on. The crucial point here, however, is that all of these different types may, or may not, have a success identity. Yet when employees have been fit into traditional management theory, they have usually been assumed to be rational, self-actualizing people. Then when the particular theory applies only part of the time, the problem is thought to be with the theory; it is not recognized that the theory fits well only for the success identity.

Fortunately, a large part of the work force does have a success identity. People with success identities get frustrated, have communication problems, and fall randomly into the Myers-Briggs types. However, to view the entire work force as success identities is to attempt to fit a number of round pegs into square holes, and to experience the frustration that this futile behavior brings. To prevent such useless effort it is necessary to accept that some members of the work force, to varying agrees, have a "failure identity."

Persons with a failure identity are those whose behavior is unrealistic.

While they too seek love and belonging, their methods for achieving these goals are the opposite of the success identity. While the success-oriented persons are able to postpone short-term pleasure for long-term gain, the failure identity is very present oriented. A success identity will respond to frustration, disappointment, or tragedy with, at best, a plan of action, or at worst, a rebound. A failure identity, on the other hand, will exhibit itself as either a "give up" person, a "symptom" person, or a "negative addict."

The give up person is the one who does just that in the face of even a small challenge. These are the people who cannot understand bumper stickers such as "when life gives you lemons, make lemonade." These are the wallflowers at parties, and the persons in the work force who avoid or refuse challenging assignments. They often expect someone else to take care of them or solve their problems, and will frequently exaggerate work accomplishments, while being ready to blame their failure on others. These are the employees about whom supervisors say, "I can't get him to do anything," or "She just doesn't give a damn!"

The symptom person is more overt in behavior. This is the person whose problem behavior exhibits itself in belligerence, aggression, shouting obscenities, and general troublemaking. This person is very self-oriented, and one who can be quickly labeled as a troublemaker. The symptom person attempts to meet his or her needs by fighting and calling attention to himself or herself.

The negative addict is the individual who turns to drugs, alcohol, or food to escape pain and create an artificial pleasure. They are self-centered and not in control of their lives. They have little self-confidence and are frequently irresponsible. They attempt to meet their needs by escaping their problems, which are many.

As you consider these different identities, I caution you to set aside personal perspectives so as not to be trapped into overly identifying with the negative identities because of your own occasional response to frustration with yelling, getting drunk, or "pigging out." It is important here to remember that the negative addict is the alcoholic, or the drug addict; and that the symptom person is the one *consistently* involved in altercations at work and feuds with neighbors, and who gives belligerent responses to constructive criticism.

The key difference between a success identity and a failure identity is control. Success identities are in control of their lives, confident, and over time experience more pleasure than pain. Failure identities, on the other hand, are not in effective control of their lives, so they experience more pain than pleasure.

In research I conducted on the relationship of identity to problem behavior in the government work place, I found that a great deal of problem behavior can be explained by identity.[36] Table 2.1 lists typical

Table 2.1
Typical Problems in the Work Place by Identity

Problem	Identity				
	Negative Addict	Symptom	Give Up	Security	Fulfilled
Tardiness	17 %	20%	0	9%	25%
Unexplained Absences	50%	34%	0	9%	0
Absent at Critical Time	50%	34%	0	27%	25%
Missed Deadline	33%	43%	33%	27%	50%
Frequent Mistakes	33%	40%	67%	27%	0
Disregard for Policies	33%	63%	83%	82%	50%
Lies	17%	35%	50%	18%	0
Exaggerates	17%	37%	83%	9%	0
Belligerence	33%	46%	17%	0	0
Drunk on job	50%	3%	0	0	0
Taking drugs on job	67%	0	0	0	0

problems in the work place with the percent of persons of each identity who displayed those problems.

THE EFFECT OF ONE PROBLEM EMPLOYEE

Unfortunately the problem employee does not act in a vacuum. Rather, problem behavior of one employee will have a ripple effect that can literally destroy the productivity of every employee in a work unit. Just one individual's problem-creating behavior can shift the organizational balance and change organizational forces from those of fulfilling purpose to those of reducing disturbance. When this happens, it will impose an enormous energy drain on you. This drain can become so powerful that organizational goals become secondary even for you.

Johnson and Johnson have aptly demonstrated how one negative person in a group can turn the whole group sour.[37] Inappropriate behavior can be contagious, and often co-workers can get drawn into covering for the problem employee, or trying to "help" to the subversion of their own best interests. One problem employee can wreak havoc in the work place.

To demonstrate what kind of havoc can take place, I'll continue the story of Marcella, which was begun early in this chapter. One day when Max, her supervisor, attempted to discuss her deteriorating performance with her, Marcella burst into tears, accused him of picking on her, taking her job, and trying to get rid of her. She then abruptly left the room, slamming the door. Within the next few days, she communicated with each of her fellow employees in an effort to build a coalition against Max.

Lionel, a co-worker, emphathized, then explained Marcella's rights as an employee if she believed she was experiencing retaliation or discrimination. First, he helped her compose a memorandum of complaint to be sent to Max's superior, Naomi. Next, Lionel met with Max to offer his assistance in dealing with Marcella. Then, Lionel went to Naomi to "warn" her that she would soon be getting a memorandum from one of the employees and told her that Max did not know how to handle the situation. Lionel's visit occurred before Max had time to talk with Naomi, who then began to doubt Max's competence and instituted a secret (and illegal) evaluation of him.

In the meantime, Marcella had told her story to the other employees. Janet advised Marcella to ignore and avoid Max and began doing that herself. Soon Janet broke out in a rash that required extensive medical treatment and for which she blamed Max.

Harold, another employee, almost became a scapegoat. Being conscientious, he quietly started coming into work early and staying late in an effort to complete both his work and that of Marcella and Janet. In one six-week period, he worked ninety-six hours of overtime. For this effort, Marcella accused Harold of racial prejudice.

Through all of this, Max was meeting regularly with Naomi, not knowing about the secret evaluations that had been requested. Naomi advised Max to get advice from the agency's attorney. He made an appointment for the following week and recorded it on his desk calendar. When he left the office to keep the appointment, Marcella searched his desk. Seeing that Max was meeting with an attorney, Marcella immediately went to Naomi's office to insist that she stop the meeting. She did.

Marcella continued her deviant behavior. She arrived late and left early. While she was at work she consistently made mistakes and implemented policy that was contrary to the philosophy of the agency and in two cases in violation of federal law. She continued to avoid or ignore Max. After about two weeks of this, Max said, "We have to talk." Marcella then physically attacked Max. He did not fight back, but called Naomi.

Naomi was out of town so Max called her boss, Sam. Sam instructed Max to immediately suspend Marcella. He did. When Naomi returned, she ordered Max to rescind the suspension. At this point, Max consulted his own attorney, who advised him to immediately take his annual leave and to file a reverse discrimination law suit. When Max returned from vacation Marcella had resigned. Two weeks later he resigned too. The effects of one problem employee, Marcella, literally destroyed the work group.

All of the issues described thus far in this chapter should demonstrate to you that the organization is a fertile environment for creating and exacerbating problem employee behavior. You probably already know that. It is important, however, for you to be aware of the conditions in the work place that can lead to an employee becoming a problem, for once you understand these conditions, you can work to prevent them.

This will free you to deal with the employees whose problem behavior is the result of a crisis over which you have no control. And you can learn to deal with them, as you will see later in this book. Before we proceed to effective ways of dealing with problem behavior, however, I want you also to consider how persons and events outside the organization can precipitate problem employee behavior.

PERSONS AND EVENTS OUTSIDE THE WORK PLACE

Unfortunately, even though you are able to create a work environment that is conducive to productivity and does not foster frustration, miscommunication, nor dissatisfaction, a problem employee may still emerge. You may remember that I said at the beginning of this chapter that an employee will usually become a problem because of a work or life crisis. Many work crises can be prevented. You, however, have no control over the employee's life away from the work setting.

Employees do not often leave their troubles at home. They do not shed them as they do their coats when they enter the door of the organization. Rather, the problems stay with them, haunting them and interfering with their productivity. Employees who bring their troubles to the work place are the most difficult ones with which you must deal, for you have no control over the cause of the problem. Accept that lack of control then learn to change the impact of the problem for the organization.

You probably know as many stories as I do about how a person's problems at home can negatively impact the work place, for no employee stands alone, unchanged by the events and actions around him or her. Rather, employees have lives outside the world of work. In those lives family and friends make demands on time and energy. Employees who are unskilled in managing these demands may well become problem employees.

You, as the human resource manager, cannot change conditions outside the organization, nor in most instances can you dictate how an employee will behave away from the work place. "However, public employees such as police officers, public schoolteachers, and persons needing national security clearance have been held to more exacting standards of off-duty conduct than those applied to the rest of society."[38] Labor arbitrators have developed six rules to help you determine if conduct away from the job is an employment issue with which you must deal. They are:

1. Does the behavior affect job performance?
2. Does the behavior affect the efficiency of fellow workers or management?
3. Does the behavior directly hurt the employer?
4. Does the behavior indirectly hurt the employer?
5. Is there clear and convincing proof of the negative impact of the employee's behavior on the employer?
6. In the case of an employee's off-duty criminal activity, does it affect job performance?[39]

Behavior that may well spill over into the organization is generally caused by substance abuse, health, or family problems. Let's talk about each of these causes as they affect the work place.

Substance Abuse

The term *substance abuse* refers to the abuse of both alcohol and illegal drugs. Substance abuse affects from 3 percent to 25 percent of American workers.[40] These employees are:

1. Four times more likely to be involved in accidents at work
2. Six times more likely to be involved in accidents away from work
3. Two and one-half times more likely to be absent from work more than a week
4. Five times more likely to file a workman's compensation claim
5. Repeatedly involved in grievance procedures
6. Receiving three times more sickness benefits
7. Functioning at 67 percent of their potential[41]

A recent study by the National Center for Health Statistics identified the average number of days workers are absent from work. You can use these figures as a barometer for gaging whether or not an employee is using an excessive number of sick days. The study, conducted between 1983 and 1985 and based on a survey of 303,000 people, found that women average 5.5 sick days annually and men average 4.3 days. The U.S. Department of Labor believes that the presence of children contributes to women's absentee rates, although the study did not take into consideration time off for child bearing.[42]

Remember, however, that excessive absenteeism is only one indicator of substance abuse, and don't automatically label an employee a substance abuser if he or she is absent from work too much. The problem may be health or family related. In my own research, I found that substance abuse explained only 17 percent of the tardiness, 50 percent of the unexplained absences, and 50 percent of the absences at critical times.[43]

If you suspect substance abuse, it is difficult to single out a single employee for drug testing. However, within the context of an overall plan that delineates your organization's substance abuse policy, drug testing is feasible. Instructions for establishing and implementing such a plan will be provided in chapter 5. A program will be more difficult for you to institute if you are the human resource manager in a government agency, however.

Because government employers are the state, they are constrained by the Constitution from mandating drug tests of civilian government employees like those permissible in the private sector. Drug testing has been found acceptable by the courts if there is a compelling public interest to justify it, the testing is based on reasonable suspicion, and tests are carried out by means set forth in written policy that safeguards the rights of the person being tested.[44]

Family Problems

A number of researchers are concerned about the "escalating conflict between work and family life."[45] It is a conflict exacerbated by the fact that 44 percent of the work force is female,[46] and that 60 percent of those women have children under the age of six.[47] It is a conflict also exacerbated by the fact that more than two-fifths of the working population are members of households where both spouses work.[48] This conflict occurs for both women and men and often results in family problems spilling over into the work place.

A graphic example of this kind of spillover is Bud, who I like to call a "good father." Bud had been an outstanding employee of a post office for six years when his attendance started deteriorating. His frequent tardiness, excessive absences, and newly acquired habit of sleeping on the job caused his supervisor to suspect substance abuse. The supervisor initiated disciplinary action and referred Bud to an Employee Assistance Program. Bud's unacceptable behavior continued. He was terminated.

Bud appealed the termination. His appeal, which ultimately reached the Merit Systems Protection Board (MSPB), generated an investigation. The investigation revealed that the reason for Bud's behavior was family problems.

Bud's wife had left him. In the ensuing divorce, Bud was awarded custody of his two children, ages seven and ten. As a result of the divorce, both children began to have emotional problems. Then Bud had an auto accident that left him without transportation. His children's problems were escalating. He was so distraught that he started seeing a psychologist. The psychologist prescribed tranquilizers, which made him so drowsy he fell asleep on the job.

In the course of the appeals process, Bud's domestic situation was resolved—his children adjusted, his car was fixed, and he stopped taking tranquilizers. The evidence Bud presented to the MSPB convinced them to give him a second chance and Bud resumed productive employment.

Health-Related Problems

Just because an employee becomes ill, don't arbitrarily think you have a problem employee on your hands. A health-related problem can hamper performance until treatment is sought. Responsible employees know that and act accordingly. Responsible employers can also provide wellness programs to enhance employee health. But sickness happens to everyone. The human body was not built to last forever, permanently immune to the ravages of disease or of age. Consider the following statistics.

Heart attacks alone cost private industry 132 million work days per year, or 4 percent of the Gross National Product.[49] Many personal habits of employees contribute to heart disease. These include high cholesterol due to improper diet, lack of physical activity, and cigarette smoking. Stress also plays a significant role in causing heart disease, and, in fact, has been implicated as a major contributing factor in 60 percent of visits to health care professionals.[50]

Some health problems are job related, as evidenced by escalating workmen's compensation claims.[51] Many others are hereditary. Still others are caused by general lack of fitness, poor sleep patterns, life-style, hobbies, and worry over family problems or family finances.[52] Whatever the cause of the health problem, however, it does not become your concern until its effects spill over into the work place in a way that hampers organizational goal accomplishment.

In chapter 5 I'll give you information on how to establish a wellness program in your organization as a measure for preventing employee health problems. I will also instruct you on how to encourage employee participation in such a program.

SUMMARY

This chapter has presented a number of reasons why perfectly competent employees become problems. It has been an effort to enable you to consider the role that your own actions and your own organization can play in creating a problem employee. Before you write off an employee as impossible, evaluate yourself and your company. Make certain that you are not a contributor to the problem.

This chapter has also been an effort to help you understand that some problem behavior is out of your control and that you cannot change the cause of all problem behavior. You will, however, learn to change the impact of that behavior on you and on your organization as you read on.

Once you have determined that you are not a part of the problem, you are ready to progress to chapter 3. In it, I'll talk about methods of dealing with the problem employee that are typically used and that don't work. You may already know some of them. Most managers do, and most managers make the same mistakes in dealing with their problem employees. Knowing what is a mistake and knowing why it is a mistake can help you learn more effective methods for dealing with a problem employee.

NOTES

1. See Wendell French, *The Personnel Management Process*, 5th ed. (Boston: Houghton Mifflin Company, 1982).

2. *Federal Register*, vol. 43, no. 166, Friday, August 25, 1978 (Washington, D.C.: U.S. Government Printing Office), pp. 38290–92.

3. Robert Hollman, "Managing Troubled Employees: Meeting the Challenge," *Journal of Contemporary Business* 8, no. 4 (October 1979), 43–57.

4. W. Randolph Flynn and William E. Stratton, "Managing Problem Employees," *Human Resource Management* 20, no. 2 (Summer 1981), 28–32.

5. Ibid.

6. Paul Wilkins and Joel Haynes, "Understanding Frustration Instigated Behavior," *Personnel Journal* 53, no. 10 (October 1974), 770–72.

7. Joseph Raelin, "An Examination of Deviant/Adaptive Behaviors in the Organizational Careers of Professionals," *Academy of Management Review* 9, no. 3 (July 1984), 413–27.

8. See, e.g., Derek Biddle and Geoffrey Hutton, "Toward a Tolerance Theory of Worker Adaptation," *Human Relations* 29, no. 9 (September 1976), 833–62; Peter Cairo, "Counseling in Industry, A Selected Review of the Literature," *Personnel Psychology* 36, no. 1 (Spring 1983), 1–18; Manfred Kets de Vries and Danny Miller, *The Neurotic Organization* (San Francisco: Jossey Bass, 1984); Mark Martinko and William Gardner, "Learned Helplessness: An Alternative Explanation for Performance Deficits," *Academy of Management Review* 7, no. 2 (April

1983), 195–204; and Joseph Raelin, "An Examination of Deviant/Adaptive Behaviors."

9. See Biddle and Hutton, "Toward a Tolerance Theory of Worker Adaptation."

10. See Raelin, "An Examination of Deviant/Adaptive Behaviors."

11. See Herbert Heneman III, Donald Schwab, John Fossum, and Lee Dyer, *Personnel/Human Resource Management* (Homewood, Ill.: Richard D. Irwin, Inc., 1980).

12. See Henry Tosi, John Rizzo, and Stephen Carroll, *Managing Organization Behavior* (Marshfield, Mass.: Pitman Publishing Co., 1986).

13. See John Kerrigan and Jeffrey Luke, *Management Training Strategies for Developing Countries* (Boulder, Colo.: Lynne Rienner Publishers, 1987).

14. Ibid.

15. This discussion is adapted from the as yet unpublished work of Jeffrey S. Luke of the University of Oregon.

16. See Chester Barnard, *Functions of the Executive* (Cambridge, Mass.: Harvard University Press, 1938 and 1968).

17. Ibid.

18. See Tosi, et al., *Managing Organization Behavior*.

19. N. A. Steackler and R. Rosenthal, "Sex Differences in Verbal and Non-Verbal Communication with Bosses, Peers, and Subordinates," *Journal of Applied Psychology* 70, no. 1 (February 1985), 157–63.

20. The discussion on barriers to communication is adapted from Willa Bruce, "Persuasion and Influence," in D. Warfle, ed., *Advanced Supervisory Practices* (Washington, D.C.: International City Management Association, 1990).

21. See Tosi, et al., *Managing Organization Behavior*.

22. See Martinko and Gardner, "Learned Helplessness."

23. See Vijay Sathe, "Implications of Corporate Culture: A Manager's Guide to Action," *Organizational Dynamics* 12 (Autumn 1983), 5–23; and Ian Mitroff and Ralph Kilmann, *Corporate Tragedies* (New York: Praeger, 1984).

24. See Kets de Vries and Miller, *The Neurotic Organization*.

25. "The Merits of Meritor," *Fair Employment Report* 26, no. 13 (22 June 1988), 97.

26. See J. R. Hackman and Edward Lawler, "Employee Reactions to Job Characteristics," *Journal of Applied Psychology Monograph* 55 (1971), 259–86; J. R. Hackman and G. Oldham, *The Diagnostic Survey: An Instrument for the Diagnosis of Jobs and the Evaluation of Job Redesign Projects* (New Haven: Yale University Press, 1974); M. M. Petty, G. McGee, and J. W. Cavendar, "A Meta Analysis of the Relationships Between Individual Job Satisfaction and Individual Performance," *Academy of Management Review* 9, no. 4 (1984), 712–21; D. Schwab and L. L. Cummings, "Theories of Performance and Satisfaction," *Industrial Relations* 10 (October 1970), 408–30.

27. See Hackman and Oldham, *The Diagnostic Survey*.

28. See Willa Bruce, "Job Satisfaction of the Nation's Municipal Clerks: Supervisors Make a Difference," forthcoming in *American Review of Public Administration*.

29. "Learning to Think Like a Manager," a CRM film (DelMar, Cal.: CRM Films/McGraw-Hill, 1983).

30. See Bruce, "Job Satisfaction."

31. See David Kiersey and Marilyn Bates, *Please Understand Me: Character and Temperament Types* (Del Mar, Calif.: Prometheus Nemesis, 1978); and Isabel Briggs Myers, *Introduction to Type* (Palo Alto, Calif.: Consulting Psychologists Press, 1980).

32. See William Glasser, *The Identity Society* (New York: Harper and Row, 1975); and Chester Karrass and William Glasser, *Both Win Management* (New York: Lippincott and Crowell, 1980).

33. See Kiersey and Bates, *Please Understand Me*.

34. The "Myers-Briggs Type Indicator" is available from Consulting Psychologists Press, Inc., 577 College Avenue, Palo Alto, CA 94306 at a nominal cost. It must be ordered and administered by a helping professional with a master's degree. An instrument for use by lay people is included in the Keirsey Bates book, *Please Understand Me*, available in paperback in many bookstores.

35. See William Glasser, *The Identity Society*, and William Glasser, *Take Effective Control of Your Life* (New York: Harper and Row, 1984).

36. See Willa Bruce, "Reality Therapy Proven to Be an Effective Management Strategy: A Report of a Computer Model," *Journal of Reality Therapy* 2 (Spring 1986), 15–24.

37. See David Johnson and Frank Johnson, *Joining Together* (Englewood Cliffs, N.J.: Prentice Hall, 1975, 1982).

38. See Ronald Sylvia, *Critical Issues in Public Personnel Policy* (Pacific Grove, Calif.: Brooks Cole, 1989).

39. Ibid.

40. See Paul Cary, "Drugs and Drug Testing in the Work Place," in John Matzer, Jr., ed., *Personnel Practices for the '90's* (Washington, D.C.: International City Manager's Association, 1989).

41. Ibid.

42. "Study Looks at Worker Sick Days," *Omaha World-Herald*, 14 May 1989.

43. See Bruce, "Reality Therapy."

44. See Sylvia, *Critical Issues*.

45. Lorraine Dusky, "Companies that Care: What the Best Employers Offer Families," *Family Circle*, 25 April 1989, 105–9.

46. See Dusky, "Study Looks At Worker Sick Days."

47. See Dusky, "Companies that Care."

48. Conference Board, *Corporations and Families: Changing Practices and Perspectives*, Report no. 868 (New York: Conference Board, 1985), 19–20.

49. R. Kreitner, "Employee Physical Fitness Programs: Protecting an Investment in Human Resources," *Personnel Journal* 55, no. 7 (July 1976), 340–44.

50. D. Brinkman, "There's Good News About Heart Disease," *Safety and Health* 139, no. 2 (1989) 53–56; E. A. Knight and W. M. Felts, "Comprehensive Health Programs Should Include Stress Management," *Occupational Health and Safety* 57, no. 11 (1988), 46–50.

51. S. Moretz, "New Developments Challenge an Old System: Can Workman's Comp Cope with Stress, Aids, and Intentional Torts? Will Exclusive Remedy Prevail?" *Occupational Hazards* 50, no. 10 (1988), 131–34.

52. See Knight and Felts, "Comprehensive Health Programs."

Chapter 3

Traditional Remedies and Why They Fail

Unfortunately, many of the management strategies we have been taught for motivating, leading, and inspiring our employees do not work with a problem employee. Chapter 2 helped you consider why problems occur both within and outside of your organization's environment. In this chapter I'll talk about the strategies, tactics, and methods that supervisors typically use for dealing with a problem employee. Although these methods are frequently what is referred to as "good management," they don't often work with a problem employee for many reasons. Therefore, they often leave the supervisor discouraged and drained.

You may be wondering why a chapter in this book is devoted to discussing methods for dealing with the problem employee that typically fail. You already know what isn't effective and you're looking for solutions. This chapter is important, however, because it will explain *why* traditional management is ineffective with a problem employee. It's important for you to know why so that you continue to utilize good management practices when they are appropriate.

Do you remember the folk saying, "Don't throw the baby out with the bathwater?" For me, that saying means don't lose confidence in the good skills you have, and don't reject the good and effective management practices that you know work for you. Rather, understand when and why to use traditional management theory *and* understand when and why not to use it.

This chapter will increase your ability to discern. You may recognize yourself in it. You may recognize some of your organization's supervisors in it. You will learn why traditional remedies for dealing with the problem employee so often fail, and you will learn what this failure can do to you and the supervisor attempting to deal with the problem employee.

TRADITIONAL MANAGEMENT STRATEGIES

A strategy is an overarching plan of operation. The dictionary defines *strategy* as, "1. the science of planning and directing military operations. 2. skill in management or planning, esp. by using strategems." It defines a strategem as "a trick, a plan, etc. for deceiving an enemy at war."[1] Thus using a strategy implies an adversarial relationship in which one side "wins" and the other "loses." This win–lose mentality permeates traditional management theory. It is probably the single most important reason that traditional management strategies fail.

Everybody likes to win. For most it is a truism that we would rather win than lose. The problem with winning, however, is that most often when someone wins others lose . . . .

Perhaps because of this win–lose mentality, organizational life typically tends to foster a destructive pattern. The boss wins—employees lose. The union wins—management loses. . . . There are situations in organizations where winners prevail and losers despair. These winners emerge by virtue of having their will imposed on others. The despair is indeed real for those who must yield and become powerless. It certainly is not pleasant to feel like a loser in one's workplace. Furthermore, if people throughout an organization feel like losers, levels of productivity can be adversely affected. . . .

Do we really need to have organizational winners and organizational losers? The answer, most emphatically is NO.[2]

Yet management theory is full of win–lose strategies for dealing with the problem employee. These strategies are typically divided into those designed to prevent problem behavior from occurring, and those designed to control (or eliminate) problem behavior after it has been recognized.

Prevention and Control

Prevention strategies are strategies that you, as a human resource manager, can use to foster a healthy organizational climate. Communicate effectively! Don't change the rules! Don't foster false expectations! Promote job satisfaction! Incorporate a balance of personality types into each work group! Establish wellness programs! Make accommodation for child care!

These are strategies that supervisors in your organization can use to minimize employee frustration. They are effective with 80 percent to 90 percent of your employees.

Control strategies, on the other hand, are often a frustration response by a manager who, disillusioned because the prevention strategies have failed, resorts to drastic efforts to repress or eliminate the problem.

Control strategies are analogous to Herzberg's positive and negative KITA, the proverbial "kick in the ass," that somehow "ought to work."[3]

Control strategies can literally be divided into "carrots" and "sticks." Carrots include goal setting and a reward when the goal is met, merit raises, a promotion, a "pat on the back," and special perquisites. When you use a carrot, you make certain your employee knows that a desired reward will be forthcoming if job performance is successful, and then you make certain that it is. Sticks are things like the threat of reprimands, the "cold shoulder," suspension without pay, demotions, transfers, and terminations. When you use a stick, you make certain your employee knows that a dreaded punishment will be forthcoming if job performance is not successful.

Tactics that have been proliferated by these strategies are the stuff of which traditional books on management and supervision are made. In them you can read and memorize how to manage in "one minute," how to "cope with difficult people," how to lead, how to motivate, etc., *ad infinitum, ad nauseam*. When you are done, your problem employee likely is still with you; and your own frustration has increased. At this point many managers resort to "ultradisciplinary measures," which include formal reprimand, short suspension, extended suspension, and termination.[4] In fact, many organizations, both public and private, provide formal guidelines for such action.

This is not to say that formal guidelines are not useful. As you'll see in chapter 8, a written policy that outlines actions that will be taken in response to specific offenses is necessary for company protection in times of litigation. The point here, however, is that these guidelines, if used precipitously, can quickly place employee and supervisor in adversarial roles in which no one wins.

Advice typically given to a manager regarding tactics for dealing with a problem employee consistently includes: (1) accept that the employee has a problem that is not likely to disappear, (2) document failing job performance, (3) confront the employee, and (4) suggest that the employee seek the help of a counselor, or accept disciplinary action.[5] Unfortunately, this is easier said than done. The advisors tell you *what* to do. They do not tell you *how* to do it.

Many of us who have dealt with problem employees believe, however, that in following such advice, most managers will handle problem employees in a way that "guarantees that they will grow worse."[6] Employee behavior can be expected to worsen for several reasons. Negative controls (sticks) are often a response by a manager to his or her own frustration. As such, they can be perceived as retaliation, and elicit an even greater exhibition of problem behavior by the employee. Punishment, while widely touted, simply is not an effective means of dealing with the problem employee.

While punishment can affect behavior, there are serious problems with using it. . . . A subordinate who is, supposedly, punished may, in fact, feel rewarded by having gotten his boss angry, or by getting attention and support of fellow workers. The second difficulty is that punishment can have undesirable side effects.

Punishment can reduce the frequency of desirable behaviors. It contributes to a fearful environment . . . can deteriorate the superior–subordinate relationship . . . can lead to counteraggression. . . . Finally, the manager can't control how other employees interpret the punishment . . . the punished employee controls the information. . . . The manager . . . is at the mercy of the misinformation and rumor.[7]

Positive controls (carrots), while well intentioned, are *imposed* without the input of the employee. They, therefore, lack employee ownership and the employee is less likely to internalize the purposes of the supervisor. The employee may feel manipulated and resent the supervisor, who may be perceived as lacking in respect. Thus controls, both positive and negative, are likely to worsen rather than alleviate the problem.

If all this sounds like oversimplification, it is meant to, for the point here is not that traditional management strategies and tactics do not work. The point is that they only work 80 to 90 percent of the time— with those employees who cannot be classified as problem employees.

Rewards

A frequently made assumption in the literature on human resource management is that there is a direct relationship between the amount of reward received by employees and organizational effectiveness. Research on this assumption, however, "shows that this is too simple a view."[8] Another frequently made assumption is that rewards increase satisfaction, motivation, and job performance. This assumption is also questionable because "people differ widely in the rewards they desire and in how important the different rewards are to them."[9]

This is certainly not to say that employees should not be rewarded equitably for the work they do. It is, however, to point out that rewards, in and of themselves, will not induce a problem employee to change behavior.

Herzberg has aptly demonstrated that the things typically included in organizational reward systems (salary raises, fringe benefits) are necessary for continued employment but insufficient for purposes of improving performance. Herzberg calls reward systems "hygiene factors" and describes them as qualities an employee expects in a work setting. If employees perceive that such factors are inequitable, they will not be motivated and are likely to be dissatisfied. The presence of reward systems, however, will not motivate, nor will they produce job satisfaction.[10]

Recent research substantiates this contention. A 1989 survey of the nation's municipal clerks revealed that although 86 percent of them are highly satisfied with their jobs, only 30 percent perceive that they have a "fair and equitable" salary.[11] In a similar survey, employees of a private metropolitan university were asked to list its strengths and weaknesses. Although salaries there are typically lower than salaries in comparable public institutions, only 21 percent of the respondents identified "low salaries" as a weakness.[12] Of course, rewards in organizations come in many forms. Pay is only a part of the reward system.

It's been my experience that problem employees can successfully manipulate a supervisor so that what the supervisor intended as punishment actually can become a reward. I remember Helen. Helen was a manager in an apartment complex in the inner city of a large metropolitan area. She had grown up in the area and was friends with many of the tenants, most of them behind in their rent. Despite organizational policy and repeated directions from her supervisor, Jon, Helen refused to institute eviction proceedings against them. As a result her accounts receivable were dangerously low. In addition, the physical appearance of the complex was deteriorating.

Jon did not know how to manage Helen. He was so intimidated by her that he would neither take action to discipline her nor to fire her. Then he hit upon a plan. He would transfer her! Now the company owned a number of housing complexes, scattered across a 200-mile radius. One of these complexes was the farthest outpost, located in a rural area, with no public transportation, no cultural activities, and no nearby shopping facilities. He decided to transfer Helen here because he thought that she would refuse to go. With that refusal he believed she would resign.

Helen fooled him. She accepted the transfer and took for herself a five-bedroom, newly remodeled apartment in the rural complex. The new apartment was far more luxurious than her previous living arrangement. Even though she no longer knew her tenants, however, soon her failure to manage again became apparent. Jon had compounded his problem. Helen was rewarded with a new apartment and less work.

PREDICTABLE COPING STRATEGIES

Of course, dealing with a problem employee is not easy. None of us likes to face having to. When you are confronted with a problem employee, you may well go through the same emotional stages that you will when confronted with a terminal illness. Certainly the presence of a problem employee in the work place is like a cancer, eating away.

You may be familiar with the stages of death and dying that have been identified by Elisabeth Kubler-Ross: denial, anger and blame, bargaining, depression and withdrawal, and finally, hope and active planning.[13] These same stages occur in communities that are facing economic decline.[14] They also are likely to occur in the supervisor confronted with a problem employee.[15]

So long as you deny that you have a problem, it is impossible to take action to correct it. Action that results from anger and blame will be counterproductive because when you are angry, it is easy to make mistakes. Angry supervisors lash out, make threats, use ultradisciplinary methods that don't work, and generally make the situation worse. That's what happened with the way Max handled Marcella in the story in chapter 2.

The worsening situation can then make you depressed, wanting to withdraw from the whole situation. It can make you give up, or resign, as Max ultimately did. It is only when you accept that you have a problem employee, and actively take the reasoned steps that will be described in chapters 4 and 5 to deal with that person, that you will be able to get yourself and the organization back to a productive mode.

Before you can begin to take appropriate action, however, you need to be aware that you, personally, have some more stages to expect and live through. Hoffer lists these stages as: (1) praying for a miracle; (2) reason will prevail; (3) pleading; and (4) bleeding.[16] Let's talk about them.

Praying for a miracle is a natural response to the existence of a problem employee. By the time you get to this point, you will have accepted that you have a problem employee and, worse, that the prevailing "how-to" books offer no guidelines for motivating or leading this type of employee. You'll be in the proverbial "catch 22." If you do not confront non-productivity, excessive absenteeism, insubordination, and/or the negative influence of the employee on the work unit, your own morale and that of other employees will deteriorate. If you do confront it, the problem employee can literally have the entire organization in an uproar. If you doubt that, reconsider the case of Marcella in the previous chapter.

Depending on his or her personality, the problem employee may induce other employees to cover up mistakes, may precipitate an accident, or may appear at work intoxicated. He or she may verbally or physically assault you, or report real or imagined indiscretions made by you in a childlike appeal to authority for support. When confronted, the problem employee may also cry and play on your sympathies, so that, in a subtle way, the responsibility for the situation is shifted to you. When confronted, the problem employee is usually so skilled in diversionary tactics that you may begin to suspect that the solution to the problem requires more effort than you're capable of, thus you pray for a miracle.

In point of fact, however, miracles rarely happen. None have been documented as occurring in organizations. When you finally realize this, you will probably move to the next predictable stage of dealing with a problem employee: reason will prevail.

Reason will prevail is the stage where you usually attempt heart-to-heart talks with your problem employee. Unfortunately, such rationalization is generally of no avail. Problem employees will likely respond to you with "I don't know what you're talking about" or "What's *your* problem?" They will express indignation, disbelief, and hostility. They may tell co-workers that you are prejudiced, or jealous, or threatened. They will likely challenge your motives, credibility, competence, and sanity, for the problem employee is not one who responds to reason. Once you realize this, the next predictable stage is pleading.

Pleading is the phase during which you will randomly beg, cajole, or threaten. By this time you will have begun to doubt yourself. You may start reading self-help books, compile a dossier of previous accomplishments, enroll in a refresher course, or become obsessed with proving yourself in ways that are not job related. You may be reading this book because you are in the pleading stage. You may be keeping detailed diaries and records in a compulsive effort to justify your own behavior. You may be looking for another job, thinking that anything would be better than trying to manage your problem employee. After a long period of agonizing, you will finally move on to the bleeding stage.

Bleeding occurs at the point in which you initiate disciplinary action. You have literally tried everything you can think of—carrots and sticks alike. You have been through a difficult self-assessment and soul searching. You have experienced feelings of guilt, inadequacy, and fear until finally you are ready to shout "No More!" Though you may be angry at yourself and feel like a personal failure, you are ready to admit that the problem is more than you can handle and to get rid of it or to pass it on.

Living through these stages is not easy. In fact, more than one researcher has found that the emotions that a supervisor trying to deal with a problem employee experiences are exactly like those experienced by an alcoholic.[17] They run the gamut from denial, through guilt, inadequacy, and fear. One management text author actually admits that he has had a 100 percent failure rate in dealing with the problem employee.[18] That is cold comfort.

TYPICAL TREATMENT

As you well know, managers are hard-pressed to know how to deal with a problem employee. Frequently, a "conspiracy of silence" ensues, in which the employee is shielded in the hope that the problems will somehow be resolved or dissolved.[19] Such a cover-up, however, puts too much faith in the employee's ability and/or desire to straighten up. It gives the worker no inkling of a manager's concern, and ignores the fact that a manager is in a position to help the employee.

Ignoring the problem employee represents a vain hope that what you ignore will go away. But the problem employee who is ignored will get worse, not better. When problem employees are ignored, when you and their co-workers try to cover for them, they inevitably think that they have you fooled or intimidated. They can cost your organization an inordinate amount of money in lost productivity.

I remember Lee. Lee was fifty-five years old and had been the manager of building maintenance for his organization for twenty-three years. In 1978, he had a major disagreement with his division head, Jonathan, over policies and procedures. Lee lost the battle, but continued the war. Building maintenance seemed to go on, not because of him, but in spite of him. He quit coming into his office, claiming he needed to be out surveying the buildings for which he was responsible. Yet a number of equipment breakdowns occurred because he had not provided for routine maintenance. He came late, or not at all, to department head meetings. If he did show up at the meetings, his comments and suggestions were so inappropriate that he became known as a "loose cannon."

Employees who worked for Lee tried to cover his mistakes because they felt sorry for him. Jonathan chose to do nothing, partly because he feared an age discrimination suit if he reprimanded Lee, and partly because he felt sorry for him. Time went on and buildings and employee morale deteriorated. Finally, Jonathan could ignore the problem no more. He dealt with it by promoting Lee to a newly created position of Maintenance Consultant and hiring Pat to manage building maintenance, with the instruction to ignore Lee. Not only did ignoring the problem not work, it increased company costs.

TECHNOLOGICAL REMEDIES

Technological remedies that have typically been used to deal with the problem employee are polygraph tests, drug tests, and searches and surveillance. These, too, are adversarial approaches to employee management. Although they are in good currency in many organizations, they are of doubtful legal status because the constitutions of twenty-two states guarantee an employee the right to privacy and the U.S. Supreme Court has ruled that a right to privacy is implicit in other provisions of the Bill of Rights.[20]

While an individual's right to privacy does not supersede an organization's need to protect health and safety of both employees and clients, invasion of that right can have negative consequences for the organization, consequences that can include successful lawsuits by the employee whose privacy is invaded. William Petrocelli provides the following judicially approved definition of the right to privacy:

It is the right to be free from the unwarranted appropriation of one's personality, the publicizing of one's private affairs with which the public has no legitimate concern, or the wrongful intrusion into one's private activities, in such a manner as to outrage or cause mental suffering, shame, or humiliation to a person of ordinary sensibilities.[21]

Thus, the successful human resource manager should approach the use of technological remedies with trepidation.

Polygraph Tests

Although once used quite frequently in pre-employment screening and often with existing employees, polygraph tests are now essentially illegal.

Non-public employers are prohibited by federal law from requiring or even suggesting polygraph tests except in very narrow circumstances. These circumstances are those that include an ongoing investigation into theft, embezzlement, or misappropriation of funds, or unlawful espionage or sabotage. Organizations that design, install, or maintain security systems or employ security personnel are also allowed to use the polygraph.[22] In all other private sector organizations, polygraph tests are illegal. Even in organizations where the polygraph test is legal, the law requires that employers not rely solely upon the results of a polygraph test in making employment-related decisions.[23]

Drug Tests

In the public sector, drug testing has become fairly common since the 1986 Executive Order of then-President Reagan.[24] In the private sector, the requirements are much less stringent. A 1988 survey by the Bureau of Labor Statistics found that only 3.2 percent of the businesses surveyed had drug testing programs. Of those who had programs, 64 percent tested current employees.[25]

While the Omnibus Anti-drug Abuse Act of 1988 (effective March 8, 1989) requires that all new federal contracts or grants must contain a provision requiring the contractor to maintain a drug-free work place, it does not require drug testing. It also applies only to drug use, possession, or distribution while an employee is on the job. Motor carriers must conduct pre-employment drug tests, periodic testing, and postaccident testing. In addition, all defense contracts involving access to classified information must contain a drug-free work place clause.[26]

More detailed information on legislation governing drug testing will be presented in chapter 8. For now, suffice it to say that drug tests are required of only a limited number of employers for specific groups of employees. While drug testing supporters have identified a number of reasons for implementing drug testing programs, opponents have listed an equal number of reasons why drug testing programs should not be instituted.[27]

The most pervasive argument against drug testing is that the percentage of errors is extremely high. In a 1981 study of thirteen laboratories used to monitor drug use by patients enrolled in methadone clinics, the Federal Centers for Disease Control found error rates of up to 67 percent![28] In fact, over-the-counter anti-inflammatory drugs such as Nuprin® and Advil® can trigger a positive test result for marijuana. Nyquil® and Contac® have chemical structures so close to that of amphetamines that they too will trigger positive drug test results.[29] Another very pervasive argument against drug testing is that lives, families, and careers can be damaged when faith is put in a simple positive test that resulted from error.

Drug tests simply do not solve substance abuse problems. This is evident in the case of the commander of the Exxon *Valdez*, who apparently had a history of alcohol-related problems. Blood tests were not administered until eight or nine hours after the nearly 11 million gallons of oil were spilled into Prince William Sound. While these tests were positive, the possibility has been raised that the commander got drunk after the spill, not before, and conflicting reports have been received from witnesses.[30]

It seems to me that both the company and the public got caught up in finding out how much the commander had to drink. By doing this, they lost sight of the real issue: An employee's inaccurate judgment cost millions of dollars and seriously damaged the environment. The reason he made the error can never be changed. It is past history. The issue now should be preventing such a mistake from ever happening again. A focus on drug testing for the past mistake can detract from the company's ability to plan for the future.

Search and Surveillance

One approach that some employers take to prevent drugs in the work place is that of search and surveillance. This approach is used sometimes when an employee is suspected of theft. Employees, however, are entitled to privacy. If you detain an employee for as little as five minutes, you could be guilty of false imprisonment. If you accost an employee in the presence of others, you could be guilty of defamation of character.[31] In your zeal to "catch" an employee with incriminating evidence, you can alienate all your employees who will resent your accusations and your failure to trust.

SUMMARY

This chapter paints a bleak picture. It is meant to. For that reason, it is short. I do not want to discourage you, but rather to demonstrate for you that you can expect the presence of a problem employee to completely disrupt your work environment and your own sense of yourself. That has happened to many others. It may have happened to you. Your own negative reactions and your own feelings of helplessness and frustration are normal and natural. They are predictable stages and, when confronted with a problem employee, you can expect to go through them, especially when you find that your usual skills and good sense are inadequate for dealing with the problems generated.

That's why I've written this book. That's why you're reading it. Together, we can discover some ways to successfully prevent and manage problem behavior in the work place. In chapters 4 and 5 I'll give you methods for dealing with the problem employee that do produce results, that have been demonstrated to be effective.

I'll caution you though that even knowing *what* to do may not prevent you from going through the stages I have described in this chapter. When confronted with a problem employee, you will still deny, get angry and depressed, hope for miracles, and plead. You may even "bleed" a little. The difference will come for you when you see the results of your efforts, when you see your problems reduced or eliminated.

By using the techniques described in the following chapters you will no longer feel helpless and out of control. You will know you are, ultimately, in charge of the situation. By developing this confidence, you can better survive the traumas created by a problem employee, both personally and legally.

NOTES

1. See David Guralnik, ed. in chief, *Webster's New World Dictionary of the American Language* (New York: Popular Library, 1973).

2. See Stephen Blumberg, *Win-Win Administration: How to Manage an Organization so Everybody Wins* (Sun Lakes, Ariz.: Thomas Horton and Daughters, 1983).

3. Fredrick Herzberg, "One More Time, How Do You Motivate Employees," *Harvard Business Review* (January–February 1968), 53–62.

4. See Martin Shain and Judith Groeneveld, *Employee Assistance Programs: Philosophy, Theory and Practice* (Lexington, Mass.: Lexington Books, D. C. Heath & Co., 1982).

5. See, e.g., William Hoffer, "How to Help a Troubled Employee," *Association*

Management 35, no. 3 (March 1983), 67–73; Eugene Pressler, "Counseling the Troubled Employee," *Management World* 10, no. 3 (March 1981), 41–42; Dorothy Schaeffer, "Counseling—No Easy Task," *Supervision* 43, no. 2 (February 1981), 5, 7–8.

6. See Chester Karrass and William Glasser, *Both Win Management* (New York: Lippincott and Crowell, 1980).

7. See Henry Tosi, John Rizzo, and Stephen Carroll, *Managing Organization Behavior* (Marshfield, Mass.: Pitman Publishing Co., 1986).

8. Edward Lawler, "Reward Systems," in J. Richard Hackman and J. Lloyd Suttle, eds., *Improving Life at Work* (Santa Monica, Calif.: Goodyear Publishing Co., 1977), 163–226.

9. See Lawler, "Reward Systems."

10. See Herzberg, "One More Time."

11. See Willa Bruce, "Job Satisfaction of the Nation's Municipal Clerks: Supervisors Make a Difference," forthcoming in *American Review of Public Administration*.

12. Dr. J. Walton Blackburn, Personal Correspondence.

13. See Elisabeth Kubler-Ross, *Death: The Final Stage of Growth* (Englewood Cliffs, N.J.: Prentice Hall, 1985).

14. Christine Reed, B. J. Reed, and Jeffrey Luke, "Assessing Readiness for Economic Development Strategic Planning," *American Planning Association Journal* 53 (Autumn 1987), 521–30.

15. Donald Phillips and Harry Older, "A Model for Counseling Troubled Supervisors," *Alcohol, Health, and Research World* 2, no. 1 (Fall 1977), 24–30.

16. See Hoffer, "How to Help."

17. See, e.g., Phillips and Older, "A Model for Counseling Troubled Supervisors" *Alcohol, Health and Research World*, 2, no. 1 (Fall 1977), 24–30; H. M. Trice and Paul Roman, *Spirits and Demons at Work* (Ithaca, N.Y.: Cornell University Press, 1972 and 1978).

18. See William Delaney, *Thirty Most Common Problems in Management and How to Solve Them* (New York: AMACOM, 1982).

19. Robert Hollman, "Managing Troubled Employees: Meeting the Challenge," *Journal of Contemporary Business* 8, no. 4 (October 1979), 43–57.

20. "Privacy at Work: Where Must Employers Draw the Line?" *Modern Business Reports, Update # 2* (New York: Alexander Hamilton Institute, 1989).

21. William Petrocelli, *Low Profile—How to Avoid the Privacy Invaders* (New York: McGraw-Hill Book Co., 1981), 112.

22. 29 U.S.C. 2001–09.

23. See David Pederson, "Wrongful Discharge and Related Claims," paper presented at the Baird Holm Labor Law Forum, Omaha, Nebr., May 1989.

24. Executive Order #12564.

25. John Taylor, "Growing Number of Firms Confront Legal Issues: Kiewit Joins Employers Testing for Drugs," *Omaha World-Herald*, 6 June 1989, pp. 1–2.

26. See Trudy Bredthauer, "Drug and Alcohol Testing in the Work Place: A Legal Perspective," paper presented at the Labor Law Forum, Omaha, Nebr., May 1989.

27. Bureau of National Affairs, *Alcohol and Drugs in the Workplace: Costs, Con-*

trols, and Controversies (Washington, D.C.: Bureau of National Affairs, 1986), 27–29.

28. H. J. Hansen, S. P. Caudill, and D. J. Boone, "Crisis in Drug Testing," *Journal of the American Medical Association* 253, no. 16 (26 April 1985), 2382–87.

29. National Treasury Employees Union v. Von Raab, #863522, November 14, 1986, reported in *Government Employee Relations Report* 24 (17 November 1986), 1574–85.

30. See "Exxon Chief: Captain not Drunk," *Omaha World Herald*, Omaha, Nebr. 17 May 1989.

31. See "Privacy at Work."

Chapter 4

Performance Monitoring: An Interpersonal Method That Does Work

Now we're ready to talk about how to manage your employees in such a way that problems can be reduced or eliminated. In this chapter I will explain Performance Monitoring, which is *the* most effective method I've found for dealing with a problem employee. It is an interpersonal method based on Reality Therapy, which was developed for use by psychiatrists and counselors by psychiatrist William Glasser in 1965.[1] I see Reality Therapy, as it can be practiced in organizations, as effective Performance Monitoring. As you incorporate Performance Monitoring into your management style, you will begin to proactively manage the problem employee.

Other effective methods for dealing with the problem employee will be explained in the next chapter. These include developing a healthy organization, policies and procedures for dealing with the problem employee in general and substance abusers in particular, wellness programs, and supervisory support systems. The Employee Assistance Program (EAP), which is also an effective method for dealing with the problem employee, will be discussed in chapter 6.

REALITY THERAPY

To learn Performance Monitoring, you first need to understand Reality Therapy, so I want to give you a little background on Glasser's views. Reality Therapy is a cognitive-behavioral technique that approaches helping by dealing rationally with problem solving. It is instructive, directive, and verbal. Those who use it focus on the present and teach others to accept responsibility for their actions by analyzing inconsistencies among their goals and behaviors. When you use a Reality Therapy approach to management, you will confront inappropriate behavior, praise positive behavior, and encourage your employees to reject behaviors that keep them from meeting their needs to gain self-worth and recognition.[2]

Glasser operates from the standpoint that "of all behaviors—thinking, feeling, doing—the easiest to change is doing, regardless of whether or not the change is made with accompanying insight."[3] You cannot know what another person is thinking or feeling—you can only guess. You can, however, observe what they are doing. When they change what they are doing, you can observe that "doing" change. "Doing" is behavior and it is behavior in the work place that you are concerned about.

To successfully manage a problem employee, you must focus on the present and assist your employees to meet their basic needs for recognition and belonging. When people are not having these needs met, they act in ways to try to meet them. For most, those actions will result in effective and productive behavior. The problem employee, however, will attempt to meet needs in inappropriate ways. It is up to you, the manager, to teach that employee how to meet needs in an acceptable way; in effect, to teach him or her how to deal with reality by "doing" what is appropriate in the organization.

Now, you probably know that there are many intellectual approaches to defining "reality." For our purposes, you need to think of reality as phenomena that have a being independent of your own volition—something that you cannot wish away.[4] When we talk in terms of dealing with reality, we recognize that actions are realistic only when they lead to an amount of satisfaction that is greater than the costs of the effort they require. Thus, an employee must be encouraged to examine his or her actions in light of that reality that cannot be wished away. You will facilitate realistic choices that can lead to greater self-actualization, and thus to motivation and performance.

To explain why people choose the behavior they do, Glasser has developed a model called "Behavior: The Control of Perception."[5] In it he explains that behavioral choices are based on internal perceptions of the way the world is, so that the behavior exhibited is a direct result of the perception being experienced. If that perception is unacceptable to the perceiver, the behavior he or she exhibits will represent an effort to change the perception to one that satisfies the basic needs to be loved and feel worthwhile. In this way people attempt to control the outside world so they can get what they need. This explanation of behavior is just the opposite of the explanation that encourages managers to use a "carrot" or "stick" to change performance, for it puts responsibility for behavior on the individual, rather than on some outside force, such as you.

This approach to understanding behavior not only places the choice of how one acts on the person acting, it also places the choice of how one feels on that person. This means that one is not "depressed," but "depressing." One is not "pleased" but "pleasing." Feelings become activities that are chosen rather than responses to some outside stimuli over which one has no control. Once you understand that both behaviors and feelings are *chosen*, you can reject excuses for inappropriate behavior.

Remember when the comedian, Flip Wilson, told us "the Devil made me do it!" Remember the employee who told you "It's all your fault!" Neither you nor the devil are responsible for other people's behavior. They and they alone are accountable and must take responsibility for their actions.

The steps of Reality Therapy have been used successfully in a large number of organizational settings.[6] Reality Therapy has eight steps. The steps are sequential and all are necessary for proactive management of the problem employee. They can be summarized as follows:

1. Establish a good working relationship
2. Focus on current behavior
3. Evaluate current behavior
4. Plan for responsible behavior
5. Get commitment
6. Accept no excuses
7. Let natural consequences take over
8. Don't give up too easily[7]

A Reality Therapist uses these steps as a part of counseling patients who come seeking help. You, however, are neither a counselor nor a physician, and *I do not advocate that you try to treat sick employees*. I don't want to lull you into thinking that understanding Reality Therapy will solve every problem you have with employees. If you have a sick employee, an employee who is a substance abuser, or an employee with numerous family problems that are impacting the work place, you will need to seek outside help. Chapter 6 will tell you how.

What is important, however, is that you are the person in the work place responsible for dealing with all employees—problem or not. When you understand Reality Therapy you can facilitate an employee in seeking professional physical or mental health services when the need arises. You can become a catalyst by which an employee can confront his or her own behavior and make a decision to change. You can enable your employee to see his or her own behavior as you see it, and then to make a decision about whether or not to continue that behavior.

PERFORMANCE MONITORING

The process you will follow as you incorporate Reality Therapy into your management style is presented in the "Flow Chart for Performance

Monitoring" depicted in Figure 4.1. In this chart, rectangles represent process symbols that contain the procedure used at this particular step, and the diamond represents a decision point. Arrows show the flow of activity between steps. This diagram illustrates that the use of Performance Monitoring is an ongoing process that will allow you to identify potential problems early on and deal with them before they can escalate.

Before talking about how the steps can be used with a problem employee, I want to note that to be completely effective these steps *in toto* should be incorporated into your management style. Performance Monitoring is not a technique to be tried after all else has failed. Rather, it is an ongoing management style, a method for facilitating productivity. While useful for dealing with the non-problem employee, it is not necessary. You can't know in advance, however, who will become a problem employee, or why or when. If you have already made Performance Monitoring a part of your management style, dealing with the problem employee will be easier. The following discussion of Performance Monitoring will assist you in incorporating it into the way you deal with your employees.

Step 1: Establish and Maintain a Good Working Relationship

No matter how many problems you have been having with an employee, you must establish a good relationship *before* you can hope to bring about change. I know that won't be easy. It's difficult to be nice and caring to someone who is literally driving you up the wall. You must remember, however, that you are in charge, and you are responsible for getting the goals of the organization accomplished. The folk wisdom that tells us that the only person whose behavior you can really change is your own has proven to be right again and again. It is up to you to provide a climate in which your employees have the opportunity to choose behavior that will enable them to successfully meet their needs *while also contributing to the accomplishment of your organization's goals.*

This first step is crucial to the incorporation of Performance Monitoring into your management style, yet it is an all-too-easy step to miss, or mismanage. A fine line exists here between "good relationship" and "superior–subordinate" relationship. Certainly, you and your subordinates are not organizational equals. This is not to say that as individuals you are innately different, nor is it to imply that you need to do one thing with "us" and another with "them." But as a manager, you must maintain your authority, while at the same time respecting and recognizing your employees as human beings.

What must happen during Step 1 is the development of a "relational-

Figure 4.1
Flow Chart for Performance Monitoring

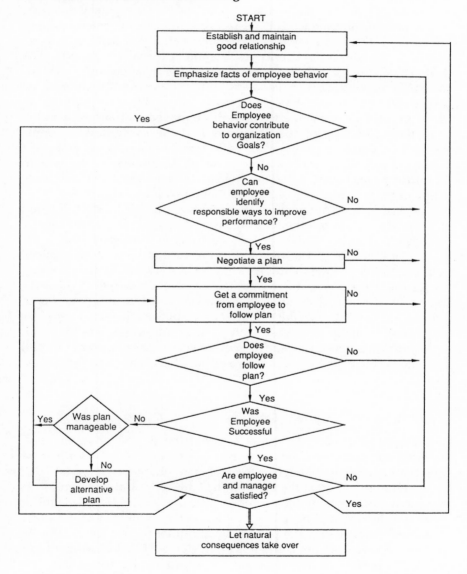

confidence," which is a belief between you and your employee that you rationally and calmly handle cooperatively and respectfully any problems that arise. Establishment of this relational-confidence will take place gradually and can be facilitated through shared activities that occur on a regular basis.[8]

To establish and maintain a good relationship with your employees you must become friends. This means you must spend time getting to know them. Even as I say this, I have to remind you that the English language provides a fluid conceptualization of the word "friend." The dictionary defines it as "one devoted to another by affection, regard, or esteem; intimate acquaintance, a supporter of a cause." You know, of course, that you cannot expect yourself, or even allow yourself, to become an intimate acquaintance of your employee, nor should you become devoted to one another by affection. Rather, your devotion must spring from, and be confined to, regard and esteem. And, you must consciously develop this regard and esteem. To implement this step in its purest form, which is making friends, violates the traditional management tenet that a boss cannot be friends with an employee.

The best advice I can give you for initiating this friendly relationship is to simply "do unto others as you would have them do unto you." This "Golden Rule" for living, I am convinced, is as applicable in the work place as it is in the world. It requires that you invest some of yourself and your time in and for your employees. It requires that you not let your frustrations and disappointment in them be reflected in your treatment of them. It requires that you ask yourself how you would want to be treated, and then treat your employees in that very same way. That's usually quite easy with most of the people who work for you. Your problem employee will require you to work harder at it. But, with the problem employee you have to work harder anyway. You know that.

Step 2: Focus on Current Behavior

In Step 2 you refuse to focus on either the distant or recent past. Rather, you must talk about the facts of your employee's *current* behavior, whether it is commendable, acceptable, or unacceptable. Ask "What are you doing?" and get the facts on the table to look at the employee's specific performance problem.

Do not discuss past mistakes. Do not accept excuses. I truly believe that you cannot change the past and you cannot predict the future. All you have is here and now, and it is on this present that you must focus as you help your employee accept responsibility for his or her own behavior.

People rarely see their own actions as having anything to do with the problem, rather they are more likely to see themselves as victims of something over which they have no control. Your role in Step 2 is to emphasize current behavior and refuse to accept excuses. Why a person did as he or she did is irrelevant. The behavior being exhibited is the issue, and self-confrontation may be a necessary step toward self-examination.

One of your roles in using Reality Therapy is to teach your employees a better way to act.

This is rarely done by lectures, but more effectively accomplished by skillful questioning. In using appropriate questions there is an implicit message: "You have power over your life. You can change. A better life is possible." . . . (Employees) begin to change their thinking from "This is an overwhelming problem" to "I believe I can handle it."[9]

Focusing on current behavior can be difficult. Most of us are nice, sympathetic people and it's easy to get caught up in listening to an employee explain why he was late, why he missed a deadline, why he broke his leg. You simply must realize, however, that "why" something happened is irrelevant. "What" is going to be done about it is crucial.

You also need to remember the stages that people go through when faced with a crisis such as a serious illness or job problem. Remember I talked about this in the last chapter: denial, fear, anger, depression, and finally, acceptance. When you confront problem employees with their unacceptable behavior those employees are likely to pass through the same stages you have. They too may "pray for a miracle," "plead," and "bleed" before any change can take place.

I remember Larry. Larry was an employee of mine who had made a mistake on a report that had cost the company thousands of dollars. This was not the first major mistake Larry had made. By company policy this mistake could cause Larry to be suspended for three days. Neither of us wanted that. I asked him to come in the office so we could talk about it. Our conversation went something like this:

Me: We need to talk about your performance.

Larry: I've never made a mistake like this before.

Me: We need to talk about what you can do about it.

Larry: Let me explain what happened.

Me: Talking about what happened isn't as important as talking about what you can do to see that you don't make a mistake like this in the future.

Larry: If you'd just let me explain. My little girl was sick and I had to take her to the emergency room the night before the report was due.

(At this point my natural inclination was to show sympathy about the child, and to lecture Larry on why he should not have put his reports off until the last minute. Most of us have a good stock speech on the importance of planning ahead and time management. I sure do, and this seemed like a good place to use it. That, however, would not have helped Larry deal with his unacceptable performance, nor would it have stopped his denial of the existence of a problem. So our conversation continued.)

Me: Larry, the reality here is that you have made a serious error on a report. Talking about why you did it will not change the mistake.

Larry: I don't understand why you're blaming this on me. Obviously you didn't do your job. If you had checked my report more carefully, you would have caught the mistake.

(See how Larry now tried to shift the blame to me. He was still not accepting responsibility for his inadequate work, rather he was trying another tack. When I wouldn't let him get by with excusing, he moved to blaming. Now my own defenses started to rise, and I wanted to give him an elaborate lecture on how competent I was and how incompetent he was. It was hard to remember that we were discussing him here, not me, but I made myself focus on the issue—his unacceptable report.)

Me: Larry, you have made serious errors in this report. you will be placed on suspension unless you work out a plan for ensuring that this does not happen again.

Larry: I think if you reread the report you'll see that mistake is yours. Here, let me show you what I was trying to do.

Me: I have already read the report and it is not acceptable work. We need to talk about what you can do to improve.

Larry: I don't know what you have against me. I've never done anything to hurt you.

(Now Larry switched from trying to blame me to accusing me of not liking him. He had moved from denial to anger. Being a rather nice, friendly person, my feelings were hurt. I wanted to reassure him how much I liked him, as I truly did. I didn't want him to be mad at me. That, however, would not have enabled him to take positive actions toward improving his performance, so, again I resisted my impulse.)

Me: Larry, we have to talk about what you can do to improve your reports.

Larry: I don't see anything that needs improving. And other people don't either. I showed my paper to the district manager and he said I did a good job.

(Now Larry moved to another predictable tactic—a referral to authority as a means of intimidation. He still had not accepted responsibility for his own actions, but I knew if I held firm he'd soon run out of excuses. I ignored my nagging fear that the district manager really had seen and approved the report. I reminded myself that the district manager did not have the time to read routine reports generated by employees at Larry's level and that decisions were left up to individual supervisors, and I continued to focus on Larry's current situation.)

Me: The errors on this report mean that you can be placed on suspension. I'm willing to talk about what you can do to improve. If you don't want to talk about that, then we're wasting our time.

Larry: Oh, alright, what do you want me to do?

(I resisted the impulse to start explaining how to research, document, and write a correct report, Larry already knew that. I resisted the impulse to review each section of the report with him and go over comments I had made in its margins. I recognized that Larry had given up three defenses: excusing, blaming, and threatening; and I recognized that he had moved through denial, anger, and withdrawal to acceptance. I knew that we were almost ready for him to move to Step 3, in which he would accept responsibility and evaluate his own performance and suggest ways to improve it.)

Me: I want you to evaluate your own performance and suggest ways that you can improve it.

Larry: You mean you'll let me redo the report?

Me: Yes. If you're willing to identify ways you can improve it and set a deadline for getting the rewritten, correct report to me.

Assisting your employee to examine behavior can be easy and rewarding. It can also be disturbing and threatening. The key, in either event, is to remain firm and committed to the process.

Step 3: Evaluate Current Behavior

In this step you evaluate current behavior. This step requires you to deliver your value judgment about performance to the employee *and* get a value judgment from the employee. When the employee is doing a good job this step is pleasant for both of you. If the employee's behavior is not acceptable to you, however, this step can be difficult, for you must get agreement that something must be done.

People are more likely to say "I've tried everything" than they are to begin immediately to suggest alternative actions. But they *must* make the value judgment that what they are doing is hurting them, and want something better, before they move to planning for improvement.

As a part of this evaluative process you must ask probing questions that facilitate the employee's thinking about what he or she wants, as well as about what he or she is doing. This leads the employee to acknowledge that what he or she is doing is not giving him what he or she wants and opens the door to planning for change.

Change, as you well know, is difficult. Jeff Luke believes that there are six laws of change. To bring about change you need to understand these laws and learn to work within them. The laws are:

1. resonance;
2. resistance;
3. incrementalism;
4. habit;
5. interconnectedness; and
6. fear.[10]

Let's talk about these laws.

Resonance. The word *resonate* comes from a musical term meaning "to be in synchronization with, to vibrate together." For change to occur, the object of change, in this case your employee, must be in agreement with you that change is necessary and be both willing and able to move with you as change occurs. That's why it's so important for both you and your employee to have a shared sense of the employee's behaviors that must change and a shared belief that the employee is capable of and responsible for changing those behaviors. This is not easy because of the other laws of change.

Resistance. All of us resist change. So often change is viewed as "the other person's thing," we are reluctant to even consider it. You probably already know that just telling someone to change doesn't get him or her to change. When that happens most of us are tempted to explain rationally the reason why we want change, and then tell exactly how to go about it. The problem is, my reasons are usually not your reasons and my wants are usually not yours.

We see resistance a lot of times with our kids, as well as with our employees. Yet as long as the other person is resisting what you know to be appropriate behavior, inappropriate behavior is likely to continue. One way to assist employees to evaluate their current behavior and decide that something must be done is to accept the resistance by saying

O.K. I can see your viewpoint. I don't completely agree with it, but I can certainly see the reason for what you are doing. But, could I ask you this? Do you believe that there is at least a possibility that what you're doing may not be the best way to handle the situation?[11]

People especially resist major, drastic change. That's why Reality Therapy focuses on one behavior, one issue at a time. That's why we have the third law of change: incrementalism.

Incrementalism. Change will only occur in small pieces. Nothing of real importance happens instantly. In this age of fast food and microwave ovens, that's sometimes hard to remember. Yet the lessons of the seasons are there for all to see. Seeds planted in the early spring do not mature until the summer. A human being takes nine months from conception to birth. We readily accept that there are no miracle diets that cause a loss of weight overnight, yet often we want our employees to change overnight. The fact is, they can't.

Changing the behavior of a problem employee is an incremental process. It happens in small steps, each change building upon the other. You must have the patience to let this happen.

I was once called in to work with an organization because the manager was concerned that his supervisors were "trigger happy."

"They want to fire people, not teach them," he said, "can you show them how to act differently?"

"Yes," I replied, "but it'll take time."

Time is our most precious resource. We must use it wisely and patiently. Recognizing that creating works of art takes time and recognizing that changing behavior takes time too is crucial to changing your problem employees.

Habit. The next law of change is habit. Change takes times because it requires that we learn to replace old, non-productive habits with new, effective habits, Have you ever started an exercise program? Do you remember how hard it was to drag yourself out on cold or wet mornings to jog or run? Do you remember how hard it was to give up your favorite television program to go over to the gym? And do you remember how much better you felt when you finally replaced the "couch potato" with the athlete? Do you remember how long it took?

Just as habits can be learned and become ingrained, they take a while to break and replace with new changed behavior. When you're dealing with a problem employee you're dealing with someone who has bad habits where work productivity is concerned. As you work to help change those habits remember that progress will take time.

Interconnectedness. All change is interconnected. No change takes place in a vacuum. Rather, every person and every event in your organization is connected to every other. To help you see how powerful this interconnectedness is, I'd like you to think about the last time you changed jobs and moved to a new city. Remember how many changes took place? Remember how many new behaviors you had to learn? You had a new city to get around in, new grocery stores, new people to meet, maybe even a new climate to adjust to. Remember how long it took you to get acclimated? Remember how the changes affected your family?

So it is with any change. Each action, each person is related to each other and as one changes, the other is forced to change in a kind of domino effect. Expect this in your organization as you start to change the way in which you deal with your problem employee.

Fear. The final law of change is fear. We, you and me included, fear change. The present is at least familiar, and we've developed the skills to cope with it. That's why we stay in bad marriages or unfulfilling jobs. We're afraid that the alternative might be worse. Your problem employee may be afraid to change. You, in fact, may be afraid to try out a new set of skills in dealing with the problem employee. "What if this doesn't work either?" you're likely to ask yourself.

All I can answer is that you'll never know until you try. And that's the only answer you can give your employee too. I remember a line I had to memorize in high school that applies here.

The coward dies many times before his death.
The brave man only tastes of death but once.

Until you and your employee are willing to confront inappropriate behavior, evaluate it, and get agreement that change is necessary, change will not occur. Dreading the confrontation is often far worse than the act itself.

I remember Carla. Carla was both a secretary and receptionist in a small company. Her office was adjacent to the manager's and contained employee's mail boxes, central files, and the copier. Carla's desk was near to and faced the exterior door. A table and several chairs furnished the area. Because of the equipment and information in Carla's office, other employees were frequently in it. Several times as many as four or five people would gather in the office and visit.

At first Laura, the manager, tried to deal with the problem in traditional ways. She asked employees not to congregate. They persisted. She decentralized the filing system and had the table and all but one chair removed. The visiting slowed; but Carla started to go to other offices to visit. Her work got behind. Budget reports due in August were not done at the end of October. Then Laura tried Performance Monitoring. Carla's responses to her were much like Larry's were to me.

When Laura first confronted Carla with her unacceptable performance, she began excusing by accusing the other employees of distracting her and taking so much of her time she couldn't get her work done. Laura insisted that they talk about Carla and not the other employees. Carla then told Laura that the whole situation was all her fault because she (Laura) didn't like Carla. Carla even screamed and cried as she accused Laura of making her a scapegoat. Laura persisted. Carla threatened to report her to the company owner for mistreatment. Laura continued to focus on Carla's performance by persisting with "What can you do about it?"

Finally, when Laura was just about to give up, Carla came into her office.

"I think I've figured out what to do to keep my work current."

"Good! Tell me about it!" exclaimed Laura, although she thought, "It's about time!"

"I'm going to rearrange my office so I won't get so many distractions," Carla explained. "I've decided that on Saturday I'll move my desk to the back, away from the door, facing the wall. Then I won't see people when they come in and stop to visit."

Laura's purpose had been achieved. Although she had been tempted to institute disciplinary actions, and had even thought about firing Carla, she was glad she had trusted Performance Monitoring morale. As you know, firing is a drastic step that brings costs in other areas, such as employee morale and in finding and training a replacement. Current employees are at least known. If they are capable, they are worth trying to save. What is required on your part is a faith that your employee with a productivity problem can and will choose to replace failing behaviors with successful ones, and the courage to confront the employee when inappropriate behaviors occur. Once your employee has accepted responsibility for his or her own behavior and begun to think of ways to improve it, you are ready to move to Step 4, in which the employee plans for change.

Step 4: Plan for Responsible Behavior

To plan for responsible behavior requires that the employee identify specific ways to improve performance and then negotiate the implementation of these improvements with you. If the employee's suggestions are reasonable and realistic, you can assist him or her in developing a plan for responsible behavior. If they are not, you must explain why not and encourage the employee to suggest other means of improvement.

Identify ways to improve performance. Identifying responsible ways to improve performance is a crucial step in changing problem employee behavior. This identification, however, is not your responsibility. It is the employee's responsibility. I think that one of the biggest mistakes we make as managers is to think we are totally responsible for our employees' behavior. If they do well, we smilingly take credit. If they fail, we castigate ourselves, wondering where we've gone wrong. For your problem employee to change to a productive employee, you must let go. Even though you may have fantastic ideas, which the employee has not thought of, for now you must keep them to yourself. Remember that when change is "the other guy's thing," it is not likely to be accepted.[12]

Negotiate a plan. The development of a plan for change in no way requires, nor is it meant to suggest, that you become an "arm-chair therapist." Rather, encouraging the employee to develop a plan for change is to acknowledge that the employee has the ability both to plan and to change. For the plan to be successful it must be concrete, small, within a specific time frame, and something that can be done immediately. The plan must be an incremental one, made and carried out one step at a time. The plan must focus on what will be done, not on what won't be done. For instance, an employee whose problem behavior is tardiness might plan "I will arrive at work at 8 A.M. *tomorrow*," not, "I will never be tardy again."

Another element in effective planning is to focus on choosing a behavior to replace the one that has been determined to be inappropriate, and that can be accomplished regardless of what others do. In the example of Carla, the successful plan was "I will move my desk on Saturday," not "I won't waste any more time by visiting." In a similar vein, an employee who has a drinking problem should not say "I'll never take another drink." Rather, he or she should say "I will attend an AA meeting tonight," and so on.

Once the plan has been made you can reinforce it by having the employee explain to you why the plan is a good one and why he or she thinks it will work. In explaining to you how the plan will work, the employee will take ownership for the plan and be more likely to move to Step 6, which is commitment.

You may work for an organization that uses strategic planning as a way of proactively dealing with the future. The same activities that your organization undertakes in strategic planning can be used by your employee in making a plan for change.

Strategic planning begins with an analysis of external threats and opportunities and internal strengths and weaknesses. This analysis recognizes the phenomenon of interconnectedness and encourages the planner to see his or her situation in a light that extends beyond himself or herself.

It's important to be careful here and not allow the employee to use external threats and internal weaknesses as excuses. Rather the employee must see them as a part of the reality with which he or she must deal. Your role is to emphasize opportunities and strengths and to ask the employee how he or she can capitalize on them to deal with the key issue, which is that part of the employee's behavior that is negatively impacting your organization. You must serve as a reality tester, confronting the employee with the facts of his or her job situation, while at the same time encouraging active planning for change.

To help the employee plan for change it is important that both of you understand the difference between strategies, goals, and objectives. A strategy is an overarching philosophy of how to attack a problem—deciding which approach to utilize. Developing a strategy involves very basic decisions about what the employee and you want from the plan. Hopefully you will both want your problem employee to once again become a productive member of the firm. If that is your strategy, then every goal and objective you set will be for that purpose.

Goals are more specific than strategies. You will have one overarching strategy. You may have several goals. All of then will be geared toward improving your employee's productivity. Each goal will require several action steps for completion. Each action step must be time bound, observable, and specific. For goals to be met, your employee must accept responsibility for taking one step at a time, and for doing this within a specific timetable. He or she must come up with the plan alone and explain to you how and why it will work. The following points will help you facilitate improved performance as a result of the plan:

1. Go over the plan in detail so that both of you understand exactly *what* is to be done.

2. Agree specifically on *when* it is to be done. It is not enough to say "soon" or "as soon as possible" or "in three weeks."

3. Specify the *quality* of the work you want. "Good work" or "better work" is not a useful standard leading to better performance. Your employee must know what "good" or "bad" means. If you can't describe it, he can't do it.

4. Specify a *quantity* standard for the employee to shoot at. Remarks like "I'd like a little more" or "You seem to be a little slow" just serve to frustrate the employee, who will then be likely to produce less rather than more.

5. Specify review points or milestones at which you and the employee will check progress on the agreed plan. If you want someone to hammer fifteen nails by 2:00 PM, don't hope for the best. The effective manager checks the second, the seventh, and the tenth nail at specific times of the day to assure that the fifteenth nail will arrive by 2:00 PM. The inefficient manager discovers at 2:00 PM that the employee didn't even have a hammer.[13]

Let the employee take responsibility for developing a plan for changing his or her behavior and presenting it to you. Once the employee has made a plan, you can proceed to Step 5.

Step 5: Get Commitment

At this step you transfer the responsibility for changing behavior to your employee. You must, however, retain involvement by continuing to show interest in the employee's success. This stage is brief and poignant. It may involve a handshake or a pat on the shoulder. You need to say to the employee, "I know you can do it. Keep me posted on how you're doing." You need also to keep yourself posted *on a daily basis*.

Another key ingredient in commitment is documentation. Never let yourself forget that this plan is a joint effort to change your employee's behavior. We hope that it will be enough to negate any thought of disciplinary action. But that specter always looms, and both you and your employee must be aware of it. It's not that you say "plan or else." Your employee must, however, be aware of the possible consequences of failure to change. You must be aware that if the employee fails to follow through and the implementation of the remaining steps of Performance Monitoring do not bring the desired changes, you will have to have maintained a written record of your conferences with your employee and the decisions made in those conferences. Let your employee know that here.

Tell the employee that the plan must be put in writing and that you will be following up to see how it's going. Let the employee know that you mean business by asking that the first step in the change process will be written documentation of the plan.

Ideally your employee will provide the documentation for you in a very short period. I prefer the next day. To cover yourself, however, you need to make and keep notes on your confrontation with the employee, and the resultant plan that has been discussed. As a part of commitment to the plan, both you and the employee should sign and date it. If the employee doesn't follow through, you have the written plan to protect you and the employee from charges that "You didn't make clear what you wanted."

Some union agreements may contain clauses that prohibit jointly signed documentation of a one-on-one discussion about job performance. If that's the case in your organization, then I advise you to keep personal notes about employee conferences. Place them in a spiral notebook in a locked drawer of your desk.

Your notes should reflect both conferences held to praise your employees *and* conferences held to discuss performance problems. You should keep notes about all conferences with all employees. In this way you defend yourself in any future charge of discrimination. If you treat all employees equally you demonstrate that such a charge is unfounded.

A mistake that many supervisors and human resource managers make is to only talk with employees when things are going wrong. If you make a habit of interacting with employees on a regular basis, you can reduce their fear of talking with you. You can also maximize the influence you have over them.

Commitment and follow-up are straightforward and need, I think, no further elaboration. So we'll move quickly to Step 6.

Step 6: Accept No Excuses

In this step you ask if the employee followed the plan and was the plan successful. Your employee's plan should have included one concrete change that he or she will accomplish by the *next day.* Make sure that when that day arrives you check to see what has been accomplished. If you observe success, compliment the employee, and make a note of the observation. If the employee doesn't follow through, you must. In this step you evaluate whether or not the employee has followed the plan. If he or she has, commend and congratulate. Let the employee know that you are satisfied with the changed behavior and continue to work on maintaining a good relationship.

If the plan has not been followed, simply accept no excuses. Don't ever let your employee explain why he or she couldn't follow through on the plan made only yesterday. Again confront by emphasizing the facts of the employee's behavior. Reiterate that the failure to follow through and do what was planned is unacceptable, and ask "What are you going to do about it?" "When can you have it completed?"

The key here is caring concern coupled with firmness and resolution. You must be as committed to following through on the results of the plan as you expect your employee to be. Sometimes that gets difficult. Certainly you have many more things to do and think about than this one employee. However, the time you invest now will pay off in the future.

If you get bogged down, just remember that this problem employee has already been taking an inordinate amount of your time and energy. Now, at least, that time and energy is focused on change. If the employee's plan did not work, above all, do not ask "why?" Just focus on what didn't work and assist the employee in developing a new, more workable plan. This step in Performance Monitoring is a "treadmill" step because it is so easy for the employee to get caught up in excusing, and it is so easy for you to get trapped into empathizing and sympathizing.[14] But it is important to remember that excuses are irrelevant; actions are important.

Employees can have such wonderful, overwhelming excuses that not accepting them can seem really cold-hearted. That's O.K. It's better to be cold-hearted than to see your employee continue to disrupt organizational productivity. It's better to be cold-hearted than to waste any more of your time. It's better to be cold-hearted than to see your employee lose his or her job.

I expect that you've already heard a lot of heart-rending excuses. In case you haven't, I'd like to tell you about Clifford. Clifford had been a surgeon in the same hospital for three years when he became a problem employee. He started being absent frequently. He failed to fulfill his agreement to conduct research and publish scholarly articles. He did not manage adequately the clerical and nursing staff under him, so patient records were inadequately kept and misfiled.

When Clifford was confronted with the fact that his behavior was impacting negatively on both job performance and the organization, he had a series of impressive excuses. His wife had left him and his brother had died. He said that these events so traumatized him that he couldn't think. Poor Clifford. Who wouldn't have job performance problems under these circumstances?

What Clifford failed to realize was the other reality in his life—if he didn't perform his job, he would lose it. If he lost the job, his problems could get worse—much worse. It was up to his human resource manager to let him know that.

The way to get people to stop excusing is to confront them with reality. You must be blunt. You must also let them know that you care about them and are willing to work with them. You can acknowledge that you understand how the employee wants to be perceived right now by affirming that you are aware of how stressed he or she is, or how overburdened he or she is, and so on, but then you must return to confronting the employee with reality and asking what he or she can do to change his or her on-the-job behavior. In this case, you could help Clifford focus on his job by asking one of several question: "I know you've been under a lot of stress. What can you do to make sure you perform your job in spite of it?" or "You're having a rough time right now. What can you do to see that it doesn't keep affecting your work?" or "I understand you're upset. Let's take a look at what you're doing and solve the problem."

What you do when you refuse to accept excuses is to strengthen your employee. You show him or her that despite it all you respect him or her and believe that he or she is capable of handling the problems *and also* doing his or her job. What you have to remember is that there is no way you can or should help Clifford solve his personal problems. The only problem that can concern you and Clifford jointly is job performance.

In Clifford's case, he had three on-the-job behaviors that were unacceptable: excessive absences, failure to do research, and failure to adequately supervise the employees under him. It is upon these behaviors that his supervisor must focus. It is for the elimination of these behaviors that Clifford must develop a plan.

It is also important to realize that when an employee has as many on-the-job behaviors to change as Clifford, it will be easy to expect him to "bite off more than he can chew." He truly cannot change all these behaviors overnight. That's reality too. He can only tackle one change at a time. Recognize that and help him plan for one change one step at a time.

The "Serenity Prayer" that is used regularly by members of Alcoholics Anonymous is as important in this step for you as it is for your employee. You might want to give your employee a copy. You might also want to memorize it. The prayer is credited to St. Anthony and states:

Give me the strength to change the things I can change,
The courage to accept the things I cannot change,
And the wisdom to know the difference.

Some readers might wonder if Clifford, who had been a model employee, should be handled differently than should those whose problem behavior cannot be attributed to a specific life crisis. The answer is "No!" Problem behavior is problem behavior and it should be confronted immediately.

If the employee fails to follow through on his or her plan, you return to Step 2 and confront the employee with his or her unacceptable behavior *and* with his or her failure to follow the plan. You let the employee know that you are disappointed in him or her, and you again ask him or her to identify what he or she is willing to do to improve performance.

Step 7: Let Natural Consequences Take Over

If you've reached this step in Performance Monitoring and your employee still hasn't changed behavior, you may think that "this stuff doesn't work" or "I'm doing it wrong." This is not likely to be the case, however. Rather your problem employees have learned over time to deal with the world by excusing, blaming, and giving up. These learned behaviors are slow to change. While your natural response might be to punish, or give up yourself, you need to hang in and have faith in the process. Part of the process is to let natural consequences occur when an employee fails to follow through on the plan for change.

It is important here to clarify the difference between natural consequences and punishment. Glasser defines punishment as an action, external to the person, which is illogical in relationship to the misbe-havior.[15] In fact, some people welcome punishment because it provides attention, even though it is negative attention. To punish is to impose a penalty from outside the person. To allow natural consequences to occur is to permit the person to face the reality of the situation, and in so doing, take responsibility for it.

It is important not to create any more pressure (punishment) than the client is already experiencing (usually a lot). Punishment is an external attempt to force a person to change but it doesn't teach the way to change...It can cause a whole series of ineffective behaviors ranging from apathy to violence.[16]

Rather than punishing, you must allow natural consequences to occur while teaching a better way to handle problems.

A body of parenting literature has grown up around the notion of using natural consequences to teach children, as opposed to punishing them, when they fail to do what parents know is best. I subscribed to this approach to parenting when my children were young, partly for their own good, partly in self-defense because I got tired of preaching and threatening. To help you understand the difference between pun-ishment and natural consequences I'd like to share a memory with you.

As in most families, my sons were expected to help with the chores. I expected them to do their own laundry. As in most families, they didn't want to. So long as I ordered them to wash their clothes they refused, or were "so busy" they just didn't have time. I ended up angry. I withdrew their privileges. They ended up angry. I spanked them. They cried. We all got upset. I tried to smooth the whole thing over and did all their laundry myself. They liked that. I got angrier.

Then I learned about natural consequences. The natural consequence of laundry not done is dirty clothes. The first time my teenage sons had no clean clothes to wear on a date, they washed their own. Allowing my sons to experience natural consequences transferred the responsi-bility for changing their situation from me to them. They were strength-ened.

So it is with employees. So long as you, the supervisor, take the responsibility for "making" them do what must be done, you enable them to continue in irresponsible behavior. You also denigrate their ability. When you neither tell people what they "must" do nor punish them for inappropriate behavior, you provide a climate of learning and growth. You provide a climate in which employees can perform and perform successfully.

Organizations tend to have a structure of rules, policies, and proce-dures that facilitate the occurrence of natural consequences in the work setting. Criteria for raises and promotions are usually spelled out. So are criteria for termination. All that you, as a supervisor, have to do is make certain the employee recognizes the reality of opportunity as well as the reality of a possible end to his or her job and let the employee make the decision about which outcome he or she wants. From this perspective, termination is not punishment, something you threaten with. It is simply a logical consequence to non-performance.

When a negative natural consequence occurs, employees are not happy about it. They are likely to resurrect all their defense mechanisms in one last-ditch effort to coerce you to smooth things over or retreat from your position of allowing the natural consequences to occur. Even as you dare not retreat, you must also resist the inclination to say, "I told you so." That phrase accomplishes nothing and frequently exacerbates already volatile feelings.

If an employee is not satisfied with the outcome of his or her actions, you must adhere to the Performance Monitoring model and, once again, emphasize the facts of the employee's behavior.

Natural consequences can also be positive, pleasant occurrences. The natural consequence of my sons' doing their own laundry was clean clothes. The natural consequence of your reading this book will be improved ability to deal with the problem employee. The natural consequences for an employee performing successfully are many: a raise, a more comfortable working environment, the satisfaction of a job well done, opportunities for advancement, a redecorated office, a comfortable camaraderie with you, a few perquisites such as the freedom to make personal phone calls, a special parking place, an "Employee of the Month" award, etc.

The key difference between natural consequences and punishment (the stick) is that natural consequences occur when you as a supervisor do nothing to create a situation that is personally uncomfortable for your subordinate, when you do nothing to demean your subordinate, and when what happens is not irreversible.[17] Your employee can get a raise or promotion *when* he or she earns it. Your employee can get another job. The key difference between natural consequences and rewards (the carrot) is that natural consequences occur when you as a supervisor allow your employees to experience the fruits of their labors, rather than try to bribe them with promises of reward.

When a person doesn't perform, don't punish. The first natural consequence of not following the plan is to renegotiate the plan. Set a limit on how frequently you are willing to renegotiate. Ask your employee how long he or she thinks is reasonable for you to wait before behavior changes. Negotiate a deadline and put the deadline in writing. Get a commitment from the employee to change within this time period. The final step of the process is don't give up too easily. Don't be taken advantage of either.

When the employee fails to make agreed-upon changes after the second or third plan, it's time for another set of natural consequences: initiation of the formal disciplinary procedure. Discussion of offenses that should prompt this measure and a sample form to use are provided in the next chapter.

Step 8: Don't Give Up Too Easily

It is important that you refuse, if at all possible, to give up on your employee. If your employee thinks you have faith in his or her ability to change, he or she is likely to have faith that change is possible as well.

Here, however, you must balance organizational reality with your desire to facilitate changed behavior in your employee. If the time you devote to your employee becomes disproportionate to the time you must devote to other employees and job responsibilities, you should plan with the employee to seek outside help before you give up entirely. If your employee's behavior is drug or alcohol related, the employee's plan should be to obtain outside professional assistance. Your support of your employee in this effort is evidence that you have not given up.

The important component of "never give up" is for you to refuse to relinquish the belief that your employee can change. It is not that you hang on to the notion that it is up to you to facilitate that change.

Throughout the process of using Performance Monitoring, you also need to realize that the employee may, at any time, choose to resign from your organization or transfer from your department. That's O.K. too. It does not mean that you or your employee or the process has failed. It means, simply, that your employee has responsibly planned to change the working situation.

The Crux of Performance Monitoring

At this point you may be wondering how Performance Monitoring can be used to deal with particular troubles a problem employee may be experiencing. The most likely troubles have been identified as falling into the following categories: social (marital, personal, etc.)—37 percent; mental health—14 percent; legal—9 percent; alcohol related—9 percent; job related—8 percent; financial—6 percent; health—14 percent; and other—2 percent.[18] While these troubles might not all spill over as problem behaviors in the work place, when problem behavior does occur these troubles are the expected precipitating causes.

In using Performance Monitoring to deal with any problem employee, however, you must keep in mind that the troubles are not your concern—the problem behavior is. Thus, you must not try to "solve" the employee's problem. Rather, you must focus on how the employee is behaving, and on what that behavior is doing to the accomplishment of organizational objectives.

Keep in mind that Performance Monitoring focuses on behavior and on teaching your employee that behavior is *chosen*, and that more effective behaviors can be chosen.[19] The crux of Performance Monitoring is the identification of employee behavior *in the work place*, and the assessment, with the employee, of whether or not that behavior is contributing to organizational goals, as well as the development of a joint plan for change.

This plan may take any number of directions. It may include steps to increase productivity or it may include an agreement by your employee to accept referral to an Employment Assistance Program. It may include an agreement to participate in Alcoholics Anonymous, and it may include a decision to seek other employment. The crucial point here is that with Performance Monitoring, you do not attempt to control the employee, nor do you coerce your employee to seek outside help. Rather, you develop a good relationship with your employee so that you can jointly plan what steps the employee will take toward increasing his or her contribution to organizational goals. By involving the employee in the plan, by expecting the employee to take responsibility for conceiving of and executing the plan, you increase the likelihood that the employee will follow through on it.[20] Whatever plan is developed, your role is to stay involved with your employee, discuss what your employee is doing to follow up on the plan, and ascertain if the plan is effective.

ACTIVE LISTENING

Active listening is a skill that you can develop to enhance the feeling of trust in any communication encounter. It is a skill that shows that you are interested in and concerned about the person with whom you are communicating. It enhances feedback in a communication episode, and it allows you to gain a great deal of information.

Performance Monitoring requires that you possess and utilize effective verbal communication skills. You will remember that chapter 2 talked about the importance of incorporating effective communication skills into your management style. Performance Monitoring asks that you go one step further in facilitating communication and use Active Listening.

As you strive to place the responsibility for behavior on the shoulders of your employees, it is difficult not to preach to them or quiz them. It is sometimes difficult to get them to respond to you in more than monosyllables. Yet as the person facilitating the problem-solving interaction, you have the responsibility to engage your employee in meaningful dialogue. You have the responsibility to communicate in such a way that you instill trust and self-confidence in your employee. You can do this with Active Listening.

Too often, when any of us talk with someone, we spend more time thinking about what our reply will be than we do in hearing what the person is saying to us. One employee complained about his manager to me in this way. "He never listens. When I talk, he talks. When I stop for breath, he stops too." Communication was *not* taking place. Listening had not occurred. Feedback was impossible.

The Formulas for Active Listening

When you listen actively, you really pay attention to what the other is saying *and* you communicate this by letting the person know you heard. Those who work in the helping professions have developed a series of formulas for ensuring that Active Listening occurs.[21] The formulas are listed below, in order of how you will use them.

Formula 1: "Parrot." Repeat what the speaker just said. That's right, I said "repeat." If someone says to you, "I'm tired," you say, "You're tired." If someone says to you, "I'll never meet the deadline;" you say, "You'll never meet the deadline."

What your repetition does is to communicate that you really heard what was said. This has the amazing effect of encouraging the other person to keep talking and giving you more information. It also communicates to the other person that you really heard what was said and are trying to understand. This instills trust in you. Sometimes the other person will say so much that you can't remember everything that was said. That's O.K. Just repeat the last sentence.

When you parrot, it is important that you keep your tone of voice matter-of-fact. If you end your parroting with a question or raise your voice in shock, the other person will perceive that you are judging him or her and become defensive. This detracts from trust-building.

Formula 2: "Paraphrase." Summarize what the speaker just said. This is a form of repetition, but it allows you to zero in on the gist of the speaker's words. The important thing for you to do is to demonstrate that you heard what was said, and that you accept the speaker's ideas and/or concerns in a nonjudgmental way. When you do Active Listening you do not judge, nor do you explain, nor do you justify. You simply *listen*, and show that you have heard.

Formula 3: "Interpret." Summarize what the speaker just said *and* add the word "because." Then say in your own words the reason(s) you believe explain the person's statement. For example, "You're late *because* your car broke down." Or, "You may not meet the deadline *because* you have so many interruptions."

Don't worry if the reason you guess is different from the person's own reason. By this time that person will know that you are truly trying to understand, so if you guess wrong they'll correct you. When they do, you simply revert to Formula 1 for a couple of sentences, then try Formula 2 again before going on to Formula 3.

By using Formula 3, you indicate that you both heard what was said and understand what was said. Once this happens you're ready to move to Formula 4.

Formula 4: "Interpret Feelings." With Formula 4, you move to the level of understanding both what is being said *and* how the person feels about what he or she is telling you. Here you take a risk and mention a feeling. "You're *worried* about being tired." Or, You're afraid you'll be in trouble if you miss a deadline."

Again, don't worry if the feeling you guess is different from the person's own feeling. If you guess wrong the person will correct you. When he or she does, you simply revert to Formula 1 for a couple of sentences, then try Formulas 2 and 3 before going on to Formula 4.

Once you really understand what the person is saying, you are in a position to respond appropriately. You can diffuse anger and you can enhance the confidence of others in you. Start today to practice Active Listening. The more you use it, the more natural and the more comfortable you will become with it.[22] The next section will show you how to use Active Listening in Performance Monitoring.

Using Active Listening

In this scenario, which illustrates how to do Active Listening, let's assume that you are dealing with an employee who has failed to complete an important report was that was due a week ago. Let's also assume that you have already established a good relationship with the employee so that you can begin with Step 2 of Performance Monitoring and confront the employee with the facts of his behavior.

You: I still don't have your report that was due last week.

Employee: It's not my fault.

[Here you must resist the inclination to say "Whose fault is it, if it's not yours?" Instead "parrot."]

You: It's not your fault.

Employee: No.

[Now the employee has thrown you a ringer. Again, resist the temptation to do more than parrot, and repeat the employee's first statement.]

You: It's not your fault.

With this, you "force" the employee to say some more. Often that takes more time than you're comfortable with waiting. Most of us are uncomfortable with silence. I am. You are. Your employee is.

You can remain in control of the situation by simply waiting until the employee speaks. In my experience, you'll have to wait no more than one minute. A minute of silence seems extremely long. A trick I've learned to keep myself from interrupting the silence is to count in my head "one thousand, one thousand and one, one thousand and two," etc. This counting keeps you occupied and maintains the silence the employee needs to decide to say some more. With this method, "one thousand and sixty" equals about one minute. I've rarely had to count this far before the employee breaks the silence with an explanation.

Employee: It's not my fault because I've had too much work to do.

You: You've had too much work to do.

Employee: Yes.

Now, the employee has offered an explanation that *might* be reasonable, and is not directly blaming you. You can again parrot, or you can paraphrase by saying:

You: Tell me about the work you're doing.

At this, the employee will likely provide you with a long list of work projects, many of them successful. This is an effort to distract you from the original purpose of your meeting, which was a missed deadline. You must come back to that issue and focus on the current behavior that is unacceptable to you. You move to Step 3 and evaluate current behavior. This requires that you provide the employee with the information that current behavior is unacceptable and why.

You: The deadline you missed caused several problems for us. [Name them.]

Employee: I said it wasn't my fault.

You: Whose fault it was is not the issue. We're here to discuss the missed deadline. I want to know when you can have the report finished.

This statement reflects that you heard what the employee said. It also moves you to step 4, "plan responsible behavior." You have refused to accept blaming and excusing and are putting the responsibility on the employee's shoulders—where it belongs.

Employee: I don't know when I can have it finished.

Here you cannot buy into the employee's expressed helplessness or indecision. You reiterate that the deadline is important and that you want to know when the report can be finished.

You: The report was due last Friday. I must have it this week. When can you have it completed?

By providing a time frame and pushing your employee to set a date for completion, you assist him or her in completing Step 4. At this point, the employee may give you a date. If the date is realistic, move to Step 5, "get commitment," by thanking the employee and shaking hands. If the date is not realistic, go back to Step 3, "evaluate current behavior," and ask for a more realistic date. If the employee asks for more resources or expresses a need for more data, keep the responsibility on the employee's shoulders by asking, "How can you get resources/data?" "By when?" Negotiate a reasonable deadline, then follow up on that day to make certain the employee has kept up his or her end of the agreement.

The key to dealing with problem employees is to focus on current behavior, insist that employees take responsibility for their own actions, and if they don't, let natural consequences occur.

Now, an employee who misses a deadline is not nearly as traumatic for you as an employee that you suspect of substance abuse. An employee who misses a deadline is not nearly as difficult to deal with as the one who seems to go from one crisis to another, or the one who is a chronic troublemaker. The key however, is that no matter what response pattern the employee exhibits, Performance Monitoring can be used. No matter what the source of the employee's problem and no matter what defense mechanism the employee exhibits, Performance Monitoring can be used. The steps are the same. So is your role.

PRECAUTIONS

Performance Monitoring is an interpersonal method of dealing with problem employees and requires that you develop the skills of empathy, confrontation, and listening. These skills will stand you in good stead as you both deal with the problem employee and implement programs that can prevent and manage problem behavior. In approaching any conversation with your problem employee, however, there are several precautions you should take. These are:

1. Document your intentions. It's always helpful, before entering a difficult situation, to jot down your objectives. You might include a timetable of the number of sessions you are willing to have with an individual before you recommend outside intervention

2. Know your own limitations, and those of your role as manager. Remember, you aren't expected to save anybody. You are responsible for an employee's performance; the final decisions affecting an employee's success or failure on the job are that employee's responsibility, not yours

3. Respect yourself and your employee enough to be absolutely clear about the performance level you expect

4. Focus, firmness, and fairness are the best tools you have. Focus on the employee's work performance and the steps that can be taken to improve it. Keep any dialogue or confrontation centered on job performance. Help the employee devise his or her own strategy for improving performance[23]

Appendix 4.A at the end of this chapter contains directions for planning an interview in which you use Performance Monitoring with a problem employee. By following these directions, you will lay a precautionary foundation from which you can incorporate Performance Monitoring into your dealings with the problem employee.

SUMMARY

This chapter has discussed a method for dealing with the problem employee that does work: Performance Monitoring, which is based on Reality Therapy, a counseling model. This model allows you to focus on the employee's behavior in the work place, rather than on trying to solve the employee's problem. It provides you with a means of assessing with the employee whether or not behavior is contributing to organizational goals and to develop a joint plan for action.

With Performance Monitoring, you can become a catalyst by which employees can confront their own behavior and make a decision to change. Performance Monitoring is not a "cure" and it cannot be used to treat sick employees. You are neither a physician nor a psychologist. You are, however, responsible for dealing with the employees in your organization. Performance Monitoring provides you with an effective means of managing your employees, as well as a technique by which an employee in need of professional or mental health services can be referred for help.

Using Performance Monitoring

Now I'd like you to think about your own problem employees--those people whose actions have probably prompted you to read this book. Since we know that from 10 to 20 percent of the work force can be classified as problem employees, you'll probably think of about one problem employee for every five people in your work force. That number can be overwhelming. So, to help you learn to use Performance Monitoring, I'd like you to choose one worker whose behavior you'd like to see change.

Picture that person in your mind. What is the employee's name? Write the employee's name below:

_____

Focus on Current Behavior
See that employee in the work setting. What does the employee <u>do</u> that you consider to be a problem? What <u>actions</u> of that employee detract from organizational goal accomplishment? Think about those actions as you consider the following list of possible problem employee behaviors. Check each one that applies to your problem employee.

<u>Problem Employee Behaviors</u>

_____ Excessive, unexcused, or frequent absences.

_____ Tardiness or early departures.

_____ Altercations with fellow employees.

_____ Causing injuries to self or others through negligence.

_____ Poor judgement and bad decisions.

_____ Unusual on-the-job accidents.

_____ Increased spoilage or breakage of equipment.

_____ Involvements with the law.

_____ Mood shifts.

_____ Other: _____
         _____

Now, for each behavior you have checked, describe the <u>specific, observable</u> actions that have prompted you to check that behavior as creating a problem in your work place.

BEHAVIOR   SPECIFIC ACTIONS

(1)_____   _____
                  _____
                  _____

(2)_____   _____
                  _____
                  _____

(3)_____   _____
                      _____
                      _____

Evaluate Current Behavior

Once you've identified the specific behaviors that indicate that you have a problem employee, you are ready to evaluate that behavior. Eventually, you will do this with the employee. But first it's important to plan for that evaluation. To evaluate the employee behaviors, you must identify how those behaviors detract from organizational goal effectiveness. Specifically, what is the effect of the behaviors you have identified on you, on other workers, and on the organization? Record those effects below.

BEHAVIOR   EFFECT ON ME

(1)_____   _____
                      _____

(2)_____   _____
                      _____

(3)_____   _____
                      _____

BEHAVIOR   EFFECT ON OTHER WORKERS

(1)_____   _____
                      _____

(2)_____   _____
                      _____

(3)_____   _____
                      _____

BEHAVIOR   EFFECT ON ORGANIZATION

(1)_____   _____
                      _____

(2)_____   _____
                      _____

(3)_____   _____
                      _____

Once you have identified the effect of the employee's problem behavior on you, on other workers, and on the organization, you are ready to formulate some evaluative statements about the employee's behavior. With these statements you will tell the employee what _behavior_ you observe and what effect that behavior has. On the next page write an evaluative statement for each unacceptable behavior you have identified:

When you
(1)_____,I_____
_____
_____.

When you
(1)_____, your co-workers (or your
supervisor) _____
_____
_____.

When you

(1)_____, the department (or the
organization) _____
_____
_____.

When you

(2) _____, I_____
_____
_____.

When you

(2) _____, your co-workers (or your
supervisor) _____
_____
_____.

When you

(2) _____, the department (or the
organization) _____
_____
_____.

When you

(3) _____, I_____
_____
_____.

When you

(3) _____, your co-workers (or your
supervisor) _____
_____
_____.

When you

(3)_____, the department (or the
organization) _____
_____
_____.

With these statements, you let the employee know that his or her behavior is creating a problem, and you let the employee know what that problem is. You are now ready to help the employee plan for responsible behavior.

Plan for Responsible Behavior

Even though, ultimately, the employee must plan for his or her own behavior change, it is important for you to decide _what_ plan you will consider acceptable. For each unacceptable behavior you have identified, you must answer two questions:

1. What will my employee have to do to change the behavior?

2. What will my employee have to do to convince me that the change has been achieved?

Use the space below to record your answers.

1.)_____
_____
_____

2.)_____
_____
_____

89

What will my employee have to do to change the behavior?

BEHAVIOR   CHANGE

(1)_____ _____
                  _____

(2)_____ _____
                  _____

(3)_____ _____
                  _____

What will my employee have to do to convince me that the change has been achieved?

BEHAVIOR   CONVINCING ACTIONS

(1)_____ _____
                  _____

(2)_____ _____
                  _____

(3)_____ _____
                  _____

You have now carefully thought through the specific problem behaviors of your employee, their effect, and the actions you expect the employee to take to bring about change. To effectively plan your interview with the employee, you should next:

1. Identify, in order of importance the problems you will address:

   (1) _____

   (2) _____

   (3) _____

2. Identify, specifically, what you expect to accomplish in the interview:

   _____
   _____
   _____

3. Identify some of the responses your employee may offer in defense of his or her behavior:

   Behavior 1:_____

   Behavior 2:_____

   Behavior 3:_____

4. Identify how you will deal with each defense offered by the employee:

   Defense 1:_____
   _____

Defense 2:_____

Defense 3:_____

5. Identify the outcome(s) you expect to take place as a result of the interview:
_____

6. What is a reasonable deadline for the employee to accomplish the outcome(s) you expect?
_____

7. What will you do if the employee does not meet the deadline?
_____

You are now ready to conduct a Performance Monitoring interview with your problem employee.

NOTES

1. See, e.g., William Glasser, *Reality Therapy* (New York: Harper and Row, 1965 & 1975); *The Identity Society* (New York: Harper and Row, 1965 & 1975); *Positive Addiction* (New York: Harper and Row, 1975); *Stations of the Mind* (New York: Harper and Row, 1980); *Take Effective Control of Your Life* (New York: Harper and Row, 1984). Glasser calls his method, as it can be used by managers, "Reality Performance Management" (RPM). His discussion of RPM is contained in Chester Karrass and William Glasser, *Both Win Management* (New York: Lippincott and Crowell, 1980).

2. See Barbara Okun, *Effective Helping* (Boston, Mass: Duxbury Press, 1976.)

3. Deborah Whitehouse "Adlerian Antecedents to Reality Therapy and Control Theory," *Journal of Reality Therapy* 3, no. 2 (Spring 1984), 10–13.

4. See Peter Burger and Thomas Luckman, *The Social Construction of Reality* (New York: Doubleday, 1966).

5. See Glasser, *Take Effective Control.*

6. See, e.g. John Banmen, "Reality Therapy Revisited," *Journal of Reality Therapy* 3, no. 1 (Fall 1983), 12–16; Alex Bassin, Thomas Bratter, and R. L. Rachin, eds., *The Reality Therapy Reader* (New York: Harper and Row, 1976); Willa Bruce "Reality Therapy as a Management Strategy: An Idea Whose Time Has Come," *Journal of Reality Therapy* 4, no. 1 (Fall 1984), 16–20; Ruth Dalbech, "Reality Therapy in School Groups," *Journal of Reality Therapy* 1, no. 1 (Spring 1981), 14–15; Donna Evans, "What Are You Doing?" *Personnel Guidance Journal* 60, no. 8 (April 1982), 460–64; Donna Evans, "Schools Without Failure in Action," *Journal of Reality Therapy* 3, no. 2 (Spring 1981), 16–21; Frederick Fahler, "Reality Therapy: A Systems Approach to Treatment in a Half-Way House," *Journal of Reality Therapy* 1, no. 2 (March 1982), 3–7; Barbara George-Mrazek, "Reality Therapy in the Air Force," *Journal of Reality Therapy* 3, no. 1 (Fall 1983), 10–11; Chester Karrass and William Glasser, *Both Win*; Larry Molstead, "Reality Therapy in Residential Treatment," *Journal of Reality Therapy* 1, no. 1 (Spring 1981), 8–13; Robert Silverberg, "Reality Therapy With Men," *Journal of Reality Therapy* 3, no. 2 (Spring

1984), 27–31; Robert Wubbolding, "Reality Therapy as an Antidote to Burnout," *American Mental Health Counselors Association Journal*, 6 no. 1 (January 1979), 39–43; Virginia Ziegler, "Reality Therapy in Continuing Education: Cohesive Culmination," *Journal of Reality Therapy* 2, no. 2 (Spring 1983), 7–9.

7. See Karrass and Glasser, *Both Win*.

8. Edward Ford, "Case Examples of the Therapeutic Process in Family Therapy," *Journal of Reality Therapy* 2, no. 1 (Fall 1982), 3–10.

9. Robert Wubbolding, "Using Paradox in Reality Therapy: Part I," *Journal of Reality Therapy* 4, no. 1 (Fall 1984), 3–9.

10. Jeffrey Luke is now director of the Bureau of Governmental Research at the University of Oregon in Eugene.

11. See Karrass and Glasser, *Both Win*.

12. Jeff Luke, personal conversation.

13. See Karrass and Glasser, *Both Win*, 67–68.

14. See Ford, "Case Examples."

15. See Glasser, *Take Effective Control*.

16. See Ford, "Case Examples."

17. See Karras and Glasser, *Both Win*.

18. See Dale Masi, *Human Services in Industry* (Lexington, Mass.: Lexington Books, D.C. Heath, 1982).

19. See Banmen, "Reality Therapy Revisited."

20. David W. Johnson and Frank P. Johnson, *Joining Together: Group Theory and Group Skills*, 2nd. ed. (Englewood Cliffs, N.J.: Prentice Hall, 1982).

21. Active Listening is based on the counseling model of Carl Rogers, and is described in "Listening Triads: Building Communication Skills," in J. William Pfieffer and John E. Jones, (eds)., *A Handbook of Structured Experiences for Human Relations Training*. Vol. I (San Diego, Calif. University Associates, 1965 and 1974).

22. Willa Bruce, "Persuasion and Influence," in Dawn Warfle, ed., *Advanced Supervisory Practices* (Washington, D.C.: International City Management Association, 1990).

23. J. B. Miles, "How to Help Troubled Workers," in John Matzer, Jr., ed., *Personnel Practices for the '90's: A Local Government Guide*, 126–133 (Washington, D.C.: International Association of City Managers, 1989).

Chapter 5

Other Methods for Dealing with the Problem Employee

The last chapter provided you with the interpersonal skills necessary for dealing with a problem employee. There are, in addition, a number of activities and programs you can undertake to supplement Performance Monitoring. These activities and programs will be discussed in this chapter.

PROMOTE A HEALTHY ORGANIZATION

As you will remember from chapter 2, problems can occur because of "neurotic" organizations. In these organizations, not just one, but most of the employees are caught up in a dysfunctional series of behaviors condoned by the organization's culture. As a human resource manager, you are in a position to promote a healthy organization by bringing about cultural change.

A healthy organization has been defined as one with a culture that motivates, utilizes, and integrates its human resources so that they are able to set and attain appropriate goals in a changing environment.[1] An organization's culture is composed of shared values, norms, and beliefs. These include the basic assumptions about the organization and how it works. These are written rules that govern behavior.

In a healthy organization, employees will believe things like, "performance is rewarded," "innovative ideas are encouraged," and "initiative is appreciated." You can develop your own list. In neurotic organizations, employees share different kinds of beliefs. In a paranoid organization, employees will mistrust their supervisor and be suspicious of their co-workers. In compulsive organizations, people will believe they must be perfect, and be afraid of innovation lest they do something wrong. Dramatic organizations are likely to have a number of prima donnas, who work for self-aggrandizement rather than the overall good.

Figure 5.1
The Action Research Model

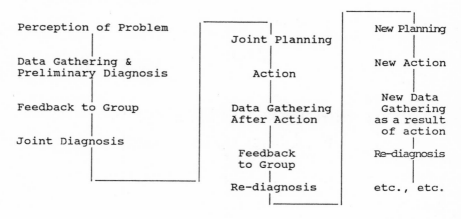

In depressive organizations, people lack motivation; and in schizoid organizations, employees seem indifferent to either praise or criticism.[2]

If you believe yours is a neurotic organization, you need to find out why—you need to diagnose the cause of the problems before you can start your organization on the road to health. The key to successful diagnosis is to utilize the collective knowledge of the people in your organization. You can access this information by surveys or a series of meetings. Ask employees to identify both the strengths and weaknesses of the organization. Ask them how they think you can capitalize on the strengths and minimize the weaknesses. A major mistake that many of us make is to think that we know what is "wrong" with an organization, or what is "right," for that matter. Employees may, however, have a totally different perspective.

A generally accepted formula for diagnosing organizational problems and bringing about change is the Action Research Model shown in Figure 5.1. Using this model requires you to adapt two assumptions: (1) the people in your organization are your most valuable source of data, and (2) the feelings of the people in your organization are as valid as the facts about your organization.

The Action Research Model is a process model in which you gather data from all organizational actors, use the data to diagnose why problems are occurring, and involve the people who provided the data in planning both the goal of the change and the techniques for bringing about that change. I would caution you here that "rational solutions work only with rational people."[3] If you believe your organization is neurotic, rational solutions will not effect the kind of change you need.

Rational solutions assume that people are rational and that they will always carefully analyze every decision, then act in a way that maximizes their own pleasure and minimizes their own pain. A rational solution implies that people can be changed through education and explanation. If they understand what you want and that the organization will be better off if they do what you want, they will change. Rational solutions require long, intricate, intellectual explanations to which irrational people pay little attention. There is, however, another way: "normative re-educative" solutions.

A normative re-educative approach assumes that people are products of cultural and value systems. It assumes that you must understand their attitudes, feelings, and beliefs—what is important to them. You must care how people feel about what you want done. When you use a normative re-educative approach, you bring about change through involving employees throughout the organization in the diagnosis and planning process. You recognize how doing what you want may make them feel and you care enough to invest the time to encourage discussion of feelings.[4]

While both the rational and the normative re-educative approaches will assist you in changing your organization, the normative re-educative approach will more effectively decrease any resistance that may occur. We know that people tend to resist changing their ideas and behavior because they are afraid—afraid that the change will bring undesirable consequences and afraid that they will be unable to deal with the change. You will minimize that resistance by recognizing why it is there and understanding that alleviating fears is just as important as rational explanation.

Often an organization (or a department in it) becomes neurotic because of the actions of key people. If, after careful diagnosis, it becomes clear to you that a supervisor, a department head, or even a top executive is the source of the neurosis in your organization, then you have a problem employee at a high level. Performance Monitoring will be an effective means of dealing with that problem employee too.

Although you may be nervous about confronting and assisting a person who is your organizational superior, you can do it by using Performance Monitoring. Remember that when you use Performance Monitoring you recognize that behavior is chosen and that different choices are possible. You recognize that if an organizational superior deals with you by procrastination or angering, the behavior is not a personal affront to you but a frustration-instigated response. You recognize that you can choose behavior of your own that will facilitate change in your superior's behavior.

To clarify this discussion, let me tell you about Arnold. Arnold was a manager in a public agency that was required to submit a grant proposal each year to obtain continued funding. He had a limited time period from the date the Request for Proposals was published in the *Federal Register* until the completed document was due in Washington. Organizational policy dictated that Arnold's supervisor, George, read and approve the proposal before it was mailed.

George had not been a supportive supervisor for either Arnold or the other managers who reported to him. He discouraged innovation and interaction, and usually blamed Arnold or one of the other department heads when problems occurred. George perceived himself as over-worked and underpaid. He frequently missed crucial deadlines. Arnold thought he was lazy. George, however, was Arnold's boss.

Arnold carefully prepared and submitted his proposal to George and explained the deadline for its arrival in Washington. He asked George to have it read and signed five days before it was due. The date came and went and Arnold had neither read nor approved the proposal.

Having heard of similar situations in which other managers had lost their tempers with George and he had threatened them with suspension, Arnold decided to use Performance Monitoring. He reiterated the importance of the deadline and asked George when he could have the proposal read and signed. George responded with numerous excuses, explaining how busy he was and how many responsibilities he had.

Arnold recognized that George wanted to be perceived as very busy and important, so he acknowledged that had heard how busy George was, but he refused to accept the excusing. He reiterated the importance of the deadline, and again asked when George could get the proposal read. George agreed to complete it in three days.

On the third day Arnold immediately went to George's office to follow up. George said he wasn't quite finished. Arnold complimented him on what he had accomplished, reiterated the deadline, and asked him when, on that day, he would finish. Arnold said "this afternoon." George said "what time this afternoon?" George said "3 P.M.." At 3 P.M. George was back in Arnold's office. The proposal had been signed.

Performance Monitoring simply requires this kind of persistence and self-confidence. It is doable though with persons at all levels of the organization. It is the first line of defense when dealing with a problem employee and it assists you to promote a healthy organization.

POLICIES AND PROCEDURES

In addition to the way you interact with an employee, the formal policies and procedures you develop for dealing with serious problems are also key to proactive problem employee management. One of the strengths of an organization is its bureaucratic insistence on established decision rules. These rules ensure fair, consistent, and equitable treatment for all who come in contact with the organization: client, customer, and employee alike. The same rules that protect your employees from arbitrary and capricious treatment protect you from unhappy legal consequences. Thus, it is incumbent upon you to ensure that your organization has, at a minimum: (1) policies and procedures for dealing with unacceptable behavior in general, and (2) policies and procedures for dealing with substance abusers.

Once you have developed a policy, it is your responsibility to see that the policy is communicated to all employees *before* it is enforced. I recommend that your policies be stated in your employee handbook. That puts both supervisors and employees on notice that these polices are meant to be taken seriously, and that they will be enforced.

Although the law varies from state to state, the trend is for the courts to treat employee handbooks as "binding agreements."[5] As a result, some authorities advise organizations not to issue employee handbooks. I think that's unfair to both the organization and the employee. No one can be expected to conform to policies they don't know exist, including you. So my advice is to write your handbook carefully, train both your supervisors and employees in what it says, and use it. It can be a powerful tool for you when problem behavior erupts.

Laws and court decisions regarding information contained in employee handbooks vary from state to state. Before you take my advice, or that of anyone else, I suggest you contact you own organization's attorney. That person will be the best source of legal guidance for you in this matter.

Policies for Dealing with Unacceptable Behavior

First of all, it is necessary for you to decide just what behavior in your employees will be considered "unacceptable," and how much of that behavior you are willing to tolerate before disciplinary action will be initiated. Table 5.1 shows the usual list of employee offenses that will require disciplinary action. Table 5.2 shows the usual list of supervisory offenses that require disciplinary action.

It is up to you and your organization to decide what you consider to be appropriate natural consequences for these offenses. I suggest that you use Performance Monitoring for each offense and set the consequences at increasingly high levels. For the first offense, get a plan for and a commitment to change from the employee. For the second offense, use Performance Monitoring to follow up and to issue a verbal warning that iterates the potential consequences for continued unacceptable behavior. For the third offense, a written warning is called for. For the forth offense, short suspension may be in order. For the fifth offense, you should explain to the employee that his or her job is in jeopardy. If you have an Employee Assistance Program, make a referral. If you

Table 5.1
Unacceptable Employee Offenses

Attendance related

      Unexcused tardiness

      Absence without leave (AWOL)

Breach of safety regulation or practice

Breach of security regulation or practice

Fellow employee related

      Sexual harassment

      Discrimination

      False, malicious, or unfounded statements

      Abusive or offensive language or gestures

      Fighting

Supervisor related

      Failure to carry out instructions

      Insubordination

Theft

Using company property for other than company purposes

Lying

Loss of or damage to company property

Sleeping, loafing, or failure to attend to duties

Negligent performance of duties

Gambling

Substance abuse

Table 5.2
Unacceptable Supervisory Offenses

All offenses listed as unacceptable for employees

Interference with an employee's right to grievance

Reprisal

Violation of an employee's Constitutional rights

---

don't, suggest that the employee seek outside help. If the employee refuses outside help, or commits a fifth offense, I believe you have no choice but to let termination be the natural consequence.

To protect yourself, your supervisors, and your organization, I suggest that you institute a "Corrective Action Report" such as the one contained in appendix 5.A of this chapter. This report should be completed as a written warning, then used again for delineating the natural consequences of consecutive offenses up to and including termination.

As you develop your polices and procedures, be aware that an employee can hang on for what seems like forever, unless you specify that no one is entitled to more than a total of four of these serious offenses before termination. I once heard of an employee who had been a problem for years. Termination was nearly impossible because the employee kept changing offenses and the organization had no polices for dealing with that.

You need to keep a central file on all employees that includes not only their performance appraisals, but also any documented policy offenses and the action taken by both employee and supervisor. This requires that you insist that your supervisors maintain records of each employee conference and the plan that resulted from that conference. It also requires that you maintain records of each conference you have about or with the employee.

You need to know, also, that in most states, an employee has a right to see what is in his or her personnel file. With regard to personnel files, most states provide the following privacy rights for employees:

1. Allow the employee to inspect his or her personnel file
2. Allow the employee to be informed of the existence of his or her personnel file
3. Allow the employee to correct what he or she considers to be inaccuracy in his or her personnel file.[6]

Do not let these privacy rights intimidate you. An employee who claims an "inaccuracy" when you and/or the employee's supervisor know that the record is correct does not have the final say in what is put in his or her personnel file. The employee, however, does have the right to include a statement of his or her perceptions, which may disagree with yours.

Policies for Dealing with Substance Abuse

Even though you have listed substance abuse as one of the serious offenses in your organizational policies on the consequences of unacceptable behavior, you should have a separate, very specific policy for dealing with substance abusers. This is especially important in light of the 1978 Supreme Court ruling that classified substance abusers as "handicapped," and therefore, protected under the 1973 federal Rehabilitation Act.[7] This act requires that you make reasonable accommodation for the handicapped. It does not require that you "extend the privileges of the Act to an employee whose current drug dependence affects performance or threatens others' safety."[8]

To help you develop a proactive policy that both provides reasonable accommodation and protects your organization and its other employees, I suggest a drug policy similar to the one reprinted in appendix 5.B of this chapter.

WELLNESS PROGRAMS

Wellness programs are those programs that offer opportunities for employees to maintain or improve health and to prevent illness. Such programs have been credited with decreasing attrition rates, lowering absenteeism rates, reducing insurance costs, and increasing employee morale.[9] Their availability in your organization will communicate a message of caring to your employees, and act as a source of prevention for employees who become problems because of inattention to fitness and other health-related issues.

Wellness programs can run the gamut from a simple aerobics dance class held in an empty conference room to an elaborate physical fitness center located on or off the premises.[10] They can include workshops on time management and stress management. They can include smoking cessation programs.[11] They can include company bowling leagues and softball teams. Their scope is limited only by your imagination and the dollars available to establish and support them.

Wellness programs do cost money; but their cost is an investment, not an expenditure. Consider the following costs of health-related problem:

- In 1985, Workmen's Compensation claims were estimated to cost the nation's employers approximately 30 million dollars, and 33 to 40 percent of those claims were attributed to back injuries[12]

- In 1976, heart attacks alone cost private industry 132 million work days per year or 4 percent of the Gross National Product[13]

- Stress-related illness costs industry an estimated 150 billion dollars annually[14]

To determine what your organization's wellness program will entail, you must first define the needs of your employees. A simple questionnaire can help you do that, as can a combing of absenteeism records for the previous one or two years to identify the reasons given for use of sick leave. The identification of employee needs will also help you decide if you are going to establish an "in-house" program, or if you are going to contract with a private firm.

No matter how good your program is, if employees do not participate the program is useless. Organizations such as construction firms or police and fire departments must have employees who are in top physical condition. For these employees, participation in wellness programs may be mandated. In other instances, employees can be encouraged to participate in wellness programs through involving them in planning the program, and through intensive marketing.

HELP PREVENT FAMILY CRISES

Until recently, organizations did not want to get involved in employees' lives away from the work place. The old myth that organizational life and family life took place in separate, isolated spheres prevailed. Workers were expected to leave their problems at home—whether or not they were capable of doing that. As we move into the 1990s, however, more and more companies are starting to realize that "what happens outside the office affects employee job performance."[15]

Family crises are major contributors to absenteeism, reduced productivity, and turnover. They occur for men and women alike, although women tend to miss more work because of crises than do men. This phenomenon has been attributed to women's traditional role of family crisis manager. Because of this role, absenteeism to deal with crises, though often considered a "woman's problem," becomes a "family's solution."[16]

One study of 5,000 employees with children under the age of eighteen found that 77 percent of women and 73 percent of men had dealt with family problems during working hours.[17] There's even a new term in our vocabulary: "three o'clock syndrome." The term "refers to reduced productivity and higher error and accident rates as employees' minds turn to their children around the time when school lets out."[18]

Thus, what appears to be a problem employee can simply be a mother, father, or spouse coping with a family problem that appears unresolvable. It is here that proactive strategies by your organization can help. Two proactive strategies you can use help assist in preventing or alleviating family crises include child care assistance and help for victims of domestic violence. Let's talk about them.

Child Care Assistance

Roughly 2,500 United States companies currently assist their employees with child care needs.[19] This is not many, for there are over one million proprietorships and partnerships in the United States. Yet a study of 415 organizations that do offer child care programs, conducted by the United States Department of Health and Human Services, found impressive results. Of those organizations that offer child care assistance:

- 90 percent reported improved employee morale
- 85 percent reported an increased ability to recruit and retain workers
- 65 percent reported decreased turnover
- 53 percent reported decreased absenteeism
- 37 percent reported an increase in the quality of their products or services[20]

You can assist your employees with child care in a number of different ways. Among the employers that offer child care assistance, 32 percent provide a referral service to licensed providers and 23 percent provide an on-site facility for which the employee pays. Only 11 percent of the companies pay the total cost of child care, while 22 percent offer an on-site cost-sharing facility, and 11 percent share the cost of off-site facilities.[21]

An example of what companies can do is the innovative package of family benefits that has been established by AT&T for its unionized workers. The package includes leave to care for sick parents and a 5 million dollar child care fund. In an agreement reached on May 28, 1989, AT&T promised to establish tax-deferred accounts that employees can use to save up to $5,000 per year for child or elder care. Parental and elder care leave provisions in the agreement guarantee a worker's job and seniority benefits for up to six months, as well as medical and dental coverage. AT&T also agreed to pay $2,000 toward the costs of adoption. This scope of coverage for child-related issues is unprecedented in a major corporate contract.[22]

Another type of child care assistance program that is being developed is one of assistance for latch-key children. You can offer workshops to teach these children how to cope in emergencies, how to deal with strangers, how to cook, how to babysit, etc. The list is limited only by your imagination and resources. As children become better able to manage alone, parental stress decreases. The children are less likely to bother parents at work with trivial issues, and the "three o'clock syndrome" is minimized.

Selecting which approach you will take depends on your own organization's needs and resources, as well as the needs of your employees and the child care services already available in your community. A good idea is to appoint a task force to assess both needs and resources, evaluate options, and make recommendations. Resources for information on establishing child care as an employee benefit are readily available.[23] You can begin now to provide your employees with what the Employee Benefit Research Institute calls "*the* fringe benefit of the 1990's"—help in caring for their children."[24]

Domestic Violence

Research has indicated that domestic violence occurs in 50 percent of American marriages. The victims are generally women, for whom "the workplace is often the only respite. . . . (This) makes the problem an on-the-job problem and, therefore, something that needs to be dealt with."[25]

A woman who has been beaten, who has suffered a blackened eye or a broken limb, or who has been the victim of verbal abuse is scarcely able to perform at her peak. Some abused women stay home because of embarrassment over how they look, and their work record shows a history of absenteeism. Others are so upset that even though they come to work their productivity is minimal.

While you are certainly not a marriage counselor, you can act proactively to minimize the impact of domestic violence on the workplace. First, however, you have to be willing to confront the possibility that an employee is being victimized at home. Here, Performance Monitoring can be an invaluable aid.

Just as you use the steps of Performance Monitoring to confront the employee with declining performance, you can use them to confront her with your observation that she is bruised, or injured in some way. As you and she process what she can do about it, you can serve as a resource for her to get help by taking the following steps.

1. Offer protection on the job within reason. You can arrange for her phone calls to be screened and you can alert security personnel for potential problems.

2. Establish a liaison with a local domestic violence shelter. Ask a representative

of the shelter to speak to top management, line supervisors, and interested employees about shelter services. Do this whether or not you are aware of any battered employees in your organization. Refer your battered employee for help.

3. Find out what resources are available in your community to acquaint battered employees with their recourse through the criminal justice system. See that your top managers and line supervisors are educated about these resources *before* they need to know about them. Get and distribute pamphlets if you can. Make certain that any employees who need the information are provided with it.

4. Ensure a work place free of references that perpetuate stereotypes about abused women. Train your employees and supervisors to recognize the nuances of sexual harassment and make certain that they understand that any form of sexual innuendo is against the law.[26]

EDUCATE SUPERVISORS

The word *educate* means "to develop knowledge, skills, and abilities; to change behavior." Education is a process, not an event. Thus, a simple presentation, though it may be necessary, is insufficient for equipping supervisors to deal effectively with the problem employee. They must be taught through interaction, demonstration, and role play. Research has consistently demonstrated that in a typical lecture, students pay attention only 25 percent of the time. When they are actively involved in learning, they pay attention 75 percent of the time.[27] Thus, when you educate your supervisors, you must provide them with opportunities to engage in discussion and problem solving.

The literature on adult education indicates that traditional methods of teaching are not often appropriate for adults. This is because adults are a heterogeneous group with diverse learning styles. Your supervisors will bring different experiences, different values, and different expectations to the learning situation. If you want the education you provide to be successful, you must deal with as many of these diversities as possible.

David Kolb has developed a model of adult education called the "Experiential Learning Model."[28] It offers a solution to the dilemma of meeting diverse needs in a way that maximizes learning. This approach to education requires that you spend as much time on the *process* of the educational experience as you do on the *content*.

Folk wisdom has always said that "experience is the best teacher." The Experiential Learning Model builds on that notion by requiring that the educational situation be structured in such a way that a common experience is used as the base for both discussion, problem solving, and theory. If all of your supervisors already have had experience in dealing

Table 5.3
Rules for Dealing with Female and Minority Employees

- Use the "right" words: Women are not "gals," "girls," or "dears." Minorities are not "boys," "girls," or "chums." Women and minorities are people too.
- Mind your own business: Questions about marital status (or plans), children, child care, birth control, or how a spouse or lover feels, thinks, or believes are clearly illegal. So are questions about sports ability, activist activities, and religious or sexual preferences.
- Keep your own values out of the work setting: Women can travel alone, are ambitious, are mobile, and can supervise men. By the way, men can travel alone, are ambitious, are mobile, and can supervise women.
  Minorities are men and women too. Treat them as equals.
- Be professional: Don't flirt. Don't tell jokes with sexual, racial, or ethnic overtones. Don't use profanity. Don't assume that women are interested in recipes and don't assume that men are interested in sports.
- Apply the same standards to all employees: A women is not a token. Neither is a minority. They do not want jobs they are unqualified for. They do want to do what they are capable of doing.
- TREAT WOMEN AND MINORITY EMPLOYEES AS YOU WANT THEM TO TREAT YOU!

with a problem employee, you can build on that commonality by having each in the educational setting describe the experience. If they don't *all* have a common experience, you can provide it through a case study, or a video/movie, or an instrument.[29]

Once a common experience is shared, trainees should reflect upon the experience by observing what happened, what they learned from the experience, and what else they need to know. At this point, they become ready for the educator to present new information in the form of a lecture. As they are able to relate experience to theory, they acquire new skills that they are ready to go back to the work site and try. A later workshop can build from these new experiences.

Educate Supervisors on Equal Employment Opportunity

To ensure that your supervisors do, in fact, treat all employees equally and fairly and to protect them from charges of discrimination in any form, it is important to educate them in both the laws and practice of equal employment opportunity. Believe it or not, the right to equal treatment was first guaranteed all United States citizens in the Civil Rights Act of 1871.

Today I doubt that there is an organization in this country that does not have a formal Equal employment Opportunity/Affirmative Action policy. Company publications and advertisements state that "We are an EEO/AA Employer," and women and other minorities are employed in areas that our grandparents would not have thought possible. Yet subtle discrimination continues to exist and female and minority employees continue to use a charge of discrimination to protest disciplinary action— even when that action is instituted for a serious dereliction of duty. Thus, it is incumbent upon you to teach your supervisors how to ensure a work place free of discrimination in any form.

Discriminatory behavior is as improper when it is not intended as when it is, and the appearance is as important as the reality. None of us is psychic. We cannot read people's minds. So we judge on what is said and what is done. The general rule, of course, is that supervisors must treat women and other minorities exactly as they do white male employees. The reality too often, however, is that supervisors unconsciously use words or behaviors that are unacceptable to minority employees. Then when problems occur, the supervisor is severely handicapped in correcting the problem. Table 5.3 lists the rules for dealing with female and minority employees. Teach your supervisors to follow them.

Education for Dealing with the Problem Employee

Education for dealing with the problem employee is also frequently available commercially. Workshops come under the rubric of "coping (or dealing) with difficult people" and do provide supervisors with an additional set of problem employee management skills. I have yet to see one, however, that covers the material presented in this book. So I encourage you to develop your own educational activities in the form of a series of workshops that use the Experiential Learning Model and are based on the material in this book.

An outline for such training is included in appendix 5.C of this chapter. At the end of chapter 6, which talks about Employee Assistance Programs, a training outline will be provided to help you conduct a workshop on how supervisors can refer employees to such a program.

SUPPORT SUPERVISORS

Another effective method for dealing with the problem employee is to provide a support system for your supervisors. Line supervisors at all levels of the organization are in a difficult position. They are the link between their subordinates and the rest of the company. As such, they often suffer from role conflict brought on by conflicting demands created by trying to balance the expectations of their employees and the needs of the organization.

Simply put, at best, line supervision is a stressful position. The line supervisor has frequently come from the ranks of the employees he or she now supervises, yet the very act of supervision separates the supervisor from the camaraderie of the people under him or her. The unit supervised may work so independently that the supervisor has little opportunity for interpersonal contact with other supervisors.

Extensive studies on the role of supervision have led researchers to conclude that because of both isolation from peers and the conflicting demands of the work place, supervisors are at high risk for stress and stress-related illnesses.[30] The consequences of these stressors, in and of themselves, can be a fertile environment for supervisors to become problem employees. When the dynamic of one problem employee in the work group is added to the already stringent demands of supervision, the supervisor is at even greater risk. The old adage that "it's lonely at the top," is never more true than when a supervisor is trying to deal with a problem employee.

A crucial proactive strategy for dealing with problem employees is for you to ensure that you offer support and guidance to the supervisors in your organization. This support and guidance should, of course, include teaching them Performance Monitoring. But the support must go far beyond that.

You may remember that classic defense mechanisms of problem employees attempt to transfer the responsibility for their behavior to someone else. This is frequently the hapless supervisor. The problem employee, in saying "It's not my fault," will often state or imply that it's the supervisor's fault. The problem employee, in saying "I'm not crazy," will frequently attempt to demonstrate that the supervisor is irrational or incompetent. Problem employees are skilled in shirking responsibility and finding a scapegoat for their problems. The supervisor is often that scapegoat.

It is, therefore, incumbent upon you, as a human resource manager, to support your supervisors when they are dealing with a problem employee. Supervisors are persons who have consistently demonstrated their competencies and skills. They have earned their positions. In so doing, they should have earned your trust.

While it is, of course, possible for a supervisor to be a problem employee, it is more likely that the supervisor will be made the brunt of problem employee resistance. A good rule of thumb in a situation where a problem employee exists is: "Assume that the supervisor is not incompetent and that the employee has a problem."

Believe Your Supervisors

There are a number of ways that you can support your supervisors. The first is simple: believe them. That statement may seem so obvious that you wonder why I make it. Yet I have often seen problem employee behavior escalate, simply because a human resource manager or a supervisor believed a problem employee's accusations instead of a supervisor's protestations.

Do you remember the story of Marcella and her supervisor, Max, from chapter 2? Marcella was able to wreak so much havoc that Max's supervisor, Naomi, began to doubt Max's competence. She instituted a secret evaluation of him, rescinded his disciplinary actions, and literally capitulated to Marcella's demands. Max lost credibility with his other employees, sought legal counsel in self-defense, and ultimately resigned. Had Naomi simply believed and supported Max the story would have had a happier ending.

Recognize Your Supervisors' Humanity

Supervisors are people too. Too often the fact that supervisors have feelings is overlooked in the rush to deal with problem employee behavior. No one can sustain the constant impact of a problem employee without suffering emotional damage. Remember Hollman's stages of coping with a problem employee? Supervisors will be praying, reasoning, pleading, and bleeding.[31] They'll go through denial, anger, and depression.[32] Don't forget that. You can and should be a support for supervisors trying to cope with a problem employee. If you aren't, your supervisors can become casualties.

Consider the case of William, who was a supervisor of air traffic controllers during their illegal strike. Concerned over the ramifications the strike was having on him, William went to the Union Hall during a meeting to plead with the strikers to return to work. He was documented as saying, "I wish you all'd come back because I'm too old and tired to be working these long hours."

Upon leaving the union gathering, he was accosted by a television crew and interviewed. During the interview, as he tried to support both his employees and his agency, he made the statement that he understood some of the strike demands. Later that night, the agency head, while viewing the news, saw and heard the interview. The next day, without discussion, he fired William for participating in union activities.

SUMMARY

This chapter has emphasized the importance of structured, consistent policies and procedures to guide you and your supervisors in disciplinary decision making. These policies and procedures should be written and distributed throughout the organization so that all employees know the logical consequences of inappropriate behavior. And they must be systematically enforced.

The chapter has also pointed out that supervisors of problem employees can become the victims of employee defense mechanisms and has urged you to both believe in your supervisors and to support them. You do not want the supervisor of a problem employee to become an unwilling sacrifice, nor a problem too.

In the next chapter you'll learn how to establish and utilize an Employee Assistance Program—the last bastion of help for problem employees, and an essential resource for you.

Corrective Action Report

Employee's name: _____ DATE: _____
Department: _____ DATE HIRED: _____
Position: _____ Time in position: _____
NATURE OF PROBLEM: _____
CORRECTIVE ACTION TAKEN:
( ) Written warning   ( ) Probation _____(months)
( ) Suspension _____ (days)   ( ) Discharge

OTHER PROBLEMS IN PAST 6 MONTHS:

	Problem	Date	Action
1.	_____	____	_____
2.	_____	____	_____

REASONS FOR CORRECTIVE ACTION (Give details, facts, specific dates, etc.
Attach any supporting documentation.)
_____
_____
_____
_____

SPECIFIC PLAN FOR CORRECTION (include referral to EAP if appropriate):
_____
_____
_____

(page 2 - back of form)

EMPLOYEE'S COMMENTS: (if none, so indicate)
_____
_____
_____

WAS EMPLOYEE ADVISED OF APPEAL RIGHTS UNDER THE GRIEVANCE
PROCEDURE?   _____Yes   _____No   Supervisor's initials_____
If "no" explain why: _____
_____

EMPLOYEE'S SIGNATURE _____
EMPLOYEE DECLINES TO SIGN _____
                         (Supervisor's initials)   DATE _____
SUPERVISOR'S SIGNATURE _____   DATE _____
NEXT LEVEL MGR/DEPT. HEAD _____   DATE _____
HUMAN RESOURCE DIRECTOR _____   DATE _____

ORIGINAL: To employee
COPIES: Department file
           Human resource manager

———————— **Appendix 5.B** ————————

Sample Drug Policy

The Purpose:

This policy shall serve as a statement of corporate concern and as a guide to this company's intentions regarding substance abuse in the work place. The company recognizes that the state of an employee's health affects his/her job performance, the kind of work he/she can perform, and may affect his/her opportunities for continued employment. The company also recognizes that alcohol and drug abuse rank as one of the major health problems of the world. It is the intent of this policy to provide employees with the company's viewpoint on behavioral/medical disorders, to encourage an enlightened viewpoint toward these disorders, and to provide guidelines for consistent handling throughout the company regarding alcohol and substance usage situations. In the final analysis, the company intends to do what it can to provide a drug-free, safe working environment; to promote the health, well-being, and productivity of its employees; and to clearly establish its intolerance for illegal behavior.

The Scope:

This policy is intended to cover all prospective employees, current employees, contractors, and vendors.

The Policy:

The company intends to give the same consideration to persons with chemical (alcohol or other drugs) misuse patterns or dependencies as it does to employees having other diseases. The company is concerned with only those situations where the use of alcohol and other drugs seriously interferes with any employee's health and job performance, adversely affects the job performance of other employees, or is considered serious enough to be detrimental to the company's business. There is no intent to intrude upon the private lives of employees.

Early recognition and treatment of chemical dependency problems is important for successful rehabilitation; service to the public; and reduced personal, family, and social disruption. The company supports sound treatment efforts: An employee's job will not be jeopardized for conscientiously seeking assistance. Constructive disciplinary measures may be used to provide motivation to seek assistance. Normal company benefits, such as sick leave and the group medical plan, are available to give help in the rehabilitation process.

Legal Drugs (including alcohol)

1. The use of any legally obtained drug, including alcohol, to the point where such use adversely affects the employee's job performance, jeopardizes the safety of coworkers, or adversely impacts on the confidence of the public in this company's ability to meet its responsibilities is prohibited. This prohibition covers arriving on company premises under the effects of any drug that adversely affects the employee's job performance, including the use of prescribed drugs under medical direction. Where physician-directed use of drugs adversely affects job performance, it is in the best interest of the employee, co-workers, and the company that sick leave be used.

   a. Any employee engaging in the misuse of alcoholic beverages on company premises is subject to disciplinary action, up to and including termination.

Illegal Drugs

1. Illegal drugs, for the purpose of this policy, include: (*a*) drugs that are not legally obtainable, and (*b*) drugs that are legally obtainable but have been obtained illegally.

2. The sale, possession, purchase, transfer, or use of illegal drugs by employees on company premises or while on company business is prohibited. Arriving on company premises under the influence of any drug to the extent that job performance is adversely affected is prohibited. This prohibition applies to any or all forms of drugs whose sale, purchase, transfer, possession, or use is prohibited or restricted by law.

   a. Any employee engaging in the sale, purchase, transfer, possession, or use of illegal drugs on company premises or while on company business is subject to disciplinary action, up to and including termination.

   b. Any employee engaging in the sale, purchase, transfer, or use of illegal drugs off the job, which could jeopardize the safety of other employees, the public, or company equipment or adversely impacts on the confidence of the public in this company's ability to meet its responsibilities is subject to disciplinary action, up to and including termination.

   c. Any employee arrested for the sale, purchase, transfer, possession, or use of illegal drugs, off the job, may be considered in violation of this policy. In deciding what action to take, the company will consider the nature of the charges, the employee's present job assignment, the employee's record with the company, and other factors relative to the impact of the employee's arrest upon the ability of the company to continue to conduct business.

Drug and Alcohol Testing

In furthering its policy to provide for the health and safety of its employees and to ensure the health and safety of others and to guard the confidence of the public in the company's ability to meet its responsibilities, the company has established the following policies for the testing of drug and alcohol use among its employees.

The company shall utilize an accredited drug testing laboratory using scientifically validated technologies where confirmation testing is performed on all presumptively positive results.

The company has the right to require body substance samples (i.e. blood, urine) from any of the following:

a. All applicants for employment

b. Any current employee who is involved in a serious near-miss accident at the work site or on duty, whether on or off company premise

c. Any current employee who exhibits significant and observable changes in performance, appearance, behavior, speech, etc. that provides reasonable suspicion of the presence of drugs or alcohol.

d. Any current employee where there is a need to establish fitness for duty as a result of an alcohol- or drug-related suspension

e. Any employee who has completed an alcohol- or drug-related rehabilitation through the EAP process and returns to work

Refusal to provide a body substance sample under the conditions described above is subject to disciplinary action, up to and including termination.

Employees who complete an alcohol- or drug-related rehabilitation through the EAP process and have subsequent positive drug tests shall undergo evaluation on a case by case basis as to the merit of further rehabilitation, leave of absence, or termination.

The results and records of drug testing are to be considered strictly confidential and are not to be discussed or shared with anyone that does not have an absolute need to know. The results and records of drug testing are to be maintained in a separate, unique file (not in employee medical records file) designed specifically for that purpose.

Company's Responsibilities

• It is the responsibility of managers/supervisors to ensure that all employees under their direction are aware of and understand the policy.

• The Human Resources Department is responsible for developing the necessary training required for effective implementation of this policy. This includes the training of managers/supervisors in documenting unsatisfactory or deteriorating job performance, absenteeism, excessive tardiness, or unsafe work practices that may be related to substance abuse. This also includes the training of managers/supervisors for intervention in those circumstances where a reasonable suspicion exists that an employee is unfit for duty (grossly unsafe work practices or suspect behavior, i.e. stumbling, slurred or incoherent speech, apparent confusion in orientation).

- The Employee Health Department is responsible for administering (or arranging for the administration of) diagnostic testing, including urine drug testing, to determine the presence or absence of drugs.
- The Employee Health Department is responsible for ensuring the confidentiality of all employees' medical records in the diagnosis of drug abuse. All records concerning urine drug testing results are a part of that record.
- The Safety Department is responsible for ensuring a safe working environment for all employees. Any employee endangering that environment will be removed and escorted to the Human Resources or Employee Health Department for disposition.
- The Human Resources/Benefits Department is responsible for assisting employees diagnosed with a substance abuse problem in fully understanding the company-offered health benefits and/or the EAP program.
- The Employee Assistance Program is responsible for providing confidential counseling to employees with drug abuse problems. The EAP will also be responsible for ordering urine drug tests for employees referred to them as a result of (suspected) drug abuse.
- The Security Department is responsible for reporting all incidents or possession, sale, distribution, or use of illegal substances to the Human Resources Department and appropriate company management.
- The company management is responsible for determining the actions to be taken against an employee determined to have used illegal drugs. (This includes the development and distribution of a policy and set of procedures).

Employee's Responsibilities

- It is the responsibility of all employees to abide by this policy.
- An employee is expected to arrive at work fit for duty. Arrival at work with performance-altering drugs or alcohol in his/her system, which have the potential to adversely affect the employee's job performance, jeopardize the safety of co-workers, or adversely impact on the confidence of the public in this company's ability to meet its responsibilities is prohibited.
- An employee taking prescription medication that may affect work performance must report this information to his/her supervisor or the Employee Health Department at the start of the work day.
- An employee is expected to perform his/her job in a safe manner. Use of a chemical substance that would interfere with personal safety or the safety of others is prohibited.
- An employee is expected to conduct himself/herself in a legal and lawful manner while on the company property or on company business. Sale, possession, distribution or use of an illegal substance on company property or while on company business is prohibited.

• Employees are expected to cooperate with the Employee Health Department in the diagnosis of a problem, including participation in urine drug testing as specified in employee policies and procedures.

Applicant's Responsibilities

• Applicants of employment to the company will be required to take a urine test for drugs. Employment is contingent on a urine drug test that indicates no performance-altering drugs or alcohol are in the applicant's system.

Source: Paul Cary, Toxicology and Drug Monitoring Laboratory, 301 Business Loop W, Suite 208, Columbia, MO 65201. Reprinted with permission. Parts of this sample policy were originally in Paul Cary, "Drugs and Drug Testing in the Workplace," *Missouri Municipal Review* 52, no. 7 (July 7 1987), 23–27. These parts are reprinted with permission of *Missouri Municipal Review*.

Appendix 5.C

"Managing the Problem Employee": A Training Workshop Outline

Goals

1. To provide participants with information on what motivates an employee to become a problem
2. To provide participants with the skills necessary to deal with a problem employee

Group size

Five to thirty participants. The activities require participants to divide into groups of three or five for discussion and role play purposes. Do not use groups larger than this. Too many people prohibit individual involvement.

Time required

Approximately eight hours, broken into two four-hour segments, scheduled from one to two weeks apart.

Materials required

1. A tablet of newsprint and an easel
2. One dark-colored magic marker for each five participants
3. Masking tape for posting newsprint
4. A copy of the "Flow Chart for Performance Monitoring" (see Figure 4.1) for each participant
5. Name tags if participants do not know one another

Materials desired

A copy of this book for each participant. They should read chapters 1 through 5 between day 1 and day 2 of the workshop. Do not give them the book until the end of day 1. Remember they need the experience and discussion before considering abstract concepts.

Process

Day 1

I. After a brief (about ten-minute) introduction in which you have workshop attendees introduce themselves to one another and state what they want from the workshop, make the following remarks:

For purposes of this training, a problem employee is defined as one whose behavior in the work place causes reduced productivity and lowered morale for self, co-workers, and supervisors. An employee may be troubled by personal problems as minor as a stubbed toe, or as major as the death of a spouse. Unless these troubles spill over into the work place as behaviors that reduce productivity, that employee is not a problem employee. Problem employees are those whose energies are directed toward the accomplishment of their own personal goals, rather than toward the accomplishment of organizational goals.

It is important to remember that all of us have been a problem at one time or another in our career. The person labeled "problem employee," however, is the one who is so frequently acting in a way that detracts from productivity that he or she actually takes up most of your time and energy. We can say, generally, that although problem employees comprise only about 20 percent of the work force, they take up about 80 percent of your time.

II. Divide participants into groups of five. Give each group a piece of newsprint and a magic marker and ask them to appoint a recorder/reporter for their group. Give them about 30 minutes to describe any problem employees they have encountered and to list all the reasons they believe these employees are problems.

III. Reassemble the large group and have each reporter post the answers from his or her group and then report back to the large group. This will provide a common base of experience and information from which you can begin to talk about problem employees.

IV. Add any reasons that you have learned from this book that are not listed.

V. Take a fifteen-minute break. Tell participants that when they return from the break, you will begin to talk about ways to deal with the problem employee.

VI. Use the structured experience titled "Listening Triads: Building Communication Skills," from J. W. Pfeiffer, ed., *A Handbook of Structured Experiences for Human Relations Training, Volume I* (San Diego, Calif.: University Associates, 1974), p. 31. This and similar handbooks are usually available in college and university libraries.

VII. Conclude the workshop by having each participant take one minute to summarize what he or she thought was the most important thing learned today.

VIII. Make the following "homework" assignments:
    1. Ask participants to try using Active Listening with their employees over the next two weeks.
    2. Assign participants to read chapters 1 through 5 of this book.
    3. Plan to reassemble for another four-hour workshop in one to two weeks. Ask participants to choose one employee with whom they would like help and write out a one-page description of that employee's behavior.

Day 2

    I. Briefly summarize day 1. Then ask each participant to name one thing that he or she found particularly helpful in reading chapters 1 through 5 of this book. List these things on newsprint and post them around the room. Tell participants that you will spend this day learning to do Performance Monitoring.
    II. Have participants fold their descriptions of their chosen employee in half and give them to you.
    III. Distribute a copy of Figure 4.1 to each participant. Review it.
    IV. Tell the group that each will role play the person in the description he or she has brought. Give them ten minutes to study the role.
    V. Divide the group into triads. Have each member choose to be "A," "B," or "C." Tell them that they will have three rounds of interaction and that each will have the opportunity to try out Performance Monitoring.
    VI. Give the following instructions:
        1. Participant "A" will be the first problem employee. "A" will spend two minutes describing himself or herself from the information in the description he or she has brought.
        2. Participant "B" will be the first supervisor who uses Performance Monitoring.
        3. Participant "C" will be the first referee. The referee's job is to make certain that the "supervisor" sticks to the Performance Monitoring model.
    VII. Begin Round 1. Stop the process after fifteen minutes. Allow five minutes for both "A" and "C" to give feedback to "B" by stating:
        1. What "B" said or did that was helpful
        2. What "B" might have done differently
    VIII. Begin Round 2. Participant "B" now becomes the problem employee, "C" becomes the "supervisor" using Performance Monitoring, and "A" becomes the referee. Round 2 also takes fifteen minutes. At the end of the time, again allow five minutes for the "supervisor" to receive feedback.
    IX. Begin Round 3. "C" becomes the problem employee, "A" becomes the "supervisor," and "B" becomes the referee. Round 3 takes fifteen minutes. At the end of Round 3, again provide five minutes for the "supervisor" to receive feedback.
    X. Take a fifteen-minute break.
    XI. Reassemble triads. Allow them sixty minutes to discuss the following questions:

1. What were your thoughts and feelings when you played the role of your problem employee?
2. What did you notice about the interaction between you as the "employee" and the person who role played your "supervisor?"
3. What were your thoughts and feelings when you played the role of "supervisor?"
4. What insights can you give the person in your triad who is the real supervisor of this employee?
5. What can you conclude about the use of Performance Monitoring with a problem employee?
   (a). When will it be helpful? Why?
   (b). When will it not be helpful? Why?
XII. Have a member of each triad report back any insights his or her group gained in the management of a problem employee.
XIII. Conclude the workshop by having each participant take two minutes to summarize what he or she thought was the most important thing learned today, and to tell how that can be used back at the work site.

***You have now set the stage for having your supervisors begin to deal with their problem employees. The training outline presented at the end of chapter 6 will strengthen their abilities.

NOTES

1. See Edgar Huse and Thomas Cummings, *Organizational Development and Change*, 3rd ed. (St. Paul, Minn.: West Publishing Co., 1985).
2. See Manfred Kets de Vries and Danny Miller, *The Neurotic Organization* (San Francisco, Calif: Jossey-Bass Publishers, 1984).
3. Ibid.
4. See Robert Chin and Kenneth Benne, "General Strategies for Effecting Human Systems," in Warren Bennis, Kenneth Benne, and Robert Chin, eds., *The Planning of Change* (New York: Holt, Rinehart, & Winston, 1969 & 1985).
5. See Thomas J. Condon, Esq., *Fire Me and I'll Sue* (Appendix A) (New York: Modern Business Reports, 1985).
6. Suzanne Cook, "Privacy Rights," in John Matzer, ed., *Personnel Practices for the '90's* (Washington, D.C.: International City Managers Association, 1989), 165–182.
7. Davis v. Butcher, 451 F. Supp. 791 (1978).
8. See Condon, *Fire Me*.
9. See D. Brinkman, "There's Good News About Heart Disease," *Safety and Health* 139, no. 2 (1989), 53–56; Samuel Klarreich, ed., *Health and Fitness in the Workplace* (Westport, Conn.: Praeger Publishers, 1987); J. S. Lang, "America's Fitness Binge," *U.S. News and World Report* 92, no. 17 (1982), 58–61; M. Leroux, "Cashing in on Wellness," *Business Insurance* 21, no. 1 (September 1981), 38–40; and R. W. Reed, D. E. Mulvaney, R. E. Billingham, and T. W. Skinner, *Health Promotion Service Evaluation and Impact Study* (Indianapolis, Ind.: Benchmark Press, 1986), 1–65.
10. See Leroux, "Cashing In."
11. An excellent resource for establishing a smoking cessation program is

William Timmins and Clark Timmins, *Smoking and the Workplace: Issues and Answers for Human Resource Professionals* (Westport, Conn.: Quorum Books, 1989).

12. A. Putnam, "How to Reduce the Costs of Back Injuries," *Safety and Health* 138, no. 4 (1988), 48–49.

13. R. Kreitner, "Employee Physical Fitness Programs: Protecting an Investment in Human Resources," *Personnel Journal* 55, no. 7 (July 1976), 340–44.

14. S. Moretz, "New Developments Challenge an Old System," *Occupational Hazards* 50, no. 10 (1988), 131–34.

15. Diane Kastiel, "Work and Family Seminars Help Parents Cope," *Business Insurance* 18, no. 22 (28 May 1984), 26–30.

16. See Arthur Emlen and Paul Koren, *Hard to Find and Difficult to Manage: The Effects of Child Care on the Workplace* (Portland, Ore.: Portland State University, 1984).

17. See John Fernandez, *Child Care and Corporate Productivity* (Lexington, Mass.: D. C. Heath and Co., 1986).

18. Dana Friedman, "Child Care for Employees' Kids," *Harvard Business Review* 64 (March–April 1986), 28–34.

19. Ibid.

20. Ibid.

21. "New Benefits Reflect Changing Workforce," *Business Insurance* 20, no. 17 (February 1986), 58.

22. "AT&T Pact Includes Family-Health Plan," *Omaha World-Herald*, 29 May 1989, p. 9.

23. Two resources for help in developing child care benefits are Catalyst, 250 Park Avenue South, New York, NY 10003, and Work and Family Information Center, The Conference Board, Inc., 845 Third Avenue, New York, NY 10022.

24. See Friedman, "Child Care."

25. Linda Schumacher, "Employee Assistance: How to Help Victims of Domestic Violence," *Personnel Journal* 64, no. 8 (August 1985), 102–5.

26. Ibid.

27. See Frank Newman, "The Restructuring of Education," *The Anteus Report* 4, no. 3 (Summer/Fall 1987), 2–6.

28. See David Kolb, *Experiential Learning: Experience as the Source of Learning and Development* (Englewood Cliffs, N.J.: Prentice-Hall, 1984).

29. An excellent source of structured experiences for a variety of training activities is available from University Associates, 8517 Production Ave., San Diego, CA 92192. Particularly helpful are the *Annual Developing Human Resources* and the *Handbook of Structured Experiences*. Both of these are produced annually.

30. C. Cooper, and J. Marshall, "Occupational Sources of Stress: A Review of the Literature Relating to Coronary Heart Disease and Mental Ill Health," *Journal of Occupational Psychology* 49 (1976), 11–28.

31. See Robert Hollman, "Managing Troubled Employees: Meeting the Challenge," *Journal of Contemporary Business* 8, no. 4 (October 1979), 43–57.

32. See Donald Phillips and Harry Older, "A Model for Counseling Troubled Supervisors," *Alcohol, Health and Research World* 2, no. 1 (Fall 1977), 24–30.

_____ **Chapter 6** _____

When the Methods Fail:
Get Outside Help

Unfortunately, none of the methods discussed in chapters 4 and 5 are successful all of the time. I am truly convinced that they are much more effective in dealing with the problem employee than are any of the traditional management methods we can use. Still, they are not failsafe. Thus, it is important that you always have a back-up plan, a way to assist your employee to improve productivity and to deal effectively with his or her problems, which are impacting the productivity of your work group. If you care about your employee, that back-up plan should be utilization of an Employment Assistance Program (EAP). It is a safety net.

If you are a human resource manager in a federal agency, your agency is mandated by Title 5 of the Code of Federal Regulations (5 CFR) Part 792 to establish appropriate prevention, treatment, and rehabilitation programs for federal employees with alcohol or drug abuse problems. Public Law 79–658 authorizes you to provide for the physical and mental fitness of federal employees. These legislative authorizations form the basis for your EAP.

If you are a human resource manager in the private sector, or if you work in a state or local government agency, the federal law can be a guide for you. Neither private sector organizations nor state and local governments are mandated by federal law to provide an EAP, however. State laws differ across the country. You should check with your attorney about specific laws that may apply to you.

This chapter will tell you about EAPs. It will tell you how to recognize an ideal EAP and how to evaluate it. It will give you advice on how to start an EAP if you do not now have access to one. Most importantly, it will tell you to teach your supervisors to refer employees to an EAP, and how to deal with the referred employees while they are participating in it. It will also show you how to increase the likelihood that your employees will take advantage of EAP services.

First, I want to define the term EAP for you. An EAP has been described variously as: (1) "a counseling service provided directly for employees and their dependents;"[1] (2) "the policies and procedures adapted by employers in order to identify problem employees;"[2] (3) "more or less structured programs that utilize technical, administrative, and professional human services and personnel people . . . to meet the needs of troubled employees."[3]

Whatever definition one accepts, it is clear that the EAP is an adjunct service to management. It is a service to help you help your employees. It is not a tool that you can use to facilitate the dismissal of problem employees. Lest you be surprised that I would even think that your organization had ulterior motives in considering an EAP, let me tell you about an organization with which I dealt.

Officials in that industry expressed a concern over increasing levels of drug and alcohol abuse among employees and approached an already established EAP about contracting for services. The officials indicated that they wanted to arrange for a counseling resource for employees and also asked the EAP to provide training to industry supervisors. When EAP staff met with them to discuss training content, the industry officials explained that they wanted the EAP supervisors trained to identify addicts or potential addicts so that these employees could be dismissed before they became problems. Such training is not the intent of an EAP. In this case, EAP staff refused to serve this particular industry.

The EAP carries with it the implicit assumption of *help for troubled employees*. The EAP is more effective and efficient in dealing with a problem employee than is a purely disciplinary method. It is more effective than you or your supervisors can be alone. The utilization of an EAP demonstrates to employees that their organization cares about them and is willing to go the extra mile. This can't help but foster employee loyalty.

It is naive, however, to deny the disciplinary nature of an EAP referral. No matter how "nice" or "caring" the EAP makes you look, it also carries an element of discipline, for the problem employee is generally "coerced" into participation with a threat of dismissal if he or she refuses to participate.[4] Remember, you will use an EAP as a last resort. In doing this you make, for your employee, what is known as a "job-in-jeopardy" referral. This means that both you and the employee must know, up front, that participation in the EAP is mandatory, and that progress toward improvement is expected.

Now of course, if employees are sophisticated enough to recognize their own troubles are interfering with their work performance, and seek help from the EAP of their own volition, the element of coercion is absent. This, however, is not always the case. The likelihood of an employee making a self-referral seems directly related to the amount of education and marketing that the program conducts, and to its reputation.

All EAPs share the following goals:

- To identify employees whose personal or health problems are interfering with their job performance
- To motivate those individuals to seek and accept appropriate help
- To address underlying stressors in the work place
- To assist both managers and employees in achieving health and productivity[5]

The typical host of an EAP is a large corporation or a large federal installation with thousands of employees. Most of us work for much smaller organizations. A general rule of thumb for determining if your organization is large enough to establish its own EAP is that guideline provided by the U.S. Department of Health and Human Services, which states that an employee population exceeding 3,000 can support one full-time counselor. For most of us it is more realistic, and less expensive, to contract with a consulting group outside the organization. But whether you have an in-house EAP or utilize the services of an outside group, you need the same information to understand, evaluate, and utilize your EAP.

THE IDEAL EMPLOYEE ASSISTANCE PROGRAM

While no EAP will be perfect, it's important for you to know the characteristics of an ideal EAP so that you will have criteria for evaluating the one available to you, or for deciding which one to choose if you plan to contract for services. An ideal EAP, like so many other ideals, is more vision than reality. It can be described, if not found.

The ideal model synthesizes characteristics of the EAPs developed by the National Council on Alcoholism and the National Institute on Alcohol Abuse and Alcoholism.[6] These EAPs have been endorsed by 70 percent of the consultants employed by the Addiction Research Foundation. The elements of an ideal EAP include events that must take place to establish it and necessary attitudes that must be developed on the part of both its management and its employees. To be successful, an EAP must be as near to the ideal as possible, and also serve an organization that is prepared to develop procedures for "documentation, coercion, referral, and follow-up."[7]

Requirements for an Ideal EAP

Shain and Groeneveld, who developed the model of an ideal EAP, have identified seventeen key characteristics that are designed to meet specific goals and that require specific activities on the part of both EAP staff and the employees of the organization that utilizes the EAP. These characteristics and the necessary activities related to them are discussed on the following pages.[8]

Written policy. An EAP, like any formal organization, should have a written policy and set of procedures. The policy should outline the procedures the organization will follow to refer a problem employee, and clearly identify the kinds of services the EAP staff will offer. It should also explicitly delineate the rights and responsibilities of both supervisors and employees, and outline the role of the EAP staff in relation to the organization's management.

This policy must clearly indicate that the EAP will be used as a source of *help*. Too often employees see the EAP as an instrument of management that will be used to find out about their personal business, rather than as an outside source of assistance that can literally save their job. A clearly stated policy about what the EAP is and is not can alleviate this worry and increase employee acceptance.

If your organization has a union, it's important to involve union representatives in policy development. Most unions are pleased to see a company utilize an EAP, as this is a means of job protection for members who might otherwise be in termination proceedings. In an ideal EAP policies and procedures clearly identify the role of both union and management in establishment and referral.

If you are the human resource manager in a federal agency, your EAP must have written policies consistent with prevailing federal requirements and regulations related to alcoholism, drug abuse, mental health concerns, rehabilitation, follow-up care, and other employee problems that affect performance.[9]

Prerequisite attitudes. In the ideal situation, organizational values will be those of help and support. An employee who exhibits disruptive behavior or inadequate job performance will be seen as a human being with a problem that can be resolved, rather than a troublemaker to be ostracized or discharged. From key executives to the lowest employee on the totem pole, the pervasive value must be one of caring. The expectation must be that people can and will be helped.

Here your role is key. Often employees must be educated to the value of an EAP. I think you must appreciate its worth, or you would not be reading this chapter. My bias is that employees want to produce and that they will produce, if given the necessary support systems to weather the storms of life and work. The EAP is one such support system. But it is only as good as it has the opportunity to be. People tend to become what we expect them to become. If you and the key managers in your organization expect that the best is possible, the best is likely to occur.

One way to demonstrate that you believe in the EAP is to make certain that its services are free for employees who utilize it. You can do this by arranging for your company's insurance policies to cover its services. Or you can arrange for your company to subsidize the services.

Any subsidy you provide will truly be an investment. Consider the experiences of other organizations. General Motors estimates that its EAP saves well over 280 million dollars per year through absenteeism reduction, and a major airline observed that it received $16.35 in return for every EAP dollar spent.[10]

Early identification. The ideal EAP will provide for early identification of problems. It cannot be used as a substitute for effective supervision and should never replace the proactive methods described in chapter 4. It should, however, be readily available and frequently utilized. The EAP staff will be more successful if it has established a program of information that encourages employees to self-refer before their problems become unmanageable. The ideal EAP markets its services and provides prevention as well as treatment. When you choose an EAP, choose one that is proactive rather than reactive.

You can facilitate the EAP's ability to be proactive by educating your supervisors about its services and about how and when to utilize it. You can also hold your supervisors accountable when they fail to observe and document failing performance. Frequently, supervisors are the biggest obstacle to early identification of problems. They ignore problems in the hope they'll go away. Remember the human propensity to "plead, bleed, and pray for a miracle?"

To help you see the value of early identification, let me tell you about Leonard. Leonard had been an employee of the same company, and a union member, for twenty-two years, when I was called in by the human resource manager. She wanted me to help her decide what to do about him. Conversation with her revealed that she had only become aware of Leonard in the previous week when his supervisor decided to fire him. A review of Leonard's departmental file showed a series of written reprimands for various unacceptable behaviors, but these reprimands had never been sent to the Human Resources Office. His performance appraisals had either reflected a "satisfactory" or a "not unsatisfactory" rating over the years. He had never received more than a cost-of-living raise, but he had never received any disciplinary action either. Finally, his supervisor, who had been with the company almost as long as Leonard, had decided to terminate him.

In the meantime Leonard had become disabled. A recent physician's statement indicated that he had kidney disease that could be expected to require dialysis soon. It was while Leonard was in the hospital that the supervisor decided to terminate him, stating that his hostility, low productivity, and frequent use of profanity could no longer be tolerated.

Now this company had, only three months prior to my encounter with it, contracted with an EAP for services. A flier had been sent to all supervisors, but no education program had been instituted and most employees did not yet know about the EAP. I suggested that instead of termination, a referral for Leonard be made to the EAP. The supervisor was opposed to such a referral, saying that if Leonard were going to change, he would have done so after one of his many reprimands. After much persuasion on my part, a reluctant referral was made—but it was made with a condition supported by the human resource manager. Leonard was given three months to be completely rehabilitated.

Now, no matter how ideal an EAP is, it cannot reverse the habits of years in three months. It cannot cure physical illness. Both Leonard and the EAP were set up to become failures. Leonard knew that and hired an attorney, in preparation for a lawsuit. I can't tell you the end of this story because I left the area before it was resolved. But you and I can both speculate that the EAP failed and Leonard sued.

Skills of identifiers. The ideal EAP will spend time and effort educating all employees, and especially supervisors, in the skills necessary to both identify problems and make appropriate referrals. Your own division of training and development can assist with this education. I'm convinced that Performance Monitoring is the best technique of confrontation and referral available. And it can be taught! In my own research, I found that an EAP alone had a 59 percent chance of eliminating the problem for which an employee was referred. In combination with a manager's use of Performance Monitoring, both before and after referral, this likelihood increased to 84 percent. This, I think, underscores the need for skilled problem identifiers.

Another reason that skilled identifiers are essential is the tendency of employees to *not* use an EAP. One study of a "broad brush" EAP found that only 4.7 percent of the company's employees used it over a five-year period. Another study found only 3.5 percent of the employees taking advantage of the company's EAP.[11] Skilled identifiers increase EAP participation. If employees do not participate, they cannot be helped.

Support for identifiers. Support for those who identify problem behavior and the need for EAP referral must be provided by both the EAP and your organization. The importance of supporting supervisors was discussed in chapter 4 as a proactive method for problem employee management and will not be repeated here. The importance of this support, however, cannot be underestimated.

Identification must be keyed to performance. The EAP is neither a panacea nor a crutch. While the ideal EAP will be available to assist employees to resolve many of their troubles, both EAP counselors and your supervisors must focus on job performance. When job performance deteriorates past a supervisor's ability to facilitate change, referral is indicated. Since your company is providing EAP services as an employee benefit, you have the right to expect that EAP staff will work with the employee to improve performance. Other services are ancillary to that. This expectation should be included in the policy guidelines that establish your organization's relationship with the EAP.

Choice. The ideal EAP does not coerce an employee into accepting its services and neither should you. For an EAP to be effective, an employee must be given the choice between accepting EAP services or risking disciplinary action up to and including termination. This choice must be made a part of the employee's reality. Help and hope are natural consequences of referral acceptance. Discipline and/or termination are natural consequences of refusal to accept the referral and cooperate with the EAP counselors.

The right to choice and the consequences of each choice must be clearly spelled out in EAP policies and procedures. An ideal EAP will not put you or your organizational supervisors in the position of having to defend the consequences of employee choice.

Self-referral. Remember the old saying, "You can lead a horse to water, but you can't make him drink?" EAPs are the water for troubled employees, and you can't make them accept it. If they themselves choose to seek help, however, they are more likely to readily accept it. Thus, an ideal EAP will make provision for employees to make self-referrals. And these self-referrals will be kept in confidence, unless the employee requests that you or a supervisor be informed.

Provision for self-referral is insufficient for successful self-referrals, however. The ideal EAP will proactively seek self-referrals. It will market its services. The paths to care must be visible, credible, and publicized. Simply sticking an announcement on a bulletin board or sending a memorandum is not enough. Colgate wouldn't sell much toothpaste if that's all it did. The ideal EAP will sell its services with the same creativity that's necessary in any advertising campaign. That's how people find out about products. That's how employees find out about EAP services.

To be accepted by employees, an EAP must be viewed as a legitimate and confidential source of help. Employee acceptance may be contingent on members of the EAP staff's being perceived as competent, and having a history of maintaining anonymity and confidentiality. That is, of course, a "Catch–22." Counselors who have maintained confidentiality will have difficulty demonstrating competence when their only witnesses remain anonymous. Thus employee acceptance may come slowly. The "grapevine," however, is effective. Given time, employee acceptance will come, and with it self-referrals. The ideal EAP recognizes this and makes no elaborate promises it cannot keep.

Availability of treatment. An ideal EAP will have easily accessible offices and it will have arrangements for in-patient care if that is indicated. Treatment facilities must be private, removed from areas frequented regularly by employees—preferably off-site. Counseling rooms in the ideal EAP will be soundproof, with concealed waiting areas. The employee who comes to an EAP usually doesn't want the fact advertised. At the same time employees do not want to take the time to go long distances to get help. Ideal EAPs will successfully balance the needs for access and anonymity.

Federal regulations require that EAPs that serve federal agencies be preferably located on-site or with easy access to the work location. If the EAP serves a dispersed employee population, it should be within a short commute of the work site. The EAP is required to have a seven-day-a-week, twenty-four hour answering service that provides a telephone number for callers requiring emergency assistance. The EAP must provide office hours that are convenient for the client population, assure that intake occurs within twenty-four hours, and provide services as immediately as possible. The office space must be private to ensure confidentiality, have sufficient rooms to accommodate the caseload, and provide adequate administrative space.[12]

Nondiscrimination. The ideal EAP will, of course, guarantee treatment without regard to sex, race, age, religion, national origin, handicap, or sexual preference. Not only should a statement to this effect be included in policies that establish the EAP, the statement should be on all advertising material and all memoranda. In the case of the EAP, nondiscrimination must extend beyond the requirements of law. Policies should explicitly state that all employees, *regardless of rank or job title*, will be treated equally.

Let's face it, some organizations have problem managers as well as problem employees. Yet managers are much less likely to refer themselves for help, as they seem to have a greater fear of reprisal.[13] EAP referral is not a two-way street, and even ideal EAPs rarely have procedures for employees to refer their supervisor for help. A recent article titled "The Executive Alcoholic and the Conspiracy of Silence" seems to capture the issue.[14] A "conspiracy" of silence is far more likely to surround top-level employees than it is line workers. The ideal EAP will structure its services in such a way that it is available for and accessible to all levels of employees.

Employee education. The ideal EAP will not only educate company employees about its services and policies, but it will provide educational services in a wide range of areas as preventive strategies. The ideal EAP will be a resource for mental health wellness programs such as stress management and time management. It may offer stop-smoking or weight loss programs. It can be a resource for you to use in presenting informational workshops on child care and domestic violence. It may provide education on, or sponsor such groups as, Alcoholics Anonymous or Al-Anon. An ideal EAP can be an invaluable educational resource for employees. In the role of educator, the EAP will have a means of establishing the credibility and reputation it needs to encourage self-referrals.

Benefits coverage. The ideal EAP will insist that your company provide comprehensive coverage of services for both mental health related illnesses and substance abuse. To encourage your company to do this, the ideal EAP will be able to demonstrate a favorable cost/benefit ratio in terms of absenteeism, accidents, and productivity. If you are just establishing an EAP in your company, this justification will be a goal. If you are contracting for EAP services, you have a right to ask for demonstrable statistics to justify your per-employee expenditure.

Protection of reputation. The ideal EAP will have well-established policies and procedures toward, as well as a reputation for, maintaining confidentiality. It must provide safekeeping for all records regarding employee treatment.[15] If an employee makes a self-referral, no inkling of that should come back to your organization, unless the employee tells you. If an employee is referred to the EAP because of job-in-jeopardy, the only information you can expect from the EAP is a confirmation that the employee accepted treatment. And that information must be kept in strict confidence, with only you and the employee's immediate supervisor privy to it. If the employee is in the unfortunate position of working for more than one supervisor, only the referring supervisor should be informed of the employee's EAP participation. To do otherwise would violate the employee's right to privacy. If the employee could be benefitted, however, by others knowing about his or her EAP participation, the employee can be asked to give written permission for such sharing of information.

Guarantee of clean slate. Any employee who utilizes the services of an EAP must be given the guarantee that this participation will not jeopardize future career opportunities after successful completion of the EAP service program. You must make that guarantee. The ideal EAP will apprise you of this same information. It will have persons on staff who are familiar with recorded cases of arbitration or litigation where this has been an issue, and who can advise you on steps to take to protect both your organization and your employee.

The guarantee of a clean slate should be publicized. Such publication and subsequent adherence to the clean slate promise will increase employee trust in both the EAP and you. Increased trust leads to increased use.

Program monitoring and accountability. Insistence on anonymity and confidentiality does not negate the necessity for record keeping and accountability. The ideal EAP will maintain service statistics and report them on a regular systematic basis. At a minimum, I think you can expect reports on numbers and types of services provided, numbers of persons served, and a per-unit cost for those services. I would want the reports on both a quarterly and yearly basis. The ideal EAP will also provide a means for you, or someone in your organization, to monitor their activities and plan with them for future services. If yours is a federal agency, the EAP must submit fiscal year reports to the Office of Personnel Management on counseling activities.

Follow-up. The final component of an ideal EAP is the requirement that it make provision for follow-up with clients so that changed behavior receives positive reinforcement.[16]

Types of Employee Assistance Programs

The "ideal EAP" discussion is a prescription, as much as a description. It is a standard by which you can measure the EAP you have access to or are considering developing. Only you can determine how near the ideal you want your EAP to be. There are always trade-offs. You must decide how many of these you are willing to make. In the real world, EAPs tend to run the gamut from the simple to the complex. The more complex the EAP, the more costly its services are. The ideal EAP is complex.

Five basic EAP types have been identified. They are: Hot line; Consortium; Contractor; Employer; and Union.

A brief description of each of these is presented below so that you can have an idea about what kind you might want to use.[17]

Hot line. The hot line is either a local or long distance telephone service available as a self-referral for troubled employees. Listeners are trained to assess problems, offer advice, and make a referral to an appropriate service provider, which the caller is urged to contact. Supervisors are available in the hot line office to assist listeners with referral information. In crisis cases, hot line staff may become actively involved in arrangements to transport the caller to appropriate long-term service providers. Records are maintained on all calls and activities, and summary reports are forwarded regularly to the sponsoring organizations.

Consortium. A consortium is a not-for-profit organization that meets the needs of small employers because it is set up to serve a number of organizations, and often the general public as well. Consortiums are most suitable for organizations with fewer than 2,000 employees. Their advantages are that they decrease company costs, facilitate maintenance of confidentiality, and often result in better utilization of other community resources. Their disadvantages are that supervisors and employees may be reluctant to deal with outsiders, consortium personnel may have little knowledge of your organization, which can handicap their effectiveness, and the different organizations that comprise the consortium may disagree on the level of desired services.

Under the current regulations governing federal agencies, one agency must serve as the consortium contracting agent for all the participating agencies. The participating agencies are then bound to the contract with the service provider through an interagency agreement with the consortium contracting agency. The agency that serves as the contracting agent may be one of the participating agencies, the Public Health Service, or the Office of Personnel Management.[18]

Contractor. A contractor is different from a consortium in that a contractor is a for-profit agency that is paid by the contracting organization. Contractors serve problem employees who may contact them in self-referral, but who will, more likely, be referred as a management response to problem behavior on the job. Although some contractors are retained to provide only substance abuse service, you can contract for the provision of whatever kinds of services you decide. The contractor can be expected to fit the ideal EAP conditions, and should be held to them.

Employer. If your organization has more than 3,000 employees, you might consider establishing an on-site EAP. While some organizations provide only a single counselor, it is possible for an employer to have an on-site ideal EAP. The benefits of doing it yourself are obvious. The services will be what you want, when you want them delivered.

If you provide the EAP yourself, you are in a much better position to control costs. In fact, Karen Hamlett of the Virgina Beach Fire Department managed to establish an EAP for the department's 321 staff members without spending a penny. For her achievement, she was named a "Personnel Winner" by *Personnel*, a publication of the American Management Association, which provides the following account:

Hamlett began the project by taking a good look at the department's employees to find out what specific problems they were facing, and how those problems were affecting them at home and on the job, and what kinds of programs and approaches would make them most likely to respond. And, starting with just this information and the telephone book, she developed an EAP that offers physicals and stress tests, televised presentations, seminars and workshops, brochures and audiovisual materials, announcements of available services, and counseling referrals—but hasn't cost the department or employees a dime.[19]

Union. Programs sponsored by unions generally evolve from a concern to protect union members. They may be as simple as peer counseling or a hot line. They may also be an elaborate ideal sponsored in conjunction with the organization. They may well result as a part of a negotiated benefit package, but once developed are likely to depend heavily on you as a human resource manager to coordinate and monitor.

EVALUATING AN EMPLOYEE ASSISTANCE PROGRAM

Factors that can affect the success of an EAP fall into two categories: human factors and program management factors.[20] In order to establish an EAP or to evaluate an existing one, you need to consider all of these factors. If they are present, your EAP is much more likely to be effective.

Human Factors

Human factors are those components of an Employee Assistance Program that can be affected by human beings—both service providers and clients. They include: (1) access ease, (2) anonymity, (3) confidentiality, (4) counselor advocacy, and (5) employee acceptance.[21]

Access ease refers to the location and availability of the EAP. Access can be constrained by location, cost, hours of operation, and encumbering policies and procedures. If neither you nor your employee can access the EAP services, they will be of little help.

Anonymity refers to the confidentiality with which an employee and his or her problem is treated. The concept of anonymity places its own constraint on access ease, for certainly an EAP located on the premises of your organization is easily accessible. An employee entering the office known to house the EAP, however, can be easily seen by other employees. Ease of access can destroy anonymity. EAP planners must somehow balance these two prerequisites of a viable program.

Once employees are in the offices of an EAP, they must be assured of privacy. Waiting areas should be secluded and offices should be soundproof. The employee who seeks help from an EAP simply does not want that fact advertised. If anonymity is not provided, he or she is not likely to return.

Confidentiality refers to the manner in which counselors affiliated with an EAP deal with the information they obtain from a client with whom they are working. Confidentiality differs from anonymity because confidentiality refers to how information gained by client participation is handled by the EAP personnel. You need to know that substantial penalties for revealing confidential information are provided in the U.S. Code.

While it is vital that an employee who seeks help from an EAP be guaranteed of confidentiality in terms of what he or she reveals about himself or herself, it is also vital that the employee who you refer for help realize that the fact that he or she has followed up on your referral will and should be reported to you, as will the regularity with which he or she keeps appointments. After all, you are using EAP services as a way of helping your employee keep his or her job. Failure to follow through on this plan for work productivity and improved performance can lead to the natural consequence of termination.

Counselors at the EAP whose services you use have a role as advocate for their clients. They should not violate anonymity or confidentiality. At the same time they should be willing to have the same faith in the employee that I've asked you to have and to support and represent the employee. The advocate may ask you to give the employee more time to change or more release time to seek help. Don't be angry when this happens. Expect the advocacy role; but remember that the bottom line must be organizational productivity. You, the employee, and the EAP counselor should have a specific time frame in which you can reasonably expect change to occur. Don't let yourself be talked out of that.

To be accepted by employees, the EAP must be viewed as a legitimate and confidential source of help. This means that the EAP must market its services and availability. It may be handicapped in this because the greatest source of legitimacy usually comes from personal testimony. Yet employees receiving services will naturally be reluctant to let others know, and you, of course, cannot brag about what the EAP did for someone. Thus employee acceptance can come slowly.

You and other managers may also be slow to accept an EAP as an adjunct to what you can do for your employees. It will be easy for you to view an EAP as interference or a waste of time. All I can say is give it a chance.

If your organization is unionized, union representatives must also accept it as a viable source of assistance to their members and as a means of maximizing their leverage in wage demands. If union members are involved in initial planning for the establishment or utilization of EAP services, they are likely to support it.

The EAP can and should encourage acceptance by providing information on general issues of productivity and mental health and making readily available pamphlets on its services. If it doesn't, ask why not.

Program Management Factors

Program management factors refer to the policies and procedures of the EAP that guide the way its staff will deal with your organization in general and the specific clients who are referred for service. These factors include: (1) confrontation support, (2) economics, (3) program flexibility, (4) interest conflicts, (5) management control, and (6) prevention aspects.[22]

For you to refer your employee for services from an EAP, you must be able to confront that employee with the reality of his or her unacceptable on-the-job behavior. If you are using Performance Monitoring, this will be easier. However, you already know that when confronted with unacceptable behavior, an employee can start excusing, blaming you, and threatening you. When that happens, it's awfully hard to hold to the courage of your convictions. Thus an effective EAP will offer training to supervisors on how to confront an employee and how to deal with the employee's reaction to the confrontation.

The EAP should also offer support for supervisors of employees who are referred for help. An employee who is participating in an EAP program will receive counseling once or twice a week, or less often. Supervisors have the right to guidance on how to manage that employee during the rest of the week. An ideal EAP should offer support groups for supervisors. "It's lonely at the top" is never more true than when you have an employee who has become such a problem that EAP involvement is necessary. You need help too. Expect it.

EAPs can be expensive. In evaluating an EAP you need to consider the following:

- Cost—you can expect this to be more than $4000 per employee
- Marginal cost of adding additional services or clients
- Methods of pricing, e.g. per client, flat fee, guaranteed minimum, etc.
- Cost vs. work force size
- Procedures in place for the monitoring and evaluation of costs
- Who pays—your organization, the employee, a third party[23]

You also need to consider how easily the existing EAP structure, methods, personnel, and payment requirements can adapt to the changing needs of your organization and your employees. A rigid program may soon be outdated. An extremely fluid program may undermine confidence because it is not consistent in the way problems are handled. You have the right to expect continuity as well as an ability to adapt to emerging needs that were not identified at the time the EAP was organized or acquired.

You need to be aware that an EAP counselor can easily become the man or woman in the middle. The counselor owes allegiance to the organization from which fees are paid and from which referrals are made. At the same time the counselor has a professional commitment to assisting the client/employee even when that assistance runs counter to organizational expectations.

In evaluating an EAP, you need to make certain how such conflicts of interest are resolved. In selecting an EAP, you need to be clear from the beginning about your reasons and expectations from it.

In evaluating an EAP, you will also want to ascertain the degree to which officials in your organization can influence the personnel, procedures, and outcomes of EAP assistance. Certainly you will not want to use the EAP as an instrument of employee control nor as a means to terminate. You will, however, need to have some say in how the EAP serves your organization. If you don't, neither you nor other managers are likely to invest the time and money necessary to make your referrals to the EAP worthwhile.

By the same token, EAP personnel must be freely informed about your organization's goals, procedures, policies, and reporting relationships. They need to know the strengths and weaknesses of various members of the organizational hierarchy. In effect, for an EAP to be successful it must be a partnership with your organization—a partnership for the purpose of assisting your employees to be all they can be.

Equally important is coordination between your organization and the EAP. You will want to make sure that you know what procedures are in place for referral to the EAP, what amount and type of response you can expect from the EAP, what assistance the EAP staff will provide to managers who refer employees, and how the use of the EAP by referred employees will be enforced. You will also want procedures for terminating the services of the EAP if managers in your organization determine that it is ineffective, inefficient, underutilized, or not needed.

In addition to working with problem employees who are referred, the EAP should maintain a prevention component that utilizes information, education, and training in a proactive effort to forestall employee problems—particularly in the area of substance abuse. The EAP must both advertise and develop credibility. If the preventive aspect is successful, the need for other services will be minimized. While this is not a likely scenario, the EAP should be willing to spend a substantial effort on problem prevention.

ESTABLISHING AN EMPLOYEE ASSISTANCE PROGRAM

The majority of the United States work force is not covered by any type of an Employee Assistance Program.[24] I think that's a tragedy. That's why this section on establishing an EAP is included in this book.

Questions That Must Be Addressed

If you are establishing an EAP, there are several questions that you must address:

• Should services be integrated i.e., should your EAP provide general counseling to deal with all problems or will you target just substance abuse?

- Should services be holistic i.e., provided to both worker and family?
- Should services be problem oriented or person oriented i.e., should they deal with specific organizational problems such as absenteeism or job dissatisfaction, or should they be directed only to specifically identified persons who are not performing?
- Should services be external to the organization, or should they be a part of the Personnel or Employee Development Department of the organization?[25]

Other questions to consider are:

- How much assistance to the manager of a problem employee should the EAP provide?
- Will the EAP assist employees whose behaviors in the work place are not the result of some identified trouble, but which detract from organizational goal accomplishment, or will it only assist troubled employees?

These questions have no simple answers. Indeed, their answers may depend as much on dollars available and size of the organization as on anything else. Yet to establish an EAP, they must be considered. I recommend that the EAP you establish be as comprehensive as possible, given whatever constraints you must work under.

Actions to Take

One of the greatest services you can provide your organization is to establish an EAP. The type of EAP and the kinds of services it will offer are limited by only your imagination and your budget, provided you have the support of both top management and line employees.

Remember Karen Hamlett? She established an EAP at no cost to her department with entrepreneurial efforts that started with an employee survey and the telephone book. After she had prepared a long list of free speakers, workshops, seminars, and telephone numbers of already existing crisis hot lines, she prepared and circulated regularly a "Health Awareness Alert" that contained this information. She also found that television cable companies were required to dedicate one cable channel for free city use. From her employee surveys, she identified appropriate professional speakers and arranged for their presentations to be taped and transmitted on the free channel. She also arranged for employee assistance issues to be included as a part of the department's ongoing in-service training program.[26]

Most of us, however, are not so creative, nor do we seem to have available the resources that Ms. Hamlett found. For us, the easiest way to get an EAP established is to contract for services with an existing provider. Before arranging a contract, however, several steps must be taken. First and crucial is the necessity to sell top management on the idea. The information presented in this book will help you with that.

Next, you need to establish a planning task force that assists you in evaluating needs and determining specifically which services you want an EAP to provide. The goal of this task force should be to develop, with employee input, a policy statement that frames the mission, goals, policies, and procedures that will govern your EAP.

Once you have completed your policy statement you are ready to issue a "Request for Proposal" (RFP). This will encourage competitive bidding and increase the likelihood that you get the program that most nearly fits your needs at a cost you can afford to pay. If possible, hold a pre-bid conference with potential vendors to discuss and clarify your needs and limitations. Directions for issuing and evaluating RFPs are provided in appendix 6.A at the end of this chapter. A summary of the requisite program elements and standards required of federal agencies are in appendix 6.B. They provide an effective guide for non-governmental organizations as well.

UTILIZING AN EMPLOYEE ASSISTANCE PROGRAM

When you decide that your problem employee has behaviors that are beyond your capability for dealing with, a referral to an EAP is in order. You must remember that this referral should not be used as punishment, it is simply the natural consequence of your employee consistently failing to follow through on the plan(s) made as a part of Performance Monitoring. Implicit, however, in this referral, must be that your employee's job is in jeopardy. You must have a clear understanding that if your employee fails to follow through on this referral, termination will follow.

As a part of establishing an EAP, guidelines for using it must be developed. The guidelines should present the philosophy behind the establishment of the EAP, enumerate the problems for which it was designed to cope, and provide directions for when and how to refer. Implicit in these guidelines must be the threat of dismissal if the employee does not cooperate.

Supervisors are often reluctant to utilize an EAP. Don't you be. Reluctance usually comes because supervisors are afraid to confront their problem employee.[27] You, however, know how to confront, and your employee is accustomed to that confrontation, if you have been using Performance Monitoring. The EAP is simply an instrument of help, a last-ditch effort to enable your employee to take charge of his or her life and return to productivity. As you confront your employee with the reality that performance has not improved, you simply offer him or her an opportunity to get outside help.

Supervisors are also frequently afraid that a grievance suit will be the result of an EAP referral.[28] Don't you be afraid of that either. Chapter 8 will tell you how to work within the legal constraints that can be an issue anytime a problem employee is present in the work place. So long as you don't use the EAP as a threat, or a reaction to some overt action on the part of your employee, you should not fear the grievance process.

Let me tell you about how one supervisor used Performance Monitoring to refer an employee to an Employee Assistance Program. Nancy had been a bookkeeper for the past three years. Her accounting and secretarial skills had been a real asset to the department. About six months ago, Nancy's husband left her. Since that time, her work had been deteriorating. Often her daily balances varied seriously with the company auditor's computer balance. Her mistakes had caused some costly financial decisions on the part of the company. Nancy's supervisor, Stan, had been using Performance Monitoring regularly with her, but she had failed to follow through on her plans for improvement. On the day of the following conversation, Stan smelled alcohol on Nancy's breath and called her into his office. Their conversation went something like this.

Stan: Nancy, I want to talk about your performance.

Nancy: There's nothing wrong with my performance.

[Nancy was beginning the typical response pattern to confrontation by denying that she had a problem.]

Stan: You haven't followed through on your plan to change, you know. Your mistakes are to the point that I'm seriously considering terminating you.

Nancy: That's not fair. You know I've got a lot on my mind right now. I haven't been feeling very well since the divorce. Then last week my cat died. (Nancy began to cry.)

[Nancy moved quickly to the next predictable response pattern to confrontation by excusing. Stan could sense himself starting to feel sorry for her as he handed her a Kleenex.]

Stan: You have been having it rough. The fact remains, though, that your job performance is unacceptable. Those mistakes you made last month cost the company a lot.

[Stan let Nancy know that he understood her being upset, but he remained on the point of the discussion, which was to confront Nancy with her behavior.]

Nancy: Well, if you'd give me some help, I wouldn't make so many mistakes. I asked you to arrange training on that new software and you wouldn't do it.

[Now Nancy switched to blaming Stan, which you'll remember is the next predictable response. Stan fought the impulse to defend himself to her and remembered that he was not the person whose performance was unacceptable. Rather he again confronted her with reality, but resisted the impulse to lecture her.]

Stan: Nancy, you told me that you would arrange for your own training and I agreed to reimburse you for the cost. I'm still willing to do that. Today, however, I want to talk about another serious problem. [Stan took a deep breath.] Nancy, I smell alcohol on your breath. You know that drinking on the job is grounds for dismissal here.

[Nancy became furious—another predictable response.]

Nancy: What I do is none of your business. You're just trying to think up ways to get rid of me. Well, I'll tell you one thing, you just try and fire me and I'll file a discrimination suit. I've watched the way you treat women in this place.

[Stan again resisted the impulse to get defensive. He knew that Nancy had no grounds for a discrimination suit. He saw what she was doing as another predictable response—appeal to authority as a means of coercion. He wanted her to know that he did care about her, and that he also had a responsibility to the productivity of the organization.]

Stan: I know you've been having it rough, and I want to help. That's why I asked you in to talk with me. I'd like to refer you to our Employee Assistance Program.

Nancy: I don't need employee assistance. Just give me time, I'll get my life straightened out.

[With this new confrontation, Nancy again moved to denial.]

Stan: Nancy, I smell alcohol on your breath. That's a major infraction of our rules, so major, in fact, that your job is in jeopardy. I have only two alternatives: I can fire you, or I can refer you to our Employee Assistance Program.

[Stan had to keep her focused on the problem and the consequences of the problem. Since the consequences had already been spelled out in organizational policies and procedures, Stan had some clout.]

Nancy: Well, I wouldn't have to drink if you'd cut me a little slack around here. Anybody'd drink, if they had to deal with all the things I have to. If you didn't call me in this office so much, I'd have time to get my work done.

[Now Nancy is excusing again, blaming Stan for her problems.]

Stan: I want to refer you for help. What do you want me to do?

Nancy: I don't care what you do, just let me alone.

Stan: I'd like to see you get help. I think help is available from our Employee Assistance Program. Will you give it a try?

Nancy: Oh, alright. What do I have to do?

As you can see from this scenario, referral to an EAP is a confrontation with your problem employee that can lead to the employee once again going through predictable stages to acceptance. These stages are denial, excusing, anger, blame, depression, and finally, acceptance. The key for use is to remain in control of your own feelings and continue the confrontation process, refusing to listen to excuses and refusing to get upset by your employee's anger and blame. The best help you can be to your employee at this point is as a caring confronter of reality.

Train Supervisors to Use the EAP

It's been my experience that one of the most difficult roles you will have in providing EAP services is getting your supervisors to refer people to them. Many supervisors are exasperated by the time an employee is at the point that an EAP referral is in order. They don't want to help the employee, they just want to get rid of the problem.

There are many reasons why the supervisor must learn to deal with the problem employee and to refer that employee for help when it's available. While the supervisor's inclination might be to simply dismiss the problem employee, recent legislation and court decisions, as well as unionization, severely limit the organization's ability to discharge. For example, an employee's discharge can be found by the courts to be invalid for any one of the following reasons:

1. The employee was discharged for reasons specifically prohibited by federal and state statutes
2. The employee was discharged for performing a statutory duty
3. The employee has been deprived of due process
4. The discharged employee had an implied contract right under the terms of employment
5. The court determines that the discharge was motivated by bad faith, malice, or retaliation, or is contrary to public policy

Not only do arbitrators overturn employer discharge decisions more than 50 percent of the time, but the laws have become so skewed in favor of the employee that the supervisor's right to terminate is literally being eroded away.[29] The case of Monge v. Beebe Rubber Co. is an example of this erosion.[30] In this litigation, the court ruled in favor of the employee because the decision to discharge him "is not in the best interest of the economic system or the public good." Due to the California Cumulative Act of 1977, your organization might even be held responsible for treatment of such employee disorders as headaches, hypertension, cardiac irregularities, weight change, depression, ulcers, etc. This legal climate makes it incumbent upon your organization to train your supervisors in the policies and procedures that protect both the employee and the supervisors. Referral to an EAP is one such policy

To educate your supervisors to the value of maximizing organizational productivity while also helping the problem employee is a crucial step in ensuring EAP referrals. Your supervisors must learn to weigh both the costs and benefits of working with, helping, and trying to change problem employee behavior against the costs to their own and other employees' morale, and, temporarily, reduced productivity. Supervisors must weigh the benefits of keeping an employee who already knows the job against the costs of finding and training a new employee. They must weigh the costs to their own psyche of dealing with the problem employee against the benefits to their psyche of believing that they ultimately have helped. To be forced into such a calculus is very uncomfortable.

Even as supervisors try to weigh costs and benefits, they will be influenced by their own value systems. They might find it more difficult to be objective about a minority, or a family's sole breadwinner, or a person they genuinely like (or dislike). Quite literally, supervisors may blame the victim or be the victim. Only a conscientious self-examination can provide supervisors of a problem employee with insight into personal values, and free them to define and confront problem behavior. It is up to you to facilitate that self-analysis.

A referral to an EAP is a conscious decision—one that requires a supervisor to admit that both the traditional and innovative supervisory strategies have failed. This creates self-doubt, and often the supervisor of an employee referred to an EAP feels like a failure. Too many supervisors seem to think that refusing to refer means they are blameless in the problem. The reality is that if they have consciously followed the techniques outlined in this book, they are indeed blameless. It is your responsibility to educate your supervisors to understand that an EAP referral is simply one more skill in their repertoire of skills.

EAP staff have an educational responsibility to your supervisors. I've seen too many occasions where EAP personnel seem to believe that simply making a presentation at a staff meeting and passing out brochures is sufficient supervisory orientation. It is not!

A simple presentation, though it may be necessary, is insufficient for equipping your supervisors to believe in the value of EAP referrals, much less to teach them how to make these referrals. You can and should expect EAP personnel to assist you in supervisory education through a workshop that teaches through demonstration and role play. An outline for a training workshop to teach your supervisors to make an EAP referral is located in appendix 6.C at the end of this chapter.

Help Supervisors Deal with the Referred Employee

Implicit in an EAP referral is the threat of dismissal for the referred employee. Thus an EAP referral requires that the referring supervisor confront the problem employee. Not only is this frequently an unpleasant experience, the employee may not appreciate the helping nature of the referral and may begin to treat the supervisor with resentment. This is one reason that it is so important that your EAP representative meet with a referred employee within twenty-four hours of the referral.

When an EAP is utilized, its services are likely to be in the form of individual counseling. A counselor will meet with the referred employee on a regular, time-limited basis. Prior to and after meeting with the counselor, the employee continues in regular employment. During this utilization period, the supervisor is not involved in employee assistance and will not know what is transpiring between the counselor and the referred employee. This situation exacerbates the supervisor's feelings of helplessness.

You can help the supervisor who is trying to cope with a referred employee by using the information in the next chapter, "Don't Become a Problem Too: Help Yourself." While it is written for you, it will be useful for your supervisors as well.

CRITICISMS OF EMPLOYEE ASSISTANCE PROGRAMS

The EAP is not the panacea it is frequently touted as being. Even if it were, there are several significant problems that you, as a human resource manager, need to consider before establishing or utilizing one. First is the logical theoretical limitation of an EAP. This limitation is that an employee cannot be confronted or coerced into EAP participation until job performance has been "officially tagged as deteriorating."[31] This may be too late to do much good.

Whether solving problems or curing diseases, there are three levels of prevention. Primary prevention occurs before the fact and involves education, inoculation, or effective supervisory practices. Secondary prevention occurs during the fact and involves crisis intervention, early diagnosis, and crisis monitoring. Tertiary prevention occurs after the fact and involves treatment and rehabilitation. Each succeeding level is less successful in eliminating the problem than the level before it.[32] Since a supervisor will likely refer an employee at the tertiary level, the opportunity for the EAP to be successful is undermined.

EAPs are not utilized as often as they should be. In an average company, about 10 percent of the employees will be referred to an EAP. Yet, it is suspected that 20 percent of all employees have an alcohol or drug abuse problem,[33] while still more have personal problems that have not yet begun to affect their job performance. If an EAP is not utilized, it cannot be effective.

Another problem with the EAP is that its structure and procedures do not lend themselves to assisting the supervisor in dealing with his or her own feelings when confronted with a problem employee. Living through the previously discussed feelings of denial, guilt, inadequacy, and fear is not an easy task. Yet these phases will likely be experienced whether or not an EAP is available as a resource. The EAP model is not structured, however, to assist the supervisor through these stages, nor does the EAP literature give cognizance to the reality of a supervisor's own feelings: feelings that may lead him or her to wonder if he or she is the problem employee.

Another gap in EAP effectiveness is created because the EAP is not designed to assist the manager of a problem employee who is simply not contributing to organizational goals. The EAP perspective assumes that the employee is experiencing some trouble which, when resolved, will alleviate the problem behavior being exhibited in the work place. Troubles that can precipitate problem behavior are marital, personal, mental, health, financial, and poor supervision. Yet an employee's problem behavior may not be the result of any trouble.

As any practicing human resource manager knows, there are a number of types of behavior in the work place that detract from the accomplishment of organizational goals. These behaviors can be exhibited by persons who are not substance abusers and who are not experiencing some marital, legal, financial, social, or health problem. The problem employee response patterns discussed in chapter 1 are examples of problem behavior for which the EAP has little to offer.

The EAP is the solution for the BIG PROBLEM and the MAJOR TROUBLE—the issues that require the intervention of a skilled counselor. The EAP is of little or no help in the day-to-day "sand in the shoes" kind of problems that plague you.

Do you know about "sand in the shoes" types of problems? Let me illustrate with a parable. There's the story told about a man who walked clear across the United States in an odyssey that required stamina to climb mountains, survive the rains and snows, and to continue on through the traffic-congested cities and the lonely highways of the plains. When he had completed his trek, he was questioned about the trip.

"How did you manage to keep going in face of the odds against you?" he was asked. "How did you have the energy to climb mountains and walk through deserts? Weren't you afraid in city slums and mountain passes?"

"The mountains, deserts, cities, and storms were a challenge. I thrive on meeting a challenge!" the man replied, then added, "it was the sand in my shoes that almost caused me to give up."

"The sand in your shoes?"

"Yes, the sand in my shoes. Those little, gritty, prickly bits of sand kept wearing away my resolve."

The EAP cannot help you shake the sand from your shoes. The proactive strategies presented in chapters 4 and 5 can.

SUMMARY

This chapter has defined and described the Employee Assistance Program. It has presented you with ways to establish, utilize, and evaluate it. It has emphasized the importance of training supervisors to avail themselves of EAP services for their problem employees and urged you to assist your supervisors when they are faced with having to cope with an employee who is referred for EAP services. The chapter concluded with criticisms of the EAP so that you will not be lulled into believing it is a panacea. Rather, the EAP was presented as one more proactive strategy for dealing with a problem employee.

Directions for Issuing and Evaluating RFPs

Once the RFPs have been received and evaluated, a one-hour presentation should be arranged for the top-ranked vendors to meet with the client's selection committee. Each vendor's presentation should be scored on a simple rating system on issues such as similarity of current clients to the group to be served, ability to deliver services proposed, retention of clients and percent of penetration of current client's work force during second and third contract years. During each vendor's presentation, the following should be kept in mind: (1) is the vendor representative a principal of the firm or a salesperson? (2) is the person representing the vendor authorized to make binding commitments? (3) what are the representative's experience with EAPs, the vendor firm and professional qualifications?

EVALUATING PROPOSALS

By their very nature, EAPs must be tailored to meet the needs of individual organizations and operated within organizational structure and climate. There are few absolutely correct responses to the following questions. Each client must strive for maximum understanding of the vendor's capabilities and then select the provider that most nearly meets the client's needs.

Organization

1. Does the vendor specialize in employee assistance or is it primarily a health care provider?
2. Is it a profit or not-for-profit firm?
3. In what professional associations is the vendor active? (e.g., the National Employee Assistance Providers Association)

Funding and Fee Structure

1. How does the vendor distribute overhead among clients? (e.g., new client and the need to add staff)
2. What percent of fee is overhead and what percent is direct service?
3. Does vendor receive public funds or grants? What percent of income is federal/state grant based? How secure is long-term funding?
4. How are fee increases determined? (pooled or individual client cost center?)
5. When are first year installation costs recouped? (distributed as overhead or next contract renewal?)
6. How does vendor provide for funding of lost business?
7. How long is fee structure guaranteed? What is projected fee structure for second and third years? Will fees increase or decrease if employee use increases?
8. Are there any unlisted service charges? If so, itemize.
9. Is fee based on number of total employees or cost per projected use?
10. Is there any limitation on number or length of visits as a cost reduction measure? If yes, itemize.
11. Who determines when employee treatment is to be discontinued?
12. Are there any extra charges for after-hour or holiday visits?

Legal Issues

1. Is proof of liability insurance provided?
2. Will a hold-harmless clause be provided to client to protect from vendor-caused claims?
3. Who owns the vendor's treatment records?
4. Does the client have input regarding vendor relocation of facilities?
5. What are the procedures for sale of vendor's practice?
6. What is client's role in vendor reduction in staff and/or increase in counselor case load; change in ration of technical, professional, clerical staff to caseload; reductions or curtailment of services?
7. What are the contract termination procedures regarding notice for employees in treatment?

Hours/Location

1. Is vendor's treatment facility convenient to the work site?
2. Percent of employees within X miles of vendor?
3. Are twenty-four hour counselors/treatment available?
4. Average time lost from work site for appointment?

5. Number/type of staff available during client's nonbusiness hours.
6. Is adequate free parking available at treatment facility?
7. How is employee confidentiality at location maintained?
8. How are shift workers handled?

Vendor Staffing

1. Will vendor permit the client to evaluate counselors and staff by on-site visits, user questionnaires and review of resumes?
2. Can client change counselor assignments if negative feedback is received from employees?
3. Are counselors qualified to provide service in treatment specialty areas?
4. Does the vendor use contract, part-time or student help? If yes, how and where?

Vendor Client References

1. Number of active contract firms.
2. Number of client firms with same or similar products and services.
3. Number of client firms serviced by vendor:

1st year   _____

2 to 5 years   _____

6+ years   _____

4. Total number of client cases processed last fiscal year.

_____   Counseling

_____   Short-term treatment

_____   Referred to other organizations

Client Staff Training

1. Is the client provided with a preview of training material with the right to script changes?
2. Is management orientation provided for?
3. Will supervisory training be conducted the initial year only or on an ongoing basis?
4. Is there an additional cost for second year or refresher training?
5. Review outline of training program: Methods state-of-the-art? Quality of materials? Vendor-developed using other organization's material?
6. Vendor flexibility in training times and location?
7. Cost of training extras? (specific list)
8. Is supervisory training "canned" or does it build on supervisors' current skill levels?

9. Is training for labor stewards provided?

10. Who pays for materials should additional training be requested?

Literature/Materials/Forms

1. Is program customized or "boilerplate" with custom cover? [Boilerplate means that the program is already established and will not be adapted to meet individual needs.]

2. What is vendor's flexibility in customizing material?

3. Is there an extra cost for tailoring program to organizational needs?

4. Is material current? (Check publication date.)

5. Did vendor develop own material?

6. Does literature reflect client organization's management philosophy?

7. Is all literature to be furnished covered in fee? (List extra charges.)

8. Does fee include design and printing of forms?

9. Are literature racks, etc. provided free?

Employee Contact

1. Is vendor's plan for employee contact comprehensive?

2. How are family members included?

3. What assurances of privacy are made?

4. Is there any evidence that vendor's plan has worked in similar companies?

5. How does vendor plan to relate to labor organization? Any prior experience?

Report/Management Information; Benefit Coordination

1. What is the frequency of reports?

2. What is the quality of the samples provided?

3. Is there any extra charge for special information needed by client?

4. How useful is information in evaluating program's success or failure?

5. Will vendor analyze client's medical coverage to ensure proper coordination for diagnostic/evaluation, treatment of alcohol/drug/psychological problems and out-patient treatment? Is there a charge?

Source: Bill Chiabotta, "Evaluating EAP Vendors," *Personnel Administrator* 30 (August 1985), 39–43. Reprinted with permission.

Summary of Elements and Standards for EAP Programs in Federal Agencies

Element 1: Needs Assessment

STANDARD: An EAP should have, both at the time the program is established and on a periodic basis thereafter, a mechanism to assess the needs for employee assistance. The EAP needs assessment should be aimed at identifying work site, environmental, programmatic, personnel, and stress-related factors deleterious to employee well-being or productivity. Program decisions should be directly related to the assessment findings and be periodically evaluated in that context.

Element 2: Program Integration

STANDARD: An EAP should be designed to assure its integration into the structures and processes guiding the overall administration and management of an agency or program. The EAP director should have access to, and involvement with, the management of the agency and serve as a consultant to address the impact of program and organizational change on the well-being of employees. An advisory board should be constituted with representatives from key divisions and offices, including both manager and employee members, to assure the responsiveness of the EAP to agency needs.

Element 3: Comprehensive Services

STANDARD: An EAP should assure the provision of comprehensive high-quality clinical services, supervisory training, management consultation, and preventive health education/health promotion services appropriate to the defined needs of an agency or program. The services must competently evaluate employees and appropriately assist them in returning to and/or remaining effective in their jobs when alcohol, drug abuse, mental health problems, or other events alter their work performance capacity. The EAP must have an established community referral network and coordinate its services with local resources, health organizations, and self-help groups as appropriate.

Element 4: Program Administration

STANDARD: An EAP should have policies and procedures in effect aimed at assuring the appropriateness, effectiveness, and efficiency of the program in meeting the needs of both management and the employee population served. The procedures must be consistent with the federally mandated requirements and with agency policies and procedures. This includes assurance of: availability of a sufficient number of qualified counselors; services provided in appropriate office space that assures easy access and privacy; a case record system in compliance with federal confidentiality requirements; guidelines for assessing or measuring the quality of care; and regular review of personnel services. An EAP must submit annual fiscal year reports to the Office of Personnel Management on counseling activities.

Element 5: Program Evaluation

STANDARD: An EAP should have a mechanism in place to evaluate the appropriateness, effectiveness, and efficiency of the delivery of services and program integration. Evaluations of the scope and appropriateness of client services, educational programs, supervisory training, and outreach activities should be performed on an annual basis and become a part of the permanent program records. Descriptive statistics should be employed whenever possible to summarize program activities and facilitate the annual evaluation. Program modifications should be made on the basis of evaluations.

Source: U.S. Department of Health and Human Services, Public Health Service, *Standards and Criteria for the Development and Evaluation of a Comprehensive Employee Assistance Program* (Rockville, Md.: Health and Human Services, 1986).

"Utilizing the EAP": A Training Workshop Outline

Goals

1. To provide participants with information about the Employee Assistance Program
2. To provide participants with the skills necessary to refer an employee to the Employee Assistance Program

Group size

Five to thirty participants.

Time required

Approximately eight hours broken into two four-hour segments, scheduled from one to two weeks apart.

Resource required

A person knowledgeable about EAP services.

Materials required

1. A film or videotape that introduces participants to the EAP. (Your EAP should have one. If not, you can select from the list at the end of this training outline)
2. A tablet of newsprint and an easel
3. One dark-colored magic marker for each 5 participants
4. Masking tape for posting newsprint
5. Name tags if participants do not know one another

Process

Day 1

I. After a brief (about ten-minute) introduction in which you have workshop attendees introduce themselves to one another and state what they want from the workshop, show the film/video.

II. Ask participants to take about five minutes to jot down three things that they learned from the film that will be useful for them.

III. Divide participants into groups of five. Give each group a piece of newsprint and a magic marker and ask them to appoint a reporter/recorder for their group. Give them about twenty minutes to share their observations with one another. Then ask them to take another ten minutes to list any questions they still have about the EAP.

IV. Take a fifteen-minute break.

V. Reassemble as a large group and have each reporter tell the others what questions his or her group has, and tape the list of questions on the wall.

VI. Have the EAP representative available to:
1. Answer the questions
2. Spend about twenty minutes describing your EAP
3. Tell participants how to make referrals
4. Tell participants about EAP procedures
   for dealing with referred employees
5. Answer any other questions that arise

VII. Conclude the workshop by asking each participant to take one minute to summarize what he or she thought was the most important thing learned today.

VIII. Tell the participants that at the next session they will work on developing the skills they will need to refer an employee to the EAP. Ask participants to read chapter 6 of this book. Also ask participants to bring a one-page description of an employee they would consider referring to the EAP. If they are not now dealing with a problem employee, ask them to describe an employee that they would want to refer if that person worked for them.

Day 2

I. Briefly summarize day 1. Then ask participants to name one thing they found helpful in reading chapter 6. List those things on newsprint and post them around the room. Tell participants you will spend this day learning to refer an employee to the EAP.

II. Tell the group that each will role play the person in the description he or she has brought. Give them ten minutes to study the role.

III. Divide the group into triads. Have each member choose to be "A," "B," or "C." Tell them that they will have three rounds of interaction and that each will have the opportunity to try out Performance Monitoring.

IV. Give the following instructions:
1. Participant "A" will be the first problem employee. "A" will spend two minutes describing himself or herself from the information in the description he or she has brought.

2. Participant "B" will be the first supervisor who uses Performance Monitoring.

3. Participant "C" will be the first referee. The referee's job is to make certain that the "supervisor" sticks to the Performance Monitoring model.

V. Begin Round 1. Stop the process after fifteen minutes. Allow five minutes for both "A" and "C" to give feedback to "B" by stating:
1. What "B" said or did that was helpful.
2. What "B" might have done differently.

VI. Begin Round 2. Participant "B" now becomes the problem employee, "C" becomes the "supervisor" making the referral to the EAP, and "A" becomes the referee. Round 2 also takes fifteen minutes. At the end of the time, again allow five minutes for the "supervisor" to receive feedback.

VII. Begin Round 3. "C" becomes the problem employee, "A" becomes the "supervisor," and "B" becomes the referee. Round 3 takes fifteen minutes. At the end of Round 3, again provide five minutes for the "supervisor" to receive feedback.

VIII. Take a fifteen-minute break.

IX. Reassemble triads. Allow them sixty minutes to discuss the following questions:
1. What were your thoughts and feelings when you played the role of your problem employee?
2. What did you notice about the interaction between you as the "employee" and the person who role-played your "supervisor?"
3. What were your thoughts and feelings when you played the role of "supervisor?"
4. What insights can you give the person in your triad who is the real supervisor of this employee?
5. What can you conclude about making an EAP referral for a problem employee?
    (a) When will it be helpful? Why?
    (b) When will it not be helpful? Why?

X. Have a member of each triad report back any insights his or her group gained about making an EAP referral.

XI. Conclude the workshop by having each participant take two minutes to summarize what he or she thought was the most important thing learned today, and to tell how that can be used back at the work site.

EAP training films: "Who Needs It," "Everybody Wins," and "Your Move" are all available from Hazelden Educational Materials. Call 1/800–328–9000 for information.

NOTES

1. See Barbara Feinstein, and Edwin Brown, *The New Partnership: Human Services, Business, and Industry* (Cambridge, Mass.: Schenkman Publishing Co., Inc., 1982).

2. See Martin Shain and Judith Groeneveld, *Employee Assistance Programs:*

Philosophy, Theory, and Practice (Lexington, Mass.: Lexington Books, D.C. Heath and Co., 1982).

3. See Donald Myers, *Establishing and Building Employee Assistance Programs* (Westport, Conn.: Quorum Books, 1984).

4. See Shain and Groeneveld, *Employee Assistance Programs.*

5. See Feinstein and Brown, *The New Partnership.*

6. See Shain and Groeneveld, *Employee Assistance Programs.*

7. Ibid.

8. This discussion is based on the "Model of an Ideal EAP," which was developed by Shain and Groeneveld and explained in their book, *Employee Assistance Programs: Philosophy, Theory, and Practice.* The model is used with permission.

9. See U.S. Department of Health and Human Services, *Standards and Criteria for the Development and Evaluation of a Comprehensive Employee Assistance Program* (Rockville, Md.: 1986). The Public Laws 91–616, 1970, and 92–255, 1972, as amended (42 U.S.C. 290dd–1 and 42 U.S.C. 290ee–1) mandate that the Office of Personnel Management, in cooperation with the secretary of Health and Human Services and other federal agencies develop and maintain appropriate prevention, treatment, and rehabilitation services for federal civilian employees with alcohol and drug abuse problems (5 CFR, Part 792). In May, 1979, the Office of Personnel Management issued guidance to federal agencies on expanding the scope of services of an EAP to include medical, behavioral, and emotional problems affecting employee performance.

10. Bill Chiabotta, "Evaluating EAP Vendors," *Personnel Administrator* 30 (August 1985), 39–43.

11. See, Myers, *Establishing and Building Employee Assistance Programs.*

12. See U.S. Department of Health and Human Services, *Standards and Criteria.*

13. Ibid.

14. Lisa McGurrin, "The Executive Alcoholic and the Conspiracy of Silence," *New England Business* 9 (June 15, 1987), 31–32.

15. In EAPs that serve federal agencies, client records must be kept in a strictly confidential manner in accordance with the confidentiality requirements of PL 93–282 and the implementing federal regulations of 42 CFR Part 21 (particularly section 2.11(n) as well as PL 93–579 (Privacy Act)). Counselors must be thoroughly knowledgeable about these regulations and are bound by the restrictions of these confidentiality and privacy regulations.

16. This discussion on the ideal EAP is based on the work of Shain and Groeneveld, and used with permission. It is described in much greater detail in their book, *Employee Assistance Programs: Philosophy, Theory, and Practice.*

17. See Myers, *Establishing and Building Employee Assistance Programs.*

18. For more information on developing a consortium for federal agencies, consult *The Development of a Public Health Service EAP Consortium,* published by the U.S. Department of Health and Human Services, Public Health Service, in Rockville, MD.

19. Barbara Solomon, "The EAP that Cost not a Penny," *Personnel* 62 (October 1985), 4–7.

20. See Myers, *Establishing and Building Employee Assistance Programs.*

21. Ibid.

22. Ibid.

23. See Chiabotta, "Evaluating."

24. Ibid.

25. Sheila Kamerman, "Book Review of *Human Services in Industry*," *Social Casework* 64, no. 7 (July 1982), 445.

26. See Solomon, "The EAP that Cost not a Penny."

27. See Donald Phillips and Harry Older, "A Model for Counseling Troubled Supervisors," *Alcohol Health and Research World* 2, no. 1 (Fall 1977), 24–30.

28. Ibid.

29. Stuart Youngblood and Gary Tidwell, "Termination at Will: Some Changes in the Wind," *Personnel* 58, no. 3 (May–June 1981), 44–53.

30. 316A 2d 549 (1974).

31. See Shain and Groeneveld, *Employee Assistance Programs*.

32. See J. Swisher, Testimony in U.S. Senate. Subcommittee on Alcoholism and Drug Abuse. Alcohol and Drug Abuse Education Programs, 1977 Hearing, 24, 25 March, 1977. Washington, D.C.: U.S. Government Printing Office, 1983. (Y4. H88:A11/977).

33. "EAPs/Wellness Programs: Separate but Equal," *Employee Benefit Plan Review* 39 (November 1984), 127.

Chapter 7

Don't Become a Problem Too: Help Yourself

One of the most important steps of problem employee management is to help yourself. Previous chapters have taught you how to confront and help the problem employee. In this chapter you will learn to help yourself.

You'll remember that problem employees precipitate a series of predictable psychological stages in those who must deal with them. That's you. The stages are denial, anger, bargaining, depression and withdrawal, then finally, acceptance and active planning.

These stages are akin to those experienced by persons confronted with catastrophic illness, or with personal or economic tragedy. These stages are painful and unavoidable. They come because they are the coping mechanisms of the mind and body. They are unavoidable and they are necessary. They are also painful.

Most people, when immersed in the emotions engendered by these stages, will begin to doubt themselves—to question their own abilities and their own integrity. They deal with the emotions in ways that do not help either the problem employee or themselves. This chapter will help you to recognize what's happening to you, and to manage your emotions and your behavior proactively, so that you will be spared some of the trauma that a problem employee can create.

In the stages of denial and anger, one prays for a miracle. In the stage of bargaining, one believes that reason will prevail and so pleads with the employee to change. As one realizes that the employee's problem behavior must be confronted before it will change, one will become depressed and want to withdraw from the whole situation as he or she mentally and emotionally "bleeds."[1] When acceptance finally comes, one feels drained and discouraged.

I have seen supervisors of problem employees stay in denial as long as ten years! This "ignore it and it'll go away" approach to the problem employee only postpones the inevitable. It also creates a de-motivating work environment for others so that organizational output is negatively impacted. Thus, even as you proactively manage the problem employee, you must proactively manage your own emotions and behaviors. You must also understand what the supervisor of a problem employee is going through.

As you prepare to help yourself, you need to know that the stages to acceptance and the coping mechanisms they generate are experienced on two levels. At one level is the reaction to the problem employee. At a deeper, more personal, more devastating level is the reaction to one's self. People begin to question their own education, their own skills, and their own abilities. This self-questioning is the most painful of all. To prevent it may be why so many people, when faced with a problem employee, stay in the denial stage so long.

UNDERSTAND TRANSITION

In order to help yourself, you need to understand what happens at the *intra*personal level as one moves through the predictable stages of coming to terms with a problem employee. First there will be a transitional period—a period precipitated by employee actions that cannot be controlled. The period of transition described here occurs whenever people are confronted with an unexpected crisis that dramatically and negatively affects their lives in some way. This period is not unique to those coping with a problem employee. It occurs for anyone confronted with the unexpected and the traumatic.

Transition has been likened by one scholar to the Land of Oz, to which poor Dorothy was blown by a tornado. This land was one of the unfamiliar, of witches and scarecrows, of unexpected twists and turns. The Land of Oz is a scary, unfamiliar place. So is the period of transition.[2]

Entering Transition

When confronted with an unpredictable crisis, people experience a number of psychic losses: (1) loss of identity, (2) loss of control, (3) loss of meaning, (4) loss of belonging, and (5) loss of a future.[3] The crisis generated by a problem employee will generate the losses in those who must deal with that employee.

The closer one is to the situation, the more frequently one must interact with the problem employee, the stronger these losses will be. The more bizarre and unexpected the employee's behavior, the greater will be the impact. While the losses will occur within anyone who must deal with the problem employee, the effect of the losses will be greater for the person who directly supervises that employee. They will all occur simultaneously and they are difficult to endure. Let's talk about them.

Loss of identity. For professionals, their identity—their sense of who they are—is inextricably intertwined with their profession. They have relied on their education, knowledge, skills, and ability to achieve the position they're in. They have demonstrated good judgment and their performance has positively contributed to organizational goal accomplishment. They are somebody. People respect their judgment. They are in control of their job and their environment.

A problem employee changes all that. Suddenly, knowledge, skills, and abilities are no longer adequate. Those who are trying to deal with a problem employee are spending 80 percent of their time and energies dealing with one individual whose behavior defies all the motivation and leadership theories they've ever studied. They begin to question themselves—to ask "Where have I gone wrong?" and "What's the matter with me?"

They expect that a person with their education and background "ought" to be able to manage any member of the work force. After all, a human resource manager or a supervisor is trained to deal with people. While wrestling with the dissonance the problem employee has created it's all too easy to conclude that one is not a good human resource manager, not a good supervisor. "If, I'm not a good human resource manager, who am I?" "If I'm incompetent as a supervisor, who am I?" An identity loss has occurred.

Loss of control. Identity loss creates a disequilibrium. If people no longer feel comfortable with whom they are, they have trouble taking charge of even those conditions and persons over which they still have some measure of control. They feel like a small, rudderless boat on a great ocean. They are being pushed and shoved by events and actions that they didn't ask for. They aren't sure where each subsequent wave will buffet them. They wonder what will happen next, and they're afraid to find out.

Because they experience such a loss of control in this one area, people begin to fear they will lose control over other facets of their job or life. They may begin to restructure their environment or redefine their job in an attempt to increase their control where they can. They will probably feel panicky.

I remember Dorothea. As she began to feel the loss of control inevitably generated by the problem employee, she surrounded herself with symbols of control. First she rearranged her office. No longer would her desk face the wall and her guest chair be near her own to communicate openness and a willingness to listen.

Dorothea turned her desk to face the door and put an effective barrier between herself and anyone who entered. She replaced the pastoral scenes on her office wall with every diploma and certificate she had ever earned to attempt to prove competence. She had a brass plate engraved with her title placed on her office door. She stole a "Do Not Disturb" sign from a hotel and hung it on her office doorknob.

Dorothea's feelings of losing control prompted her to display pathological behavior. But she is not unique. Loss of control is a scary thing.

Loss of meaning. The problem employee will prompt those who manage them to agonize with questions like, "Why me?" "Doesn't what I've accomplished count for something?" They will frequently be disoriented, as they try to bring some meaning to the experiences they are undergoing. They may seek out such books as *When Bad Things Happen to Good People.*[4] They may start to read the Bible. They may return to school. They may begin to search for a new job—even a new career.

As people experience a loss of meaning, they must find a replacement for it. They wonder if they will be able to. They wonder if the search for meaning is worth the time and effort, and they wonder how they will survive without meaning to what they have done and what they are doing.

Loss of belonging. Frustration with a problem employee will also precipitate a loss of belonging. Where once the supervisor and human resource manager felt a part of an organization and knew their roles in it, they have come to question their ability and the contributions they can make. They may begin to withdraw from organizational functions, be uncomfortable in staff meetings, and stop participating in organizational activities such as picnics or bowling leagues. They will feel isolated and alone. They may think people are talking about them behind their back. They may cease to trust others and begin to see them as allies of the problem employee and enemies of themselves.

People trying to cope with a problem employee may try to strengthen their sense of belonging in areas of life outside the organization. They may become more involved with their family. They may take on a new hobby or join a new club. They may become overly busy outside the organization so they won't have to deal with what's going on in it. They will feel left out, like a "rebel without a cause" because they do not belong in the organizational scheme of things as they once did. The problem employee has seen to that.

Loss of a future. If the problem employee has wreaked enough havoc, those who must manage him or her may fear a loss of a future. They have lost confidence in their own abilities and start to doubt their relationships in the organization. They may think that failure to prevent their employee's problem behavior communicates to superiors that they are incompetent or no longer able to perform. They may begin to see themselves as representatives of the Peter Principle at work and believe that they have truly reached the highest level of their incompetence. Their future looks bleak.

Moving through Transition

The passage through transition is a movement from the crisis created by the problem employee toward a new and different future. It is a journey through a kind of psychic never-never land on an uncharted course. It is slow and it is painful.

In the Old Testament, the word for "wilderness" is also the word for "sanctuary." The Plains Indians called their journey . . . a Vision Quest. And this is not just a so-called primitive idea. The no-man's land between what was and what will be is a time when we are most in touch with our creative unconscious and most able to break out of the old thought forms and see things in wholly new ways. . . . You're going to have moments (or days or weeks) of discouragement . . . you may feel that you've (been) hung up on a big rock . . . (been) shut up in a little room with a large beast.[5]

While dealing with a problem employee one is struggling in the "no-man's land" described above. Past experiences and tried and true techniques have failed. New approaches and techniques must be learned, new kinds of decisions made, new kinds of skills mastered. And one must learn these new ways while at the same time experiencing the stages of denial, anger, bargaining, and depression.

Until the no-man's land is conquered and the stage of acceptance reached, no one can say that the problem employee has been effectively managed. So long as the deep *intra*personal anguish continues, one experiences a troublesome sense of unrest—a kind of guilt—a gnawing uncertainty about what might have been.

Moving through transition can take longer than anyone would ever expect. If one is not prepared for dealing with a problem employee, if one does not know that such a creature exists, the shock of discovery deepens the anguish. The key seems to be in preparation.

Surviving Transition

You'll remember that I said that transition occurs whenever people are confronted with an unexpected crisis that dramatically and negatively affects their lives in some way. This period is not unique to those coping with a problem employee. It occurs for anyone confronted with the *unexpected* and the *traumatic*.

The best way to survive transition and keep from becoming a problem employee too, then, is to accept that approximately 10 to 20 percent of the work force are problem employees and to institute the proactive strategies described in this book for managing these employees. Your understanding and preparation can assist your supervisors as well. Any supervisor who is trying to manage a problem employee will be in a very difficult period, a period that you can now recognize as a transition zone.

The time one spends in the transition zone seems to be directly related to the intensity of crisis experienced, the difficulties encountered in crisis resolution, and the amount of support available. We generally expect that to pass through the transition created by the death of a loved one takes about two years. Recovering from the impact of a problem employee may take that long as well.

It may take longer, for the person trying to manage a problem employee does not have the kinds of support systems so often available to the widowed or orphaned. No one sends flowers. No one cries with you. Some blame you. Others castigate you. You berate yourself. You have no opportunity to mourn and no formal ceremony to bury the issue.

If your encounter with a problem employee has been very traumatic, it may literally haunt you a long time. The "ghost" of your own problem employee may be still alive in the hallways of your head and heart for many years, as you rethink, requestion yourself, and reexperience the wilderness.

HELP YOURSELF

Using proactive strategies to manage the problem employee is crucial to ensuring that when you are confronted with a problem employee you do not become a problem too. Equally crucial to successful survival is that you proactively manage yourself.

Here, as with the problem employee, Performance Monitoring is the most effective method I've found. Its emphasis is on taking positive control of your life by recognizing that all behavior is chosen, and that you can choose what you do and how you act and react. Behavior choices influence feelings and thoughts as surely as feelings and thoughts influence behavior.

Picture for a minute a four-legged stool. The stool is perfectly balanced. Now imagine that the stool represents your total behavior. One leg is *feeling*. One leg is *thinking*. One leg is *doing*. One leg is *physiological response*. The stool cannot stand if one leg is removed. The stool will be out of balance if one leg is shortened or lengthened. The stool legs are a part of the whole. So it is with behavior. Behavior is a composite of feeling, thinking, doing, and physiological reaction.[6]

"There is tremendous value in learning as much as we can about how we behave—especially how we can control our behavior."[7] To help you understand this, I'd like you to think about how you might react if you were faced with a problem employee who verbally abused you and physically threatened you.

When you called the employee into your office, your purpose was to talk about the employee's deteriorating performance. Your intent was to be helpful, and you were conscientiously trying to confront the employee's behavior while planning with him to make the necessary change. Instead of perceiving you as the competent, helpful person you are, the employee turned on you, cursed you, and accused you of discrimination. When you suggested that you talk later, after he had calmed down, the employee grabbed a paper weight off your desk, threw it at you, and stormed from the room. Because you still have to deal with the employee, you will begin to generate components of behavior that seem sensible to you.

What may make immediate sense to *do* is to go home, drink a few beers, and plan how to avoid the employee on the morrow. What you may *think* is sensible is to condemn yourself for not approaching the employee in the "correct" way or to decide that you are not competent. You will also generate a series of *feelings* that make sense right now— blame, anger, depression, resentment—a whole group of feelings that seem appropriate responses to the encounter. You may also have a *physiological* reaction such as stomach cramps, heartburn, and sweating palms. These symptoms, added to your *thinking*, *feeling*, and *doing* comprise your total behavior, which, if anyone asks, you will probably describe as "upset" or "miserable."

To help yourself, you must understand that you have chosen the misery. Now you might ask, "How could I be happy after what I've just been through?" I would have to answer that you can't just automatically choose "happy." But you can get yourself to "happy" by recognizing that *feeling* is only one component of your totality of behavior. It's almost impossible to choose physiological responses consciously. It is about as difficult to choose to be happy in the face of discouraging odds. But

there is a very important lesson to be learned. *Because we always have control over the doing component of our behavior, if we markedly change that component, we cannot avoid changing the thinking, feeling, and physiological components as well.*[8] [Emphasis in original.]

Knowing that you have the capacity to make choices, and knowing that the choices you make directly influence how you feel, think, act, and react is a powerful tool for helping yourself. This knowledge also, paradoxically, is a tremendous responsibility. You can no longer blame others for how you deal with them or for how you react to them.

There are some scholars who believe that our values and attitudes directly influence our behavior. They believe that "correct" behavior will only come from "right" attitudes, and that if one does the "right" thing for the "wrong" reasons, ultimately the thing done will be worthless. I don't agree with that. I believe that you can change your attitudes by changing your behavior. I want you to believe that too.

The easiest part of behavior to change is *doing*. One cannot *do* without also beginning to think, feel, and react differently. The new behavior, which is out of synchronization with the old feelings and thoughts, creates a dissonance that the subconscious will act to resolve. That resolution comes through altered feelings, thoughts, and reactions. So, when you choose to *do* (or behave) differently and act on that choice, your mind and body will automatically adjust to reduce the disequilibrium. In essence, *doing* something you enjoy will cause you to *feel* better.

Help Yourself through Transition

To help yourself through the transition forced upon you by the problem employee requires that you consciously take control of yourself. People in the helping professions consistently operate under the axiom that "the only person's behavior you can truly change is your own." Change that, and other changes follow.

Change coping mechanisms. Let's assume, for a moment, that you are the person described above who starts to cope with the reaction to the problem employee by drinking a few beers and planning how to avoid the employee on the morrow; as you condemn yourself for not approaching the employee in the "correct" way, you feel blame, anger, and resentment, and experience stomach cramps, heartburn, and sweating palms. Instead of giving in to the misery that all this generates, you can choose a different behavior. In the short term, you can go to a party or a movie, have sex with your significant other, weed the garden, paint, or take a weekend excursion. For the long term, you can return to school for an advanced degree, join a "little theater" or historic preservation group, or get active in community improvement. The list is endless— limited only by your imagination and the *doings* that you truly enjoy.

"Wait a minute!" you may say. "That only avoids the problem."

To which I reply, "Not at all. You already know how to deal with the problem. What you must do also is deal with yourself. Choosing behaviors that turn misery to pleasure simply allows you to regenerate to face another day."

Put thoughts and feelings into words. You can also help yourself through the transition with words that describe what you're going through. If you're an auditory communicator, then find a person you trust and *talk*. If you're a visual communicator, start a journal and *write*. Put your thoughts and feelings into words. Describe the employee's behavior. Describe your own. Identify every "right" action you took. Describe how the employee responded. Describe what you might have done differently. An outline for an Administrative Journal is contained in appendix 7.A. If you are an auditory communicator, use the outline to guide your discussions about what's happening to you because of the problem employee. If you are a visual communicator, buy a spiral notebook and make faithful entries into your journal.

The Administrative Journal outline was derived from the notion that the most significant learning about organizations in general, and management in particular, comes from your own experience. Too often, worry over a problem employee, concerns for deadlines, and conflicting demands give you little time to reflect and learn from the reflection. Keeping an Administrative Journal provides "a practical way of transcending the immediate situation and engaging in more extensive learning."[9] It will help you turn your encounter with a problem employee from a crisis to an opportunity.

In your journal, identify the losses you are experiencing. Name them. Describe how the loss makes you feel. Identify at least one *doing* that you can use to change the feeling. Identify your fears. Name them. Identify at least one *doing* you can use to change the fears.

Think of a worst-case scenario—the absolutely worst thing that can happen to you because of the problem employee's actions. Describe it. Say what its outcome might be. Decide what you can *do*, if that outcome occurs.

Grow. Think about how this transition fits into the path of your own development. If you had to give it a title, like a chapter title, what would you call this present transition? "Growing Up at Last?" "Coming to Terms with the Universe?" "A Star is Born?" Or what?[10]

When you're confronted with a problem employee, look at that confrontation as an opportunity for growth. The Chinese symbol for "Crisis" is also the symbol for "Opportunity." Every event, every activity, every issue has two sides. It's all too easy to see only the negative side: the crisis. But the problem employee also provides you with opportunities— opportunities to learn new skills, to rethink old issues, to become stronger, and to rethink your career choice. There are many others. Stop and list at least three opportunities that your problem employee has provided for you. Take them and grow.

MANAGE STRESS

Stress is caused by your body's response to a stimulus that disturbs or interferes with your normal physiological equilibrium.[11] Stress is an internal part of life. It is created by conflicts, frustration, and pressure. Stress is also created by triumph, joy, and elation. The winner of a race will experience as much stress as the loser, for stress can be either "distress" or "eustress."[12]

Distress is created when unpleasant things happen. The other form of stress (the "eu" is for euphoria) occurs after a pleasant or exhilarating experience. The problem employee will generate distress for you. You can create eustress by successfully managing the way you deal with that employee.

Stress can creep up on you unexpectedly. I once heard a person's ability to tolerate stress compared with a frog in a pot of boiling water. If the water is cold when the frog is put in, then gradually heated to boiling, the frog can survive to high degrees of temperature. If the water is almost boiling when the frog is dropped in, the frog dies instantly. Either way, the frog's death is assured.

Your body adapts to stress in the same way the frog adapts to increasing water temperature. As stress increases, you adapt and adapt— until stress becomes serious distress. One physician has produced a detailed catalog of the danger signals of distress. This list is contained in Table 7.1.[13]

Stress can make you both physically and emotionally ill. It has been estimated that from one-third to one-half of all patients seeing physicians are suffering stress-related problems.[14] In an attempt to cope with stress, the American public consumes over 295 million dollars' worth of tranquilizers, another 195 million dollars in sleeping pills, and over 286 gallons of hard liquor per year.[15] Medical problems such as coronary heart disease, strokes, hypertension, emphysema, diabetes, cirrhosis, ulcers, colitis, arthritis, skin rashes, allergies, and asthma have all been related to stress. You need to protect yourself from these stress-related illnesses, and you can.

"You are stressed because you are stressable. That is, *it is your reaction to a situation that stresses you, not the situation itself.*"[16] (Emphasis in original.) Using Performance Monitoring with yourself will enable you to choose the response you make to any situation, including a stressful one. First, however, you must develop an awareness of what your body does when it *reacts* to stress.

Most of us have a low level of self-awareness. We live in our bodies, but we don't often listen to the messages they send us. One exercise to develop awareness of the signals your body is sending is to try to answer the following questions:

• What is my resting pulse rate?
• What is my blood pressure?
• When is my energy level at its peak?

- When my energy decreases, what precipitates the decrease?
- What are my biggest time wasters?
- What are my own symptoms of stress? Joint pain? Pounding heart? Sweating palms? Stomach cramps? Headache?
- What job conditions create stress for me?
- What behaviors of others create stress for me?

Once you recognize the signals your body provides, you can take actions to:

- Reduce or eliminate the stressors
- Change your perception of the stress
- Manage your physiological state
- Improve your coping ability
- Counteract stress[17]

Reduce or Eliminate the Stressors

A number of techniques have been developed to help you reduce and eliminate conditions that prompt your body to respond with distress.[18] You can teach yourself to reduce stress with Performance Monitoring. It will help you take control of your life.

Table 7.1
Danger Signals of Stress

General irritability	Pounding of the heart
Dryness of throat & mouth	Emotional instability
Overpowering urge to cry	Inability to concentrate
Weakness and dizziness	Extreme fatigue
Anxiety	Trembling & nervous ticks
Easily startled	Nervous laughter
Stuttering	Grinding teeth
Insomnia	Excessive sweating
Frequent urination	Frequent diarrhea
Migraine headaches	Irregular menstrual periods
Pain in the neck & back	Change in appetite
Substance abuse	Nightmares
Neurotic behavior	Psychosis
Accident proneness	Increased smoking

Table 7.2
Actions to Help Reduce Stress

Say "No!"

Delegate one responsibility at work to someone else.

Delegate one responsibility at home to someone else.

Conduct shorter meetings.

Reduce the overtime you put in at work.

Join a club.

Participate in a new sport.

Participate in a new hobby.

Save for a vacation.

Take a vacation.

Escape for a weekend.

Implement time management.

Avoid an irritating person.

Start an exercise program.

Allow yourself to be idle once in awhile.

Read a good book.

Live by the calendar—not by the stopwatch.

Table 7.2 contains a list of behaviors you can choose to help you reduce stress. Consider the list and choose one behavior from it that you are willing to *do*. When you have accomplished your first choice, choose another. Remember that your goal is to help yourself survive the stress created by a problem employee. You can change the way you feel by choosing one behavior that helps you feel good.

Change Your Perception of the Stress

Remember that stress is not created by an event, rather it is created by your *reaction* to the event. What is challenging and exciting for one person might be seen as extremely difficult and painful by another. All of us have experienced days of operating effectively followed by days of feeling stress and anxiety when responding to the same types of pressure. It is possible to reduce the distress you experience simply by changing your perception of the situation. Use Performance Monitoring with yourself to ask, "What are you *doing*?" "Is it helping?" "What can you *do* to see this situation differently?"

Learning to look on the bright side, especially when you're trying to deal with a problem employee, isn't easy. But it can be done, in suc-

Table 7.3
Actions to Help Change Perceptions of Stress

- Set goals that you have more than a 50% chance of meeting.
- Compliment yourself at least once a day.
- Compliment someone else at least once a day.
- Recall your basic values as a means of getting trivia in perspective.
- List the things and people you are thankful for.
- List your priorities in order.
- Recognize that you are not Super Person.
- Remind yourself that you are not responsible for stressors.
- Accept the things you cannot change.
- Change the things you can change.
- List your accomplishments.
- Describe your talents.
- Have a philosophy for living a purposeful life with a moral code. This can be attained through organized religion or from another direction. However you get there, get there.

---

cessive steps, over time. Table 7.3 contains a list of positive steps you can take to change your perceptions from negative to positive. You can think of others. Begin to change the way you perceive events to which you react with stress. Choose one activity that you're willing to undertake to begin to change your perceptions of stress.

Manage Your Physiological State

Without help from you, your body may react to stress in a way that makes you physically ill. If you are experiencing physiological symptoms whose onset you can pinpoint to your encounters with a problem employee, then you can help yourself react differently. Of course, if you become ill, you should consult a physician. Many times, however, the symptoms of illness appear as a result of your body's reaction to stress. You can often relieve the symptoms of stress by following the tips in Table 7.4. Try one, or two. Expect to feel better.

Improve Your Coping Abilities

An obvious method for dealing with pressures is to become more efficient in getting all of your job and home responsibilities accomplished. As you free yourself from the worries of too much to do with too little time, you gain the energy you need to cope with a problem employee. A number of books on time management have been written. Read one. Then follow the tips on "Ways You Can Save Time," which are listed in Table 7.5.

Table 7.4
Actions to Manage Your Physiological State

- Learn to relax without drugs. Try an evening stroll or a hot bath.
- Get enough rest.
- Establish a decompression routine between work and home. Try spending 10 minutes in the park. Take 20 minutes to read without interruption.
- Take mini-vacations during the day. Put your feet up for 5 minutes. Look out the window. Breathe deeply.
- Eliminate sugar and caffeine from your diet.
- Get up from your chair every two hours. Take a stretch break.
- Think before you act.
- Park at the far end of the parking lot.
- Scribble or doodle occasionally.

Table 7.5
Ways You Can Save Time

- Carry blank 3 × 5 cards with you. Jot down ideas as they come to you.
- Plan each day and set priorities.
- Use the 80/20 rule: 80% of the value comes from doing 20% of the work.
- Generate as little paperwork as possible. Handle each piece of correspondence only once.
- Have a place for everything and keep everything in its place.
- Do not waste time feeling guilty about what you did not do.
- Do not waste time regretting mistakes.
- Do spend the time to take actions to manage your stress.

Counteract Stress

Some activities preclude stress. When involved in them, you are unable to feel stressed. To a great extent, the specific activity you choose is up to you. Some general advice for counteracting stress includes:

- Develop positive addictions: jogging, swimming, walking.
- Be good to yourself. Go to a movie. Visit a friend. Eat ice cream.

- Balance your work and recreation. Develop an absorbing hobby: ceramics, yoga, guitar playing, gardening, whale watching.
- Read books that demand concentration.

In general the principles of balance and moderation will be useful for you. You need to accept that every day has three important parts: work, relaxation, and sleep. Too many times, we forget the relaxation part. Yet to survive a problem employee, you must strike a balance between all three parts. When one period intrudes on another, it produces stress and fatigue. If worries from your job creep into your relaxation hours, they will also creep into your sleep and dreams. You'll wake up still feeling tired.[19]

PLAN FOR IMPROVEMENT

You can use Performance Monitoring with yourself to plan for improvement. Remember that the trauma created by a problem employee creates both crisis and opportunity. As you've read through this chapter, and considered ways to help yourself, I hope you've seen a number of opportunities to improve your own life. You can take charge of your life by planning to maximize those opportunities. Making and following the plan can alleviate the pain you experience from your encounters with a problem employee. A plan for improvement provides you with a *doing* that can enrich your life.

Using Performance Monitoring with yourself is much akin to using it with your employees. The steps are the same:

1. Focus on current behavior. Ask, "What are you *doing*?"
2. Evaluate current behavior. Is your behavior producing the results you want?
3. Plan behavior that will produce the results you want
4. Make a commitment to your plan
5. Accept no excuses
6. Let natural consequences take over
7. Never give up![20]

To help you make a plan for improvement, appendix 7.B contains a form that you can use, and directions for completing the form. By using the form to identify what you want and what you're *doing* to get it, you can use the opportunities created by your problem employee to better your life.

SUMMARY

Problem employees can wreak havoc in the lives of those who must manage them. The closer you are to the problem, and the more unexpected and traumatic that employee's behavior is, the greater will be the impact on you personally. This chapter has alerted you to the changes you will go through as you come to terms with problem employee management. It has provided you with tips on how to survive the changes in your own life created by a problem employee. You have been given tips on how to manage your stress. This chapter has also provided you with techniques for using Performance Monitoring to successfully manage yourself.

Appendix 7.A

The Administrative Journal

The Administrative Journal has four sections and an appendix. Work in all sections of the journal, each day if possible. Don't feel compelled to write in the sections in any particular order. Just start wherever it seems most comfortable for you and work back and forth in your journal as your thoughts and interests dictate. This will enable you to view your experiences from different vantage points. In so doing, you can both learn and grow. The journal sections are:

- Outer Experience
- Reflections on the Outer Experience
- Inner Experience
- Reflections on the Inner Experience

OUTER EXPERIENCE

In this section, objectively record your particular experiences each day. The description doesn't have to be lengthy. Make your entry only long enough to help you recall the details when you return to this section later. Be as objective as possible in this section, as you answer the questions of "Who?" "What?" "When?" and "Where?"

REFLECTIONS ON THE OUTER EXPERIENCE

The purpose of this section is to help you look for clues to understand the outer experience you have described. Reflect on the experience and try to remember other similar experiences. Think back to any material you have read or studied that will help you understand the outer experience you have described. What did the experience have to do with what you have learned in this book? Based on this experience, what general advice could you give someone else on dealing with the problem employee? Record your thoughts.

INNER EXPERIENCE

This is the subjective section of your journal. In it record how the experience made you *feel*. Record how you reacted emotionally, physically, intellectually, and spiritually. If you became angry or hurt, say so. If you felt energized and in control, say so. Record how your reaction affected you.

REFLECTIONS ON THE INNER EXPERIENCE

Now reflect on the emotions you are experiencing. What is their significance for you? How do they compare to other emotions you have experienced at other times in a similar situation? What do your feelings about the inner experience tell you about yourself? What resources are available to help you understand your inner experience better? What poetry or literature or music can provide insight? Why? How? What insight did you gain from your experience?

APPENDIX

The appendix to your journal will help you see the big picture. You will record in the first four sections of your journal on a daily or weekly basis. Those sections provide an ongoing account of your experiences and your learning from them. The appendix, however, is a summary, a place to reflect on what the information you have recorded can do for you. Start it at a marker event such as the first encounter you had with a problem employee. As you feel the need, record your reactions to such issues as:

- The phase of life and work you are now in
- The patterns of the experiences you have recorded
- The kinds of learning you are experiencing
- In terms of your personal growth, what do you want from this period in your life? What are you getting from it?

Source: This Administrative Journal outline is adapted from Robert Denhardt, *Theories of Public Organization* (Monterey, Calif.: Brooks/Cole, 1984), 188–197.

Appendix 7.B

Directions for a Plan
for Improvement

Figure 7.1
Plan for Improvement

		PLAN FOR IMPROVEMENT			
Date	What do I want?	What am I doing now?	Is it helping or hurting?	What is my plan to do better?	Am I committed to following my plan?
Date	Did I follow my plan today?	What excuses did I give for not following my plan?	What were the consequences?	Review what I want	What is my next plan? Never give up!

Source: Patricia Haines, "Reality Therapy for Self-Help," *Journal of Reality Therapy* 2, no. 2 (Spring 1983), 21–23. Reprinted with permission.

INSTRUCTIONS FOR USING THE PLAN FOR IMPROVEMENT

Date:

(of first entry)

What do you want?

In simple terms, list what you really want. What goal do you wish to achieve or what problem do you wish to solve?

What are you doing now?

List specific actions you have taken to reach your goal or resolve your problem. Thinking about it or realizing that something must be done does not constitute action. Recognizing that a problem exists is not even half the battle. It is perhaps one-fourth. After recognition comes the true test of dedication to change.

Is it helping or hurting?

Write ways in which your actions are helping to relieve the problem, or ways in which your choice of actions is not working.

What is my plan to do better?

Make a plan with specific actions which will help you achieve your goal or alleviate your problem. Write only those actions you are willing to do.

Am I committed to follow my plan?

Are you committed to faithfully and consistently follow the actions stated in your plan? Think about it before you write "yes" in this column. Your answer here reflects how badly you want to achieve your goals or solve your problem.

Date:

(of each subsequent day)

Did I follow my plan today?

Answer "yes" or "no." An answer of "sometimes" really means "no." Therefore, list it as a "no." A "no" answer reflects a lack of commitment to following your plan and to achieving your goal.

What excuses did I give for not following my plan?

What excuses did you give yourself for not following through with your plan of action? Write them down, then recognize that they are excuses, not reasons.

What were the consequences?

What happened as a result of not following your plan? Perhaps the most significant result is "no change for the better" or "matters became worse."

Review what I want

If you did not follow through with your plan, you should look at your goal. Again decide if that is what you really want.

What is my next plan?

If you decide you really want your original goal, make another plan of action to achieve it. Go through this same process until the goal is reached. Goals should be flexible. Therefore, if necessary, change your want and amend the goal.

Never give up!

Never give up on yourself. You can fulfill your needs for love and belonging, worth and recognition, fun and freedom to choose by using this plan for self-improvement.

NOTES

1. "Reason will prevail," "praying for a miracle," "pleading," and "bleeding" are the frequently quoted behaviors identified by Robert Hollman in "Managing Troubled Employees: Meeting the Challenge," *Journal of Contemporary Business* 8, no. 4 (October 1979), 43–57.

2. William Bridges, "Transitions," a speech presented at the 1987 National Conference of the Council for Adult and Experiential Learning, San Diego, CA, June, 1986.

3. See William Bridges, "How to Manage Organizational Transition," *Training* 22 (September 1985), 28–32.

4. See Harold Kushner, *When Bad Things Happen to Good People* (New York: Avon Books, 1983). This book has been so popular that the 1987 edition is a deluxe, hard-bound gift edition.

5. William Bridges, "Twenty-five Helpful Hints on Handling Transition Successfully," a paper presented at the 1987 National Conference of the Council for Adult and Experiential Learning, San Diego, CA, June 1986.

6. See William Glasser, *Take Effective Control of Your Life* (New York: Harper and Row, 1985).

7. Ibid., 47.

8. Ibid., 51.

9. See Robert B. Denhardt, *Theories of Public Organization* (Monterey, Calif.: Brooks/Cole Publishing Co., 1984).

10. Bridges, "Twenty-Five Hints."

11. See Benjamin Kleinmuntz, *Essentials of Abnormal Psychology* (New York: Harper and Row, 1974).

12. James Gallagher, 31, no. 2 "Coping with Stress," *Association Management* (February 1979), 95–99.

13. Gabe Mirkin, "How to Cope with Job Stress," *Nation's Business* 67, no. 1 (January 1979), 69–72.

14. James Manuso, "Executive Stress Management," *Personnel Administrator* 24, no. 11 (November 1979), 23–26.

15. Eugene Randsepp, "Coping with Job Related Stress," *Supervision* 43, no. 3 (March 1981), 10–14.

16. See Helene Lerner and Roberta Elins, *Stress Breakers* (Minneapolis, Minn.: CompCare Publications, 1985).

17. See Alfred Alschuler, Jacqueline Carl, Robert Leslie, Ingrid Schweiger, and Diann Uustal, *Teacher Burnout* (Washington, D.C.: National Education Association, 1980).

18. See Anne Riley and Stephen Zaccaro, *Occupational Stress and Organizational Effectiveness* (Westport, Conn.: Praeger Publishers, 1987), for a discussion of stress management systems and how those systems can be used to benefit both the organization and its employees.

19. This discussion on stress management is adapted from J. Walton Blackburn, Mma Kalu, and Supachai Yavaprabhas, *Stress and How to Deal With It—A Manual for Managers and Supervisors* (Blacksburg, Virg.: Center for Public Administration and Policy, 1981). Used with permission from Dr. Blackburn.

20. Patricia Haines, "Reality Therapy for Self Help," *Journal of Reality Therapy* 2, no. 2 (Spring 1983), 10–23.

Chapter 8

Legal Issues in Problem Employee Management

A final key proactive strategy for problem employee management is to understand the laws that affect human resource management. Problem employees, when you confront their unacceptable behavior, often attempt to coerce you by threatening a lawsuit or a grievance. You cannot stop anyone from suing, nor should you try. You can, however, minimize the likelihood that the suit will be successful by understanding the law and recognizing that justice truly is blind. Laws protect you as well as your employees. If you understand the law and work within it, you will not be intimidated by the threat of a lawsuit.

The purpose of this chapter is to assist you in understanding the legal issues surrounding problem employee management. *It is not intended to replace legal advice. A qualified attorney should be consulted for additional information.*

Today's employee management is governed by a series of executive orders, federal laws, and court decisions. In addition, there is an alphabet soup of state and local laws within which you must operate. This chapter cannot cover them all. It is meant to be only a general guide for alerting you to the kinds of legal issues you can face in dealing with a problem employee. It cannot speak to specific issues that you may have to confront. It should, however, make you more alert and more self-confident in your dealings with a problem employee.

The first supervisor I ever had gave me some of the best advice I ever got. "Cover your own back," she said. This chapter will help you "cover your back"—protect yourself and your organization. It will not protect you from litigation, nor will it tell you what to do if an employee initiates legal action. You should have an attorney for that. The chapter will, however, make you more knowledgeable about legal issues and possible legal ramifications of your actions.

EMPLOYMENT AT WILL

As much as you might like to terminate a chronically problematic employee, your right to do this is being eroded. In the early days of employee–employer relations the "employment at will" doctrine held. It has been recognized by the American court system since 1877. This doctrine holds, essentially, that an employer can terminate an employee at any time with or without notice or vulnerability, in the absence of a limiting law or a written agreement with the employee. It is a doctrine based on mutuality: If an employee can quit at any time, an employer can terminate at any time. It is a doctrine fast being eliminated by the legal system.

Wrongful Discharge

In addition, at least twenty-one states recognize another common law doctrine, that of "wrongful discharge." Wrongful discharge is the countervailing doctrine to employment at will. A wrongful discharge is one that violates the law. It means, simply, that an employer cannot terminate an employee without just cause and due process. In essence, the doctrine of wrongful discharge prohibits employers from being "trigger-happy." They cannot fire at will.

There are three judicially created conditions that imply wrongful discharge. These are: breach of an implied contract, breach of public policy, and breach of an implied covenant of good faith and fair dealing.

Let's talk about these conditions of wrongful discharge.

Breach of an implied contract. Courts have consistently found that statements in an employee handbook constitute a legal and binding contract. So do policy memoranda and notices. I strongly believe in the necessity for an employee handbook that spells out both the employee's and the organization's rights and responsibilities. However, you should put no promises or guarantees in an employee handbook that you will not be able to keep.

The courts have consistently ruled that an employee is justified in relying on the promises made in an employee handbook.[1] If you guarantee a progressive discipline system, make certain it is used before you initiate termination proceedings. If you provide a grievance procedure, follow it. Do not make such statements as "employees have a long and secure future," unless you are certain this is true. Do not state that "no employee can be terminated without just cause" unless you are prepared to ensure that termination is preceded by lengthy and copious documentation of the cause for a termination decision.

Both the Michigan and the New Jersey Supreme Courts have suggested that *if* an employee handbook contains a disclaimer that specifically states that the employee handbook is not intended to be a binding contract, then it is not a binding contract.[2] The trick to getting around the treatment of an employee handbook as a binding contract seems to be in the wording and distribution of a disclaimer.

A disclaimer that has successfully held up in court is that which Sears, Roebuck and Company places on all its job applications and employment contracts:

In consideration of my employment, I agree to conform to the rules and regulations of Sears, Roebuck & Co., and my employment and compensation can be terminated with or without cause, and with or without notice, at any time, at the option of either the Company or myself. I understand that no store manager or representative of Sears, Roebuck & Co., other than the president or the vice-president of the company, has any authority to enter into any agreement for employment for any specified period of time, or to make any agreement contrary to the foregoing.[3]

In addition to this statement, to protect your company further, make certain that the disclaimer is signed by the employee, and that it is conspicuously placed in the handbook.

The inclusion of a disclaimer to protect your company, however, has the potential for a quite different set of negative consequences. Employees who must sign such a disclaimer may feel that your company is not a good place to work. Those statements you use to "cover your back" in the event you want to discharge a problem employee can denigrate your ability to foster good employee relations. With a disclaimer you are, in effect, saying that the company "is free to make whatever promises and representations it wishes, yet cannot be held to any of them."[4]

It seems to me that you will be better able to proactively manage all your employees by developing and distributing an employee handbook, which you recognize (as many of the courts have) as a binding legal agreement. Put in it reasonable and just policies and procedures that clearly state both the company's and the employee's rights and responsibilities. Then train your supervisors to equitably follow those policies and procedures. Include formal disciplinary procedures and the employee behaviors that will activate them.

The key to avoiding or winning a lawsuit that charges wrongful discharge due to a breach of employee contract (implied or written) is to develop a contract in the form of an employee handbook that is reasonable, clear, and followed. Have your attorney check the wording of your employee handbook to minimize the likelihood of wrongful discharge; and remember that employees have the right to expect that you mean what you say and say what you mean.

Breach of public policy. The second type of wrongful discharge is known as the "public policy exception" to the employment at will doctrine. This exception is based on tort theories. A tort is a wrongful act or damage that does not involve a breach of contract, and for which a civil action can be brought. Thus, a wrongful discharge that breaches the employment at will doctrine arises when an employer discharges an employee for a socially undesirable motive. This type of wrongful discharge is not recognized in all states.

Examples of discharges that the courts have found violate public policy include:

• An employee who is discharged for refusing to give false testimony on behalf of his or her employer[5]

• An employee who is discharged for refusing to engage in criminal activity[6]

• An employee who is discharged for filing a Workman's Compensation claim[7]

• An employee who is discharged for performing jury duty[8]

Clearly, termination for the above reasons does not make sense. If the truth were known, I expect that the employee discharged in these cases had a history of unacceptable behaviors that had not been documented. Their discharges could have been as much a frustration reaction on the part of a supervisor or a human resource manager, with the reason given for discharge only the one that "broke the camel's back."

Breach of an implied covenant of good faith and fair dealing. The third type of wrongful discharge is known as the breach of an implied covenant of good faith and fair dealing. At the time of this writing, only seven states (Alabama, California, Massachusetts, Montana, Nevada, Oklahoma, and Oregon) recognize a violation of an implied covenant of good faith and fair dealing as a condition of wrongful discharge.[9] A termination is more likely to be seen as a breach of an implied covenant when the employee has been with the organization a long time.

In Massachusetts, the termination of an employee who had been with a firm for forty years was ruled to be a violation of the implied covenant of good faith and fair dealing.[10] A California Court of Appeal decision, three years later, "suggested that *any* termination of a long-term employee without just cause would violate the implied covenant of good faith."[11] According to an analysis by Rand Corporation, the California decision "created a potential lawsuit in every employment discharge, entitling the discharged employee to tort damages, including punitive damages and damages for emotional distress."[12]

The key seems to be how the courts will define "long-term employee." In the Massachusetts case, the employee had been with the firm for forty years. In the California case, the employee had been with the firm for eighteen years. In another case that came before the same California court, seven years was determined to not be "long term."[13]

While damages for employee discharge as a breach of an implied contract of good faith have only been awarded in a few states, the existence of this emerging doctrine should serve as a note of caution for you. To cover your back you may want to consider what many other organizations have done to protect themselves. They have:

instructed company interviewers to avoid any talk of job security or even of "promotions from within," and they scoured their employee handbooks and other company documents of dangerous language. Terms such as "permanent" or "career" or "probationary" were excised. Indications that dismissal would only be for just cause were eliminated. Promises of fairness or equitable treatment were taken out. Even pleasantries such as "Best wishes for a long and happy relationship" were scrapped.[14]

You, of course, know that you can only terminate for just cause that is documented and that is in line with your human resource management policies and procedures. To terminate for other reasons is not only irresponsible, but leaves you open to a lawsuit that you cannot win.

Legislative Protection

Legislation enacted in the twentieth century has given protection to employees from at will termination in several instances:

- An employee cannot be terminated for forming or joining a union, or participating in collective bargaining
- An employee who is a union member (or employed in a unionized organization in a job represented by the union) cannot be terminated without adherence to the due process provisions of the union contract
- An employee cannot be terminated for "whistleblowing," i.e. reporting a supervisor or an employer who is violating some law or policy, even though the report may later be determined to be false
- An employee cannot be terminated because of age, race, sex, national origin, religion, or handicap (and in some states, marital status or sexual preference)
- An employee in the public sector civil service system cannot be terminated without adherence to the due process provisions of the system

To say that you cannot terminate under the conditions that may be construed as a breach of public policy or a breach of an implied contract or a breach of an implied covenant does not mean you cannot terminate. It means only that you cannot terminate without a valid reason, and that the reasons on this list are not valid.

Let's talk about the ramifications of these exceptions to the employment at will doctrine.

Union activity. As you think about legislation that impacts your ability
to deal with a problem employee who is a union member, you need to
be aware of the provisions of the Norris-LaGuardia, Wagner, and Landrum-Griffin Acts, three of the major federal laws that govern organizational and union conduct. All of these laws constrain your ability to
deal with a problem employee when a union is present. Each of them
requires that organizations engage in specific behavior in dealing with
union activities.

The Norris-LaGuardia Act prohibits your use of the federal judiciary
to interfere with union activity and prohibits you from requiring that
your employees refrain from union membership. This means that if, in
your judgment, an employee has become a problem because he or she
is trying to organize a union, you need to tread very carefully.

The Wagner Act recognizes an employee's right to engage in union
activities. If a majority of employees in your organization desire union
representation, it requires you to collectively bargain with the union
regarding wages, hours, and terms and conditions of employment. The
Wagner Act makes it incumbent upon you to work cooperatively with
a union that represents a problem employee. If your employees are
represented by a union, you can include policies and procedures for
dealing with them in your union negotiations. This will help you avoid
difficulties with the union.

The Landrum-Griffin Act requires that union members be entitled to
due process both within their union and within their company.[15] Due
process requires that no action is taken against an employee in an arbitrary and capricious manner. Employees who are facing discipline or
termination are entitled to be informed of any charges against them and
to face their accusers. This means that you cannot abruptly discharge
an employee on the basis of a secret report. It also means that employees
have the right to face the person accusing them and to defend themselves
against those accusations. Due process also requires that you follow the
procedures negotiated in the union contract for all disciplinary action or
termination.

Union membership provides a job security that does not exist in an
employment at will environment. Knowing this, a problem employee
who is a union member will often try to play the union steward against
you or the supervisor like a recalcitrant child tries to set parent against
parent. The key to proactively managing a problem employee who is
also a union member is to work cooperatively with the union. See it as
your ally. Include union representatives in disciplinary policy development, and in the establishment of an Employee Assistance Program.

Union stewards and union members have unique opportunities to help you help a problem employee and avoid litigation. Union stewards can encourage employees to check with them if they observe a co-worker who appears to be troubled or in need of assistance. Union stewards may be the first ones to notice employee cover-up for a problem worker and they can communicate the dangers of this cover-up through a union newsletter or at union meetings.

Even as the presence of a union in your organization constrains your ability to deal with problem employees by simply terminating them, it enhances your ability to institute proactive strategies. It is simply in the best interest of both the union and the organization to work together.

Whistleblowing. Whistleblowers can be found in both the private and the public sector. Their value lies in their willingness to expose fraud, waste, and abuse. They are rarely popular, however, and are frequently labeled as problem employees. They have been called "malcontents," "informants," "bag ladies," and "mental health patients," for the fine line between whistleblowing and irrational, vindictive complaining is difficult to discern.[16]

In addition to the protection provided by the First and Fourth Amendments to the U.S. Constitution, whistleblowers are protected from retaliation under approximately twenty-five federal laws.[17] The most recent legislation protects federal workers. The Whistleblower Act was signed into law by President Bush in April 1989. It "assures the confidentiality of federal employees who blow the whistle, gives them the right to appeal a measure which seems retaliatory, and increases the powers of the Office of Special Counsel which protects their rights."[18]

Private sector workers are now covered by a potpourri of laws, none of which protects all of them all of the time. To rectify this, Senator Howard Metzenbaum (Democrat/Ohio) has introduced legislation that would provide protection for all whistleblowers (including state and local government employees) not currently covered by federal law.

The heart of whistleblower protection is to keep an employer about whom the whistle is blown from taking retaliatory action against the employee. To not take what can be construed as retaliatory action can be difficult, for the employee does not have to produce direct testimony or evidence as proof of retaliation. Rather, circumstantial evidence can be considered proof.[19]

In effect, an employee that you consider to be a problem employee may be engaging in behavior protected under whistleblower legislation. This can be graphically illustrated by the case of an employee who was a passport officer. He had submitted a number of memoranda, increasingly critical and replete with invectives, accusing the Department of State of mismanagement in respect to its program of detecting fraud in passport applications. This employee had been observed removing file folders from the fraud file cabinet and had refused to comply with direct written and verbal orders to return the files. He had threatened to use force to take the files. As a result, he was discharged on the basis of insubordination and removal of government files. He appealed the termination. The administrative law judge who heard the appeal concluded that the discharge was a reprisal for whistleblowing.

You can reduce the chances that your organization will be judged retaliatory in whistleblowing litigation by making certain that you do not engage in the following general categories of facts or circumstances that are used to establish inference of discriminatory motive:

1. Employer's hostile attitude toward matter underlying the employee's protected conduct
2. Employer's knowledge of protected conduct
3. Nature of protected conduct
4. Special conditions of employment following protected conduct and leading up to discharge
5. Disparate treatment of discharged employee prior to protected conduct
6. Previous expressions of satisfaction with work record
7. Disparate treatment of similarly situated employees
8. Termination procedure
9. Timing of discharge
10. Threats or retaliation against other employees for similar conduct.[20]

This list is, of course, not exhaustive; but it will give you an idea of the kinds of behavior you and your supervisors must avoid to prevent a decision that you retaliated due to whistleblowing.

DISCRIMINATION

The concept of equal employment opportunity came into being in 1964 with the passage of Title VII of the Civil Rights Act, which was amended by the Equal Employment Act of 1972. Under this legislation, discrimination in all terms and conditions of employment is prohibited on the basis of race, color, national origin, religion, and sex. This prohibition applies to private employers with more than fifteen employees, union, employment agencies, state and local governments, and educational institutions. The Age Discrimination in Employment Act of 1967 prohibited discrimination against employees over age forty and the Rehabilitation Act of 1973 prohibited discrimination against the handicapped. All of this legislation simply requires that you treat all employees equally.

Persons covered under anti-discrimination laws are known as a "protected class." Frequently members of a protected class, who are also problem employees, will use the status to intimidate you or threaten you with a lawsuit. Frequently supervisors of such employees will react to the threat by backing down from their supervisory responsibility to facilitate productive behavior. You should not fear either a lawsuit or the threat of a lawsuit.

Frequently employees who are discharged will attempt to claim discrimination even though none exists.

Charges of discrimination have been filed by long-haired and/or bearded male workers, and by females who allegedly were fired for rejecting their male superiors' sexual advances, gaining weight, getting married, getting pregnant, or refusing to shave their legs.[21]

A charge of discrimination requires that the person making the charge present evidence that demonstrates reasonable cause for believing that discrimination has occurred.[22] As a result of a June 1989 Supreme Court decision, you, as an employer, can justify what appears to be a discriminatory impact, if you can establish that the action you took was based on reasonable and usual business practices.[23]

The best way to handle a discrimination charge is to have in place an established grievance procedure. This procedure should give the employee an opportunity to present his or her side of the situation in which discrimination is charged to persons in the organization other than those directly involved. A sample grievance procedure is contained in appendix 8.B at the end of this chapter.

The grievance process begins by requiring the employee to bring his or her complaint to the immediate supervisor first. It is the supervisor's responsibility to attempt to negotiate a satisfactory resolution. If that is not possible, the complaint should come to either you, as the human resource manager, or to an Affirmative Action officer. The way a grievance is handled in these early stages dictates how far it goes and how much ire it causes.

To ensure that the grieving employee gets a fair hearing, there are a number of things that you must do. You should instruct supervisors to do them as well.

Listen!

Dealing with a complaining employee is not pleasant. It's hard to keep your own feelings under control. The best technique for listening is Active Listening, which was explained in chapter 4. With Active Listening, you can discuss the matter and not argue it. This will put you in a helping role instead of an adversarial one.

Get the Complete Story

Getting the complete story requires learning both the facts that caused the employee to charge discrimination and learning how the employee feels about the situation. A supervisor who receives the initial complaint must get the complete story from the employee. If the complaint gets to you, you must get the complete story from *both* the employee and the supervisor.

Work to Resolve the Problem

Once you hear the story, ask the employee to specifically state what he or she believes will be necessary for the problem to be considered resolved. Don't try to come up with a solution alone. Ask the employee and supervisor what they think will be appropriate, then decide what to do.

Don't Make Snap Judgments

After you have heard both sides of the complaint, thank the employee and state when you will have a decision. You will need time to carefully weigh alternative responses. If you make a commitment on the spot, you may later regret it.

Act Promptly

Your grievance procedure should contain a stringent time frame in which you must try to resolve the complaint. Adhere strictly to that time limit.

In the private sector, if you cannot resolve the employee's complaint at the organizational level, the employee can take the complaint to the Equal Employment Opportunity Commission (EEOC), or may elect to take you to court. In the federal government, the complaint must go to the Merit Systems Protection Board for an attempt at resolution before the employee seeks outside resolution. State laws vary as to what actions a state or local government employee can take in pursuing restitution for alleged discrimination.

When an employee takes a charge of discrimination to the EEOC, the commission will listen to both the employee's and the organization's side of the story and attempt conciliation. If the employee cannot demonstrate reasonable cause or if the charge of reasonable cause is successfully rebutted, the Equal Employment Opportunity Commission will dismiss the complaint. At any point in this process, the employee has the right to be represented by an attorney. If a complainant cannot demonstrate reasonable cause, however, most attorneys will not agree to represent them.

There are two schools of thought on what you should do if you or someone in your organization is charged with discrimination. The first school suggests that you cooperate fully with the Equal Employment Opportunity Commission (EEOC). It suggests that you share your documentation and be open about your defense. This school puts an emphasis on conciliation that can be obtained with the input of EEOC representatives. At the federal level (and in some states), in most instances the employee does not have the right to sue until conciliation has been attempted and failed.

The second school of thought suggests that upon a charge of discrimination, you immediately seek legal counsel, even if the EEOC will be involved. Most attorneys will advise you not to share your defense with the EEOC. Once an attorney gets involved, your relationship with the employee is likely to move from a conciliatory one to an adversarial one. The attorney's advice will be geared toward helping you cut your losses.

The problem comes in choosing which school of thought to buy into. If you cooperate with the EEOC, you may weaken your position if a dispute does go into court. On the other hand, the EEOC may be able to help resolve the dispute without the costs entailed in extensive litigation.

It will generally not be up to you alone to choose between the EEOC and litigation. If your organization carries liability insurance, as many organizations (both public and private) do, the insurance carrier will become an important actor in the resolution process. It will want you to take whatever action ultimately costs less.

Although discrimination laws vary from state to state, reasonable cause is typically demonstrated in one of two ways: "The first is to show a discriminatory intent behind a particular practice, and the second is to show that the effect of a particular practice is discriminatory."[24] Although the determination of intent may seem to require an ability to read minds, intent can be established simply by showing that two employees or two classes of employees were treated differently. The most frequently used approach to demonstrate reasonable cause is discriminatory effect that "is demonstrated by presenting statistical evidence of what is known as *disparate* or *adverse* impact."[25]

This means that for a problem employee to successfully recover damages from you or your company for alleged discrimination, the employee must be able to prove that he or she was treated *differently* than similarly situated other employees. For example, if a female employee is discharged for absenteeism, and she can demonstrate that male employees with an equal number of absences still hold their jobs, then discrimination will be determined to exist. On the other hand, when you present evidence that *all* employees, regardless of race, sex, age, creed, or national origin are treated *identically* when they have excessive absences, no reasonable cause to suspect discrimination exists.

This doesn't mean employees won't claim discrimination. It just means that if you treat all employees equally and document that treatment, discrimination will not be proven. It also means that your best defense against discrimination charges are statistics that demonstrate equal treatment and show neutral legitimate consideration. A June 1989 Supreme Court decision has made your job easier than in the past. In the case of Wards Cove Packing Company v. Atonio, the Court shifted the burden of proof in suits alleging discriminatory patterns in hiring and promotion from the defendant (i.e. the organization) to the plaintiff. It ruled that the plaintiff bears the burden of disproving an employer's assertion that adverse employment action or practice was based on a legitimate neutral consideration. This means that in charges of discrimination, you are no longer guilty until proven innocent, but rather innocent until proven guilty.

If you are charged with discrimination, it is still prudent, however, to use only objective records and reports in your defense. Creativity generally will not be appropriate.

Take, for instance, the case in which a light-skinned black clerk-typist brought a discrimination charge against her darker-skinned supervisor at the Internal Revenue Service. Instead of showing that all clerk typists received the same treatment, the IRS's defense was that there was no cause for action because the two women were of the same race. The U.S. District Court for the State of Georgia ruled that the suit should proceed to trial because this defense takes a "naive world view."[26]

THE SPECIAL CASE OF SUBSTANCE ABUSERS

Generally, upon discovery that an employee has possessed or used alcohol or drugs at work, private employers would be free to discharge an employee at will unless: (1) rules setting forth the policy and company disciplinary procedure are found to constitute an employment contract modifying the at will relationship, or (2) discharge would violate a duty imposed by statute. . . .

In the event that a grievance is filed by an employee whose discharge is covered by a collective bargaining agreement, the burden of proof required to show "just cause" may vary with the arbitrator. . . . Unless a plant rule prohibiting the use or possession is found to be "unreasonable, arbitrary, capricious, [or] discriminatory," an arbitrator will ordinarily enforce a rule which is uniformly applied.[27]

In the public sector, however, substance abusers have far more rights. The Rehabilitation Act of 1973 applies generally to federal employees, federal contractors, and to recipients of federal funds and includes substance abuse as a part of the definition of "handicap."[28] While alcoholics and drug abusers *in need of rehabilitation* are excluded from the protection of the act, two Supreme Court decisions have limited the ability of federal employers to discharge an alcoholic employee. Specifically, the Court has ruled that federal employers can only dismiss an alcoholic who refuses treatment or repeatedly fails in treatment. In addition, federal employers are required to "exert substantial affirmative efforts to assist alcoholic employees toward overcoming their handicap before firing them for *performance deficiencies related to drinking*." (These standards for dealing with alcoholics apply equally to drug abusers.)[29]

Drug and Alcohol Testing

Legal requirements. The Omnibus Anti-Drug Abuse Act, which became effective March 8, 1989, applies to the recipients of all new federal contracts or grants over $25,000. While the act does *not* require drug testing, it does have a number of specific actions you must take in relation to prevention of substance abuse. These are:

• Publish and distribute to all employees a statement that prohibits the manufacture, sale, possession, or use of any controlled substance while at work. The statement must specify the disciplinary sanctions for violation.
• Establish a drug-free awareness program that informs employees of the dangers of substance abuse, and lets them know about any available drug counseling or Employee Assistance Program services.
• Require employees, as a condition of employment, to report a drug conviction for a violation occurring at the work site within five days of the conviction.
• Notify the contracting agency within ten days after the employee's conviction.
• Discipline any employee convicted of a drug violation occurring at the work place *or* require that employee to participate in a rehabilitation program.[30]

The Department of Transportation drug testing regulations became effective December 21, 1988, and apply to interstate commerce drivers of commercial motor vehicles with a gross weight of over 26,000 pounds. These regulations require motor carrier corporations to establish Employee Assistance Programs. Under these regulations, a driver is disqualified from operating the commercial carrier if he or she uses a controlled substance *on or off* duty. The regulations *require* five kinds of tests:

1. Pre-employment test
2. Periodic tests that occur as a part of the also-required biennial medical examination

3. A test if observable actions cause suspicion of substance abuse

4. Post-accident testing within thirty-two hours of an accident that results in death, bodily injury, or property damage more than $4,400

5. Random testing of 50 percent of drivers annually[31]

If your organization has a contract with the Defense Department, you are required by Department of Defense regulations to "institute and maintain a program for achieving the objective of a drug-free workforce." You are also required to provide an Employee Assistance Program and supervisor training, as well as drug testing of employees who are in positions that grant access to classified information. The regulations specifically make clear that state law will govern the way in which drug testing is administered.[32]

Legal constraints. Recent developments suggest that you may be faced with restrictions in implementing a drug testing program if you are not required by law or regulations to do so. Many state courts have ruled that drug testing is unconstitutional, arguing that it violates the constitutional right to privacy and to be free of unreasonable search and seizure.

In a case involving customs workers in Louisiana, a federal judge ruled that "drug testing is no minor frisk or pat-down. It is a full scale search that triggers application of Fourth Amendment protection."[33] However, a federal appeals court overturned this decision, stating that it is reasonable to expect those who enforce drug-related laws to demonstrate that they are drug free.[34]

The key to establishing a drug testing program that will survive a court test is to make certain that the program is not a punitive one and that it is administered equally to all employees after a specific policy statement that includes the following safeguards against charges of rights violation:

- Safeguard against a "defamation of character" charge. Results of all testing must be kept confidential and not communicated to a third party without the express written permission of the employee.
- Safeguard against an "unreasonable search" charge. Ensure that the test is given in a careful, consistent, and dignified manner.
- Safeguard against a "negligence" charge. Use only a qualified testing facility that has built-in precautions against the possibility of error in testing.
- Safeguard against an "assault and battery" charge. Any touching, such as the drawing of blood, constitutes technical "battery." Safeguard against the charge by getting the employee's written consent before the test is administered.
- Safeguard against a charge of "discrimination." Require the test uniformly of all employees.
- Safeguard against a "breach of contract" charge. Specify in your employee

handbook and/or other personnel management policies and procedures when, where, how, and why the drug test will be required. Include these same specifications in your contract with a union.

• Safeguard against a "wrongful discharge" charge. Make certain that your drug testing procedure is both valid and reliable. In the event of a positive test result, a second test should be required.

EMPLOYEE ASSISTANCE PROGRAMS

Although the Employee Assistance Program is a generally demonstrated means of helping the problem employee and many organizations are mandated by law to provide one, the EAP is not legally risk free. It is possible for an employee to bring Fourteenth Amendment charges against either your organization or the EAP if you have not carefully covered your legal "back." With the EAP, as well as with a drug testing program, it is possible for an employee to charge defamation of character, discrimination, negligence, or breach of contract. It is also possible for you to safeguard your organization with proactive strategies.

• Safeguard against a "defamation of character" charge. Maintain records of EAP referrals in a file separate from the employee's personnel file. Do not disclose that the employee has been referred. Do not ask for, or expect to receive, any report from the EAP other than that the employee has or has not kept appointments. Make certain that EAP administrators and counselors understand and uphold the employee's right to privacy. Whether liability will be imposed in a defamation of character case depends mainly on the purpose of the disclosure. If the disclosure is made for the purpose of ensuring safety and is limited to a very few people who need to know, you are not as likely to be held liable.[35]

• Safeguard against a "discrimination" charge. Make certain that EAP services are available to all employees, regardless of age, race, sex, religion, national origin, or handicap. State this in your policies. Make certain that a disparate number of members of a protected class are not referred for services. If you have a supervisor who seems to be referring only women, or only blacks, you need to scrutinize the referrals carefully to make certain that discrimination is not occurring.

• Safeguard against a charge of "negligence." Make certain that EAP counselors are competent, trained, and, if appropriate, licensed. Insist that periodic evaluations of performance are conducted. Require that counselors have malpractice liability insurance.

• Safeguard against a "breach of contract" charge. Remember that statements contained in your employee handbook are considered contractual. This includes statements about what the EAP can and cannot do, and how and when it will be utilized. Simply promise nothing you cannot deliver.

ISSUES OF PARTICULAR CONCERN IN THE PUBLIC SECTOR

If you are a human resource manager in the public sector, you, your employees, and your supervisors are all protected under the law from unreasonable acts that deprive constitutional rights. Equal protection under the law was first codified by Congress on April 20, 1871 in 42 U.S.C. Section 1983. This law has become known as the Ku Klux Klan Act and states:

Every person who, under color of any statute, ordinance, regulation, custom, or usage of any State or Territory or the District of Columbia, subjects, or causes to be subjected any citizen of the United States or other person within the jurisdiction thereof to the deprivation of any rights, privileges, or immunities secured by the Constitution and laws, shall be liable to the party injured in an action of law, suit in equity, or other proper proceeding for redress.[36]

Because the language in Section 1983 states "under color of any statute, ordinance, regulation, or custom," it applies only to employees of the government. Section 1983 was identified by Congress as an "Act to enforce the provisions of the Fourteenth Amendment to the Constitution of the United States, and for other purposes." The Fourteenth Amendment prohibits equal protection violations, due process violations, and violations of the First, Fourth, Fifth, Sixth, and Eighth Amendments to the Constitution. For your information, these amendments are included as appendix 8.A at the end of this chapter. Recent personnel action lawsuits against government employers have been brought under Section 1983 and the Fourteenth Amendment, jointly.

Despite the wide-ranging coverage of Section 1983, as a basis for legal action in personnel disputes it lay dormant for almost ninety years until the Supreme Court Decision of 1961,[37] which

set out several significant rules regarding Section 1983. First, every Fourteenth Amendment violation by state and local government officials can serve as the basis of a Section 1983 damages action. Second, Section 1983 must be interpreted against the "background of tort liability" which makes a person responsible for the natural consequences of his or her conduct. Third, a Section 1983 damages action is available in federal court for Fourteenth Amendment violations even though the plaintiff has available a state law remedy against the official or employee because he or she has also violated a state law.[38]

While Section 1983 had always allowed lawsuits if a Fourteenth Amendment right was violated, the 1961 Court decision allowed suits to be brought against an employee of a local government who had violated the plaintiff's Fourteenth Amendment rights. In 1978, another Court decision held that local governments are "persons" and can, therefore, also be sued for damages under Section 1983.[39] Then, in 1988, the 1976 Civil Rights Attorney's Fee Awards Act was determined to entitle plaintiffs to a reasonable attorney's fee in addition to any other damages awarded.[40] A 1989 Court decision, however, ruled that states are not persons and cannot, therefore, be sued for damages.

All of this means, literally, that a local government can be sued by employees who believe their Section 1983 rights have been violated. A state or federal government cannot be sued. Just because an employee sues, however, does not mean the employee will win the lawsuit. You need to be informed, but not afraid.

A local government employee can also sue a supervisor or you by charging discrimination. If this happens, you need to know that when you act in your official capacity, and act in good faith, you have what is known as "qualified immunity" from Section 1983 tort liability. A tort is a wrongful act or damage that does not involve a breach of contract, and for which a civil action can be brought. If you act in good faith with a problem employee and objectively and consistently apply personnel policies and identified sanctions, then you as an individual are immune from tort liability even if the employee sues for damages from you, personally.

In the public sector you can protect your organization from loss by developing and enforcing policies and procedures that ensure that all employees: are treated equally; are guaranteed due process if discipline or discharge is instituted; and are guaranteed a pretermination hearing during which the employee has the opportunity to defend his or her actions.

Equal Treatment

To say that you are required by law to treat your employees equally seems like an oversimplification. An example of unequal treatment seems in order. Suppose you have a policy that states that an employee will be terminated after six unexcused absences occur in a six-month period. A number of white employees have six unexcused absences and they are lectured or temporarily suspended. Then a black employee misses six days of work without an excuse. You terminate that employee. You have been guilty of unequal treatment. To ensure equal treatment, you must be certain that your policies, and the way in which those policies are enforced, are color-blind, as well as blind to sex, religion, age, and national origin.

Due Process

As explained earlier, due process in organizations requires that no action is taken against an employee in an arbitrary and capricious manner. Technically, a public employee's due process rights are violated if you try to deprive that employee of his or her property. While the notion of a job as "property" is an evolving issue, for all practical purposes an employee has a "property right" to a job if that job has a real or implied guarantee of continuing. Generally speaking, a civil service system, a union contract, or any documents that imply guarantee of employment, provide an indication of a property right to that employment.

Pre-termination hearing. Due process requires you to provide an employee you are trying to terminate with a pre-termination hearing.[41] At the hearing, the employee is entitled to be represented by the person of his or her choice. This may be an attorney. It may be a union representative. Persons at the hearing who represent management's point of view should include, at least, the person who appointed and the person who terminated the employee. The laws that govern specifically who must and who may attend the hearing vary from state to state.

LEGITIMATE AUTHORITY

As you can see, the law does not deny you your legitimate authority as an employer. It simply provides employees with the opportunity for legal redress *if* you violate their rights.

Courts of law have fully supported employers in cases where employees have been fired for insubordination or for excessive absences. Employers also have usually found themselves on safe ground when the employees clearly have violated some stated company policy.

In all those cases where the employers prevailed, there was one central characteristic: The employee had violated some clearly stated rule or policy. And the employer had acted specifically on the basis of that violation.[42]

You do have the legitimate authority to discipline and terminate your employees. You must, however, take these actions within the law.

SUMMARY

This chapter has presented you with some of the legal issues that impact problem employee management. These include Fourteenth Amendment protection, the doctrine of employment at will, and the concept of wrongful discharge. The chapter has also discussed the special legal constraints created by union agreements, and the legal issues surrounding substance abusers and the Employee Assistance Program. It has also provided instructions on how to deal with a charge of discrimination.

While the problem employee is more likely to attempt resorting to use of legislation than are other employees, if you utilize the information presented here you should be able to proactively act to minimize litigation. Although some states have additional protective legislation, the key is to remember to treat all employees *respectfully, consistently, equally,* and *objectively*. If you do that, you will be able to successfully and proactively manage all your employees in a way that will maximize organizational productivity. You will satisfy the courts *and* you will feel good about yourself.

Constitutional Amendments That Govern Employee Rights

AMENDMENT I (Freedom of speech). Congress shall make no law respecting an establishment of religion, or prohibiting the free exercise, thereof; or abridging the freedom of speech, or of the press; or the right of the people to peaceably assemble, and to petition the Government for a redress of Grievances.

AMENDMENT IV (Protection from unreasonable searches). The right of the people to be secure in their persons, houses, papers, and effects, against unreasonable searches and seizure shall not be violated, and no warrants shall issue, but upon probable cause, supported by oath or affirmation, and particularly describing the place to be searched and the persons or things to be seized.

AMENDMENT V (Due process). No person shall be held to answer for a capital, or otherwise infamous crime, unless on a presentment of indictment of a Grand Jury, except in cases arising in the land or naval forces or in the militia, when in actual service in time of war or public danger, nor shall any person be subject for the same offense to be twice put in jeopardy of life or limb; nor shall be compelled in any criminal case to be a witness against himself, nor be deprived of life, liberty, or property without due process of law; nor shall private property be taken for public use without just compensation.

AMENDMENT VI (Right to be informed of charges and right to be confronted by witnesses against him). In all criminal prosecutions, the accused shall enjoy the right to a speedy and public trial, by an impartial jury of the State and district wherein the crime shall have been committed, which district shall have been previously ascertained by law, and to be informed of the nature and cause of the accusation; to be confronted with the witnesses against him; to have compulsory process for obtaining witnesses in his favor, and to have the assistance of counsel for his defense.

AMENDMENT VIII (Protection from cruel and unusual punishment). Excessive bail shall not be required, nor excessive fines imposed, nor cruel and unusual punishments inflicted.

AMENDMENT XIV (Citizenship rights cannot be abridged). All persons born or naturalized in the United States, and subject to the jurisdiction thereof, are citizens of the United States and of the State wherein they reside. No State shall make or enforce any law which shall abridge the privileges or immunities of citizens of the United States; nor shall any State deprive any person of life, liberty, or property, without due process of law; nor deny to any person within its jurisdiction the equal protection of the laws.

Sample Grievance Procedure

The grievance procedures that follow are established in order to provide each employee and applicant for employment with an opportunity to request and receive review of any grievance relating to wages, hours, and/or terms and conditions of employment that the employee believes has arisen as a result of discrimination because of his or her race, age, color, disability, religion, sex, national origin, veterans' status, or marital status. (Include in this list all protected classes in the law of your state.)

ELIGIBILITY

Any employee, believing that she or he has a grievance resulting from a perceived injustice through the action of another employee, a supervisor, or other person acting for this organization may bring a grievance under these procedures. Equal employment opportunity information, counseling, and/or informal discussion of a grievance will be provided by _____ (designate an Affirmative Action officer or other position in the Human Resource Office) to any employee who wishes to have this service prior to filing a complaint. At any time that an employee shall have questions about this procedure, or shall require assistance in preparing and filing documents, _____ (designate an Affirmative Action officer or other position in the Human Resource Office) shall assist the employee.

RETALIATION

Employees and job applicants who request a review in accordance with the outlined grievance procedure may expect a fair hearing without fear of harassment or retaliation. The right of the employee or applicant to representation shall be recognized at all steps of the procedure. The employee or applicant shall bear the expense of his or her representation.

Any retaliatory action of any kind taken by any employee of this organization against any other employee or applicant as a result of the person seeking redress through these procedures, cooperating in an investigation, or otherwise participating in any proceeding under these procedures is prohibited, and shall be regarded as a separate and distinct grievable matter.

STEP 1: INFORMAL PROCEDURES

Each employee having a grievance concerning his or her wages, hours, and/ or terms and conditions of employment, which the employee believes to be a direct result of discriminatory action predicated on the employee's race, age, color, disability, religion, sex, national origin, veterans' status, or marital status, shall bring the grievance to the attention of his or her immediate supervisor within twenty (20) working days after the alleged discrimination took place.

Upon bringing the matter to the immediate supervisor's attention, the supervisor and the employee shall proceed to informally discuss the grievance in an effort to resolve it in a mutually satisfactory manner. Before the employee leaves this meeting, the supervisor shall prepare a brief written summary of the complaint. The statement shall then be read, reviewed, and signed by the employee with the understanding that this is an informal complaint, and that the statement has been prepared merely to record the discussion.

In the event that an employee believes that the discussion of the grievance with the immediate supervisor would be useless for the employee, the employee need not follow Step 1, but may, in lieu thereof, file a written formal grievance directly with the _____ (Affirmative Action officer or human resource manager).

STEP 2: FORMAL COMPLAINT

If the employee and his or her immediate supervisor are not able to reach a mutually satisfactory resolution to the employee's grievance, the employee may file a written complaint with the _____ (Affirmative Action officer or human resource manager). This written complaint must be filed within five (5) working days from the date on which the employee met with the supervisor. The written complaint must contain a full description of the alleged underlying discrimination upon which the grievance is based *and* the redress sought.

Within ten (10) working days after the receipt of the complaint, the _____ (Affirmative Action officer or human resource manager) shall contact the employee's immediate supervisor, and such other administrative personnel in the employee's department as may be deemed appropriate. During this same ten-day period, the _____ (Affirmative Action officer or human resource manager) shall give the employee an informal hearing on the grievance, make a thorough investigation of the facts surrounding the alleged grievance, and attempt to arrive at a mutually satisfying resolution.

Within the next ten (10) days, the _____ (Affirmative Action officer or human resource manager) shall prepare a written report that shall include:

• A copy of the grievance submitted by the employee

• A written summary of the results of the investigation

• A description of the alleged discrimination

- A determination as to the existence of the discrimination and the validity of the grievance

- A statement of recommended action.

A copy of this report shall be forwarded to the employee, the employee's supervisor, the human resource manager, and _____ (a designated organization official).

Within ten (10) days after receipt of this report, the human resource manager, in consultation with appropriate officials, shall determine whether or not to implement the recommended action and set a reasonable date for implementation, and shall then notify the employee of the determination.

STEP 3: REVIEW BOARD

If the employee is not satisfied with the decision reached in Step 2, or if the decision is satisfactory but is not implemented by the date indicated, the employee has ten (10) days to request a formal hearing before the Review Board. This request must be submitted in writing to the Chair of the Review Board.

Within ten (10) days of the request for review, the Board shall:

- Review the grievance in its entirety

- Discuss the grievance with the employee and with the appropriate supervisor and administrative staff

- Undertake an independent investigation that may include a hearing at which the employee, supervisor, and any relevant others may be allowed to present their version of events leading to the grievance. In the event a hearing is held, a written transcript of the hearing must be maintained, and it shall be appropriate to utilize recording devices to ensure accuracy.

Upon completion of the investigation and hearing, the Board shall, within ten (10) working days, submit a report and recommendation to the employee, the human resource manager, and _____ (a designated organization official). The report shall include:

- A copy of all written reports received by the Board

- A written summary of the Board's investigation

- The Board's decision

- The Board's recommendation

- An indication of whether or not the Board's recommendation is acceptable to the employee.

The _____ (designated organizational official) shall have ten (10) working days from the day on which the report is received to render a decision. The decision shall be communicated in writing to the employee, the employee's supervisor, the Board, and the human resource manager. This decision shall be final and binding so far as internal grievance procedures are concerned.

NOTES

1. Cynthia Scherb, "The Use of Disclaimers to Avoid Employer Liability Under Employment Handbook Provisions," *The Journal of Corporation Law* 12 (Fall 1986), 105–21.

2. Toussaint v. Blue Cross and Blue Shield, 408 Mich. 579, 292 N.W.2d 880 (1980) and Woolley v. Hoffmann-LaRoche, Inc., 99 NJ, 284, 491 A.2d 1257 (1985).

3. See Scherb, "The Use of Disclaimers," 113.

4. Ibid.

5. Peterman v. IBT, 344 P2d 25 (1959).

6. Tammy v. Atlantic Richfield, 610 P2d 1330 (1980).

7. Savoduik v. Korvittes, Inc., 488F. Supp. 822 (NY 1980).

8. Nees v. Hocks, 536 P2d 512 (OR 1975).

9. Robert Landers, "Fired For No Good Cause: Is It Legal?" *Editorial Research Reports* 2, no. 20 (25 November 1988), 597–611.

10. See David Cathcart and Mark Dichter, eds., *Employment-At-Will: A 1986 State-By-State Survey* (Washington, D.C.: National Employment Law Institute, 1987).

11. See Landers, "Fired for No Good Cause."

12. Ibid.

13. Ibid.

14. Ibid.

15. See Herbert Heneman III, Donald Schwab, John Fossum, and Lee Dyer, *Personnel Human Resource Management* (Homewood, Ill.: Richard D. Irwin, Inc., 1980).

16. See, U.S. House of Representatives, Report of the Civil Service Subcommittee of the House Post Office and Civil Service Committee, House Report 99–859, 99th Congress, 2d. Session, p. 17 (Washington, D.C.: Government Printing Office, 1986).

17. See Stephen Kohn and Michael Kohn, *The Labor Lawyer's Guide to the Rights and Responsibilities of Employee Whistleblowers* (Westport, Conn.: Quorum Books, 1988).

18. Sheila McCormick, "Whistleblowers Receive Consideration on Capitol Hill," *Public Administration Times* 12, no. 8 (2 June 1989), 3.

19. Kohn and Kohn, *The Labor Lawyer's Guide*, 77.

20. Ibid.

21. Clyde Summers, "Protecting All Employees Against Unjust Dismissal," *Harvard Business Review* 58, no. 1 (January–February 1980), 132–39.

22. See M. Hill, "Sex Discrimination under Title VII and the Constitution," *Labor Law Journal* 29 (1978), 570–81.

23. Ward's Cove Packing Co. v. Atonio, *Labor Law Journal* (1989).

24. Heneman, Schwab, Fossum, and Dyer, *Personnel Human Resource Management*, 56.

25. Ibid.

26. Walker v. Secretary of Treasury, DC NGA., No. 1:87-cv–1789-CAM, April 11, 1989.

27. Jennifer Adams, "At Work While Under the Influence," *Marquette Law Review* 70 (Fall 1986), 88–119.

28. 29 U.S.C. 701–96 (1982).

29. See Adams, "At Work," 110.

30. "Anti-Drug Abuse Act of 1988" (PL100–690, 18 November 1988).

31. U.S. Department of Transportation, "Drug Testing Programs, Workplace Procedures," Federal Register 53:223 (21 November 1988), 47002.

32. Department of Defense Federal Acquisition Regulation Supplement, "Drug-Free Work Force" *Federal Register* 53:188 (28 September 1988), 37763.

33. National Treasury Employees Union v. Von Raab, #86–3833, April 22, 1987, reported in *Government Employee Relations Report* 25 (27 April 1987), 611, 612.

34. National Treasury Employees Union v. Von Raab, 816 F.2d 170 (1987) Cert. granted, #86–1879.

35. John Monroe, "Employee Assistance Programs—The Legal Issues," *Employee Relations Today* 15, no. 3 (Autumn 1988), 239–43.

36. 42 U.S.C. (20 April, 1871), Section 1983.

37. Monroe v. Pape, 365 U.S. 167 (1961).

38. See Sheldon Nahmod, "Municipal Liability: What Should Be Done About Section 1983?" A Policy Working Paper of the National League of Cities (Washington, D.C.: National League of Cities, 1987).

39. Monroe v. Department of Social Services, 436 U.S. 568 (1978).

40. 42 U.S.C. 1988.

41. Board of Cleveland Education v. Loudermilk (1985) 84 L Ed 2nd 494.

42. See Thomas Condon, *"Fire Me & I'll Sue!" A Manager's Survival Guide to Employee Rights* (New York: Modern Business Reports, Alexander Hamilton Institute, 1984, 1985).

Index

About the Author

WILLA M. BRUCE is Assistant Professor of Public Administration at the University of Nebraska, Omaha. She previously taught Personnel Administration in the College of Business at Virginia Polytechnic Institute and State University.